MW00587770

Paul and the law

Titles in this series:

An index of Scripture references for all the volumes may be found at
http://www.thegospelcoalition.org/resources/nsbt

NEW STUDIES IN BIBLICAL THEOLOGY 31

Series editor: D. A. Carson

Paul and the law

KEEPING THE COMMANDMENTS
OF GOD

Brian S. Rosner

APOLLOS

INTERVARSITY PRESS
DOWNERS GROVE, ILLINOIS 60515

APOLLOS
An imprint of Inter-Varsity Press, England
Norton Street
Nottingham NG7 3HR, England
Website: www.ivpbooks.com
Email: ivp@ivpbooks.com

InterVarsity Press, USA
P.O. Box 1400
Downers Grove, IL 60515-1426, USA
Website: www.ivpress.com
Email: email@ivpress.com

InterVarsity Press®, USA, is the book-publishing division of InterVarsity Christian Fellowship/USA® <www.intervarsity.org> and a member movement of the International Fellowship of Evangelical Students.

Inter-Varsity Press, England, is closely linked with the Universities and Colleges Christian Fellowship, a student movement connecting Christian Unions throughout Great Britain, and a member movement of the International Fellowship of Evangelical Students. Website: www.uccf.org.uk

First published 2013

Set in Monotype Times New Roman

Typeset in Great Britain by CRB Associates, Potterhanworth, Lincolnshire

Printed and bound in Great Britain by Ashford Colour Press Ltd., Gosport, Hants.

USA ISBN 978-0-8308-2632-2

UK ISBN: 978-1-84474-891-4

British Library Cataloguing in Publication Data
A catalogue record for this book is available from the British Library.

Library of Congress Cataloging-in-Publication Data
A catalogue record for this book is available from the Library of Congress.

P	19	18	17	16	15	14	13	12	11	10	9	8	7	6	5	4	3	2	1
Y	29	28	27	26	25	24	23	22	21	20	19	18	17	16	15	14	13			

To Andrew Cameron, Richard Gibson
and Philip Kern

Contents

Tables

Series preface

New Studies in Biblical Theology is a series of monographs that address key issues in the discipline of biblical theology. Contributions to the series focus on one or more of three areas: (1) the nature and status of biblical theology, including its relations with other disciplines (e.g. historical theology, exegesis, systematic theology, historical criticism, narrative theology); (2) the articulation and exposition of the structure of thought of a particular biblical writer or corpus; and (3) the delineation of a biblical theme across all or part of the biblical corpora.

Above all, these monographs are creative attempts to help thinking Christians understand their Bibles better. The series aims simultaneously to instruct and to edify, to interact with the current literature, and to point the way ahead. In God's universe, mind and heart should not be divorced: in this series we will try not to separate what God has joined together. While the notes interact with the best of scholarly literature, the text is uncluttered with untransliterated Greek and Hebrew, and tries to avoid too much technical jargon. The volumes are written within the framework of confessional evangelicalism, but there is always an attempt at thoughtful engagement with the sweep of the relevant literature.

Anyone who follows long-standing debates over Paul and the law, over the use of the Old Testament in the New (especially in Paul), over the cogency or otherwise of various theological systems (e.g. Lutheranism, various forms of covenant theology, dispensationalism), over the origins of the common tripartite classification of biblical law (moral, civil and ceremonial), knows that Paul's understanding of the law lurks behind many other theological debates. Add to the topics already mentioned the relationships between Christian Jews and Christian Gentiles, the unity of the new humanity in Christ, Paul's apparent flexibility when he evangelizes Jews in Jerusalem and Corinthians in Achaia, and, in historical theology, the validity or otherwise of the 'third use' of the law, not to mention the sheer avalanche of books and articles on these and related topics, and one readily perceives why a book on Paul and the law is likely to be of perennial interest.

So what is the distinctive contribution of the volume you are holding in your hand? Brian Rosner's strength lies in showing with patience and clarity how the apostle Paul articulates an array of complementary but quite different stances towards the law. That these diverse stances can be integrated he does not deny, but his focus is on letting the crucial passages in Paul speak for themselves. Whether one is persuaded by each exegesis is not as important as listening attentively to the diversity of emphases within Paul's own writings, before attempting the grand synthesis. This is a book to read slowly and appreciatively, a book to ponder.

D. A. Carson
Trinity Evangelical Divinity School

Author's preface

Most scholars come at Paul and the law as interpreters of Romans and Galatians. My background and perspective are somewhat different. Although I have taught the exegesis of both letters, most of my research has been in three different areas: 1 Corinthians, Paul's ethics, and the Jewish background to Paul's letters. With these interests to the fore, I am as much concerned about what Paul does with the law, especially for questions of conduct, as I am with what Paul says about the law.

I have been pondering the subject since the beginning of my doctoral studies in the late 1980s and in one sense this book is an attempt to complete that project. As one reviewer of my published dissertation complained, *Paul, Scripture and Ethics* 'does not account for Paul's approach to the Mosaic law'.

My goal is to bring some neglected evidence to the discussion and to defend some proposals that sharpen and build on the work of others. I have sought to write something fresh and readable, which examines enough trees to sketch a reliable guide to the wood, along with a map of the broader lie of the land (for subjects related to the law, like justification and ethics).

The book's ideas have been test run in a variety of settings and my indebtedness to others is too big to spell out in full. Special thanks are due to Roy Ciampa and Michael Bird, who kindly read and commented on parts of the manuscript. Don Carson, the editor of the *NSBT* series, provided invaluable guidance from the outset. Phil Duce of IVP was supportive along the way. Eldo Barkhuizen's copy-editing was done with painstaking care and diligence. My wife, Natalie, gave encouragement at every stage.

I am especially grateful to Moore Theological College for the privilege of giving the 2011 Annual Moore College Lectures on Paul and the law. The book's final test run was in that context. The book was largely completed in my last semester at Moore before moving to Ridley Melbourne, where I am now happily ensconced. It is dedicated to three of my closest Moore colleagues and friends, Andrew Cameron, Richard Gibson and Philip Kern.

The subject of Paul and the law is notoriously complex. Nonetheless, I am convinced that the hermeneutical solution to the puzzle of Paul and the law that this book expounds is exegetically compelling, takes Paul's historical context into account and retains at full strength Paul's twin emphases on the free grace of God in salvation and the demand of God for holy living.

A revised and expanded version of my 2010 article 'Paul and the Law: What He Did Not Say', *JSNT* 32: 405–419, appears in chapter 3 and is used with permission.

Brian S. Rosner

Abbreviations

1QS	*Community Rule / Manual of Discipline* (Dead Sea Scrolls)
4Q266	*Damascus Document*[a] (Dead Sea Scrolls)
4Q525	*Beatitudes / The Demons of Death* (Dead Sea Scrolls)
'Abot R. Nat	*'Abot de Rabbi Nathan*
AB	Anchor Bible
ABRL	Anchor Bible Reference Library
AD	Anno Domini (after Christ)
AGAJU	Arbeiten zur Geschichte des antiken Judentums und des Urchristentums
Ag. Ap.	*Against Apion* (Josephus)
Alleg. Interp.	*Allegorical Interpretation* (Philo)
Ant.	*Antiquities of the Jews* (Josephus)
AV	Authorized (King James) Version
Bar.	Baruch
BBR	*Bulletin for Biblical Research*
BC	before Christ
BDAG	W. Bauer, F. W. Danker, W. F. Arndt and W. F. Gingrich, *A Greek-English Lexicon of the New Testament and Other Early Christian Literature*, 3rd ed., Chicago: University of Chicago Press, 2000
BECNT	Baker Exegetical Commentary on the New Testament
BZ	*Biblische Zeitschrift*
BZNW	Beihefte zur Zeitschrift für die neutestamentliche Wissenschaft
CBQ	*Catholic Biblical Quarterly*
CD	*Damascus Document* (Dead Sea Scrolls)
Dec.	*On the Decalogue* (Philo)
Dial.	*Dialogue with Trypho* (Justin Martyr)
DPHL	*Dictionary of Paul and His Letters*, ed. G. F. Hawthorne and R. P. Martin, Downers Grove: IVP; Leicester: IVP, 1993

Dreams	*On Dreams* (Philo)
Embassy	*On the Embassy to Gaius* (Philo)
Esd.	Esdras
ESV	English Standard Version
ExpTim	*Expository Times*
Gk.	Greek
HBT	*Horizons in Biblical Theology*
HCSB	Holman Christian Standard Bible
Hebr.	Hebrew
Hist. eccl.	*Historia ecclesiastica* (Eusebius)
ICC	International Critical Commentary
IJST	*International Journal of Systematic Theology*
JETS	*Journal of the Evangelical Theological Society*
JJS	*Journal of Jewish Studies*
JSNTSup	Journal for the Study of the New Testament, Supplement Series
JTS	*Journal of Theological Studies*
LCL	Loeb Classical Library
lit.	literally
LXX	Septuagint
Macc.	Maccabees
Migr.	*On the Migration of Abraham* (Philo)
Moses	*On the Life of Moses* (Philo)
MT	Masoretic Text
Names	*On the Change of Names* (Philo)
NAB	New American Bible
NASB	New American Standard Bible
NDBT	*New Dictionary of Biblical Theology*: *Exploring the Unity and Diversity of Scripture*, ed. B. S. Rosner, T. D. Alexander, G. Goldsworthy and D. A. Carson, Downers Grove: IVP; Leicester: IVP, 2000
NET	New English Translation
NICNT	New International Commentary on the New Testament
NIDOTTE	*New International Dictionary of Old Testament Theology and Exegesis*, ed. W. A. VanGemeren, 5 vols., Grand Rapids: Zondervan; Carlisle: Paternoster, 1997
NIGTC	New International Greek Testament Commentary
NIV	New International Version
NJB	New Jerusalem Bible

NLT	New Living Translation
NovT	*Novum Testamentum*
NovTSup	Novum Testamentum Supplements
NRSV	New Revised Standard Version
NT	New Testament
NTS	*New Testament Studies*
OT	Old Testament
PNTC	Pillar New Testament Commentary
Prov.	*On Providence* (Philo)
Pss Sol.	*Psalms of Solomon*
RSV	Revised Standard Version
Sacrifices	*On the Sacrifices of Cain and Abel* (Philo)
SBLSymS	Society of Biblical Literature Symposium Series
Sifre Deut.	*Sifre Deuteronomy*
Sifre Num.	*Sifre Numbers*
Sir.	Sirach
SP	Sacra pagina
Spec. Laws	*On the Special Laws* (Philo)
TDNT	*Theological Dictionary of the New Testament*, ed. G. Kittel and G. Friedrich, tr. G. W. Bromiley, 10 vols., Grand Rapids: Eerdmans, 1964–76
T. Jos.	*Testament of Joseph*
T. Jud.	*Testament of Judah*
TNIV	Today's New International Version
TNTC	Tyndale New Testament Commentaries
tr.	translated, translation
TSAJ	Texte und Studien zum antiken Judentum
TynB	*Tyndale Bulletin*
UBS4	United Bible Societies Greek New Testament Editorial Committee, *A Textual Commentary on the Greek New Testament: A Companion Volume to the United Bible Societies' Greek New Testament*, 4th rev. ed., Stuttgart: United Bible Societies, 1994
VC	*Vigiliae christianae*
WBC	Word Biblical Commentary
Wis.	Wisdom
WUNT	Wissenschaftliche Untersuchungen zum Neuen Testament
ZNW	*Zeitschrift für die neutestamentliche Wissenschaft und die Kunde der älteren Kirche*

Chapter One

'Circumcision is nothing'
The puzzle of Paul and the law

Paul's views on the law are *complex*.
(Ben Witherington III)[1]

Paul and the law – The subject is *complex*.
(Donald A. Hagner)[2]

Current discussion of Paul's view of the law . . . has
become extraordinarily *complex*.
(D. A. Carson)[3]

There is nothing quite so *complex* in Paul's theology as the
role and function which he attributes to the law.
(James D. G. Dunn)[4]

There is a general agreement that Paul's view of the law is
a very *complex* and intricate matter which confronts the
interpreter with a great many puzzles.
(Heiki Räisänen)[5]

Understanding Paul's relationship to the Law of Moses is fraught
with difficulty.[6] Not only is the subject notoriously complex and much
studied (some would say studied too much), but major positions are
also entrenched. Difficulties begin with questions of definition, of

[1] Witherington 1998: 66, italics added.
[2] Hagner 2007: 104, italics added.
[3] Carson 2004a: 393, italics added. Hafemann (1993: 671) has written similarly,
'Paul's understanding of the Law is currently the most debated topic among Pauline
scholars.'
[4] Dunn 2008: 441, italics added.
[5] Räisänen 1987: xii, italics added. Cf. N. T. Wright 1991: 211, commenting on the
law in Rom. 8:4, 'This is complex.'
[6] Cf. Kruse 1996: 287: 'Anyone who seeks to understand Paul's approach to the law
. . . encounters many problems.'

both the extent of Paul's corpus and the meanings of 'the law', and are exacerbated with numerous problems of interpretation of the key texts, decisions about which lead to vastly differing syntheses of Paul's teaching. Like a big jigsaw puzzle with most of the pieces missing, and the box lid thrown out, there seem to be numerous possible configurations, none of which fits every piece. Some doubt whether Paul himself knew what he was talking about.

Those who write about Paul and the law are typically greeted with a barrage of accusations, ranging from unthinking conservatism to complete eccentricity, from advocating licence to imposing legalism, from cheapening grace to ignoring the demands of God.[7] If few scholars know exactly what they think about the subject, most can tell you what they do not think.

Indeed, it is tempting to agree with 1 Timothy 1:7, which judges that those who want to be 'teachers of the law' do 'not know what they are talking about or what they so confidently affirm' (TNIV). Many would counsel with Titus 3:9 that it is best to avoid 'arguments and quarrels about the law, because these are unprofitable and useless' (TNIV)![8] Those who write on Paul and the law may feel an affinity with Hebrews 5:11: 'We have much to say about this, but it is hard to explain because you are slow to learn' (NIV 1984). However, given the failure to arrive at a consensus at many points on the subject this would hardly be a fair retort!

Too much, however, is at stake to ignore the topic. It is not only the study of Paul and his letters that depends on a clear understanding of the apostle to the Gentiles' stance towards the Jewish law; his teaching concerning salvation, salvation history, Israel, the church, anthropology, ethics and eschatology are all inextricably linked to his view of the law. Needless to say, no serious examination of Paul's relationship to the Law of Moses can afford to underestimate the complexity of the subject, which is after all a subset of one of the biggest questions in the study of early Christianity, namely the parting of the ways between the nascent movement and the mother faith.

The reason understanding Paul and the law is so critical to the study of the New Testament is that it touches on the perennial question of the relationship between the grace of God in the gift of salvation and

---

[7] Cf. Bassler 2007: 'No aspect of Paul's thought is as hotly disputed as his view of the law.'

[8] These warnings are of course not about valid questions of interpretation but concern false teaching. But the sentiment is frequently expressed in response to the subject of Paul and the law.

the demand of God in the call for holy living. Misunderstanding Paul and the law leads to distortions of one or both. From the beginning, even in Paul's day, his teaching on the law has raised hackles on one of two fronts. People think either that the free gift of salvation has been compromised, or a solid basis for the demand of God for obedience and a holy life has been removed. If justification is not by works of the law, does that not lead to licence? If one removes the law, is the result not lawlessness? Do those without the law not end up as outlaws? And if we are still under the law in some sense, does that not compromise the free gift of salvation?

With reference to the history of research, Richard Hays warns, 'Like the stone steps of an ancient university building, the topic of "Paul and the Law" has been worn smooth by the passing of generations of scholars.'[9] John W. Martens uses a different metaphor to make the same point: 'Scholarship on Paul and the law is a vast array of acres and acres of cultivated fields.'[10]

Three theological positions in particular have a strong interest in Paul's view of the law. Each tends to focus on an emphasis in Paul's letters that is clearly present, but plays down other aspects of the subject. Broadly speaking, *Lutheranism* holds that Paul believed that Christ abolished the law and that the law is the counterpoint to the gospel. The primary role of the law is to lead us to despair of any hope of obedience leading to God's acceptance and to drive us to seek God's mercy in Christ. For the most part the law is not seen as playing a big role in the Christian life (although Luther himself made effective use of the law in his catechisms). Secondly, the *Reformed* view agrees that salvation is by grace and not by obeying the law, but once saved we are under the moral law and must obey it in order to please God. Thirdly, the so-called New Perspective on Paul, which is really a new perspective on Paul in relation to Judaism, thinks that the problem of the law for Paul is not that salvation is by grace and not works, but that Paul's opposition to the law was simply that it was used by Jews to exclude Gentiles from the people of God; Jewish ethnocentrism is the reason Paul opposed the law. There is something to learn from each of these perspectives. In my view the challenge is to hold on to their valid insights in a manner that does justice to the full range of evidence and, with important qualifications, does not deny the validity of other perspectives.

[9] Hays 1996b: 151.
[10] Martens 2003: xiii. To me, rather than a well-cultivated field it feels more like a minefield!

However, the present study does not focus on the history of interpretation. Nor do I document the pedigree of every position I defend; this is not merely to avoid the toil and tedium, but to prevent prior treatments obscuring a fresh appraisal of the primary sources themselves. Neither does this book offer a comprehensive investigation and typology of the usage of 'law' in Paul's letters; much can be missed by focusing too tightly and too early on the explicit evidence to the neglect of other lines of enquiry that set such things in context.[11]

Instead, my goal is to bring some neglected evidence to the discussion and to defend some proposals that sharpen and build on the work of others. Every researcher approaches the subject with a particular profile that impacts the shape of his or her investigation. Most scholars come at Paul and the law above all as interpreters of Romans and/or Galatians. This is understandable, given the fact that the vast majority of Paul's references to *nomos* occur in these two letters. To use a metaphor, if the 'law is the main subplot of Romans',[12] in Galatians the law is personified and appears as a main character in the drama.

The exegetical problems in connection with the law in Romans and Galatians alone are well known:

- Is Christ the end of the law or its goal, or both?
- Are we no longer under the law's jurisdiction or just its condemnation?
- Do believers fulfil the law or does Christ do it for us?
- Is 'the law of Christ' the law reconfigured, or a new set of commandments, or something else?
- Are we under the moral law? Must we keep the Ten Commandments?
- Are 'works of the law' identity markers separating Israel from the nations, or works demanded by the law?
- Is Paul's opposition to doing the law just his concern that it marks off Jews from Gentiles?

To make matters worse, the standard positions on these questions are entrenched. Paul and the law is the New Testament studies version of the Battle of the Somme, the 1916 World War One allied attack on

[11] Cf. Barclay 2011: 37: 'In the history of scholarship on "Paul and the law" by far the greatest attention has been paid to Paul's theoretical statements on our topic, with numerous attempts to plot the location of the law in relation to faith, Christ, grace and works on the complex map of Pauline theology.'
[12] Dunn 1997: 131.

the Western Front in France: lots of close fighting in trenches, with no clear winners, hardly any progress, many casualties and no sign of an armistice or even a détente. My strategy, to extend the metaphor, is not to enter the fray head on, but to come in from a different direction. More precisely, it is not Paul and the law that is the Battle of the Somme, but Paul and the law fought on predictable lines in Romans and Galatians that fits this unflattering description. There is much vital evidence that has been neglected. Many books on the subject concentrate exclusively on what I cover just in chapter 2!

My background and perspective are somewhat different. Although I have taught the exegesis of both Romans and Galatians, most of my research has been in three different areas: 1 Corinthians, Paul's ethics, and the Jewish background to Paul's letters.[13] With these interests to the fore, I am as much concerned about what Paul does with the law, especially for questions of conduct, as I am about what Paul says concerning the law (the exclusive focus of many studies). Driving the investigation is the question, according to Paul, *how does the law relate to the issue of how to walk and please God* (cf. 1 Thess. 4:1)? Even if Paul's answer may at first sight seem very un-Jewish, the question itself sits comfortably in a first-century Jewish setting.

Many book-length investigations of Paul and the law seek to be exhaustive in their treatment of the relevant Pauline texts and/or the history of interpretation. An unintended consequence of this is that they are also exhausting to read, and ironically readers are put off developing a comprehensive grasp of the subject. On the other hand, chapters on Paul and the law in various textbooks, while concise, tend to skip over the problems and are therefore unsatisfying. Even the most casual readers of Paul's letters recognize real difficulties in understanding the subject and object to simplistic generalizations and a selective review of the evidence. Most students and ministers, and even scholars, cannot remember what they think about the key texts, let alone have an idea of how they all fit together. The result is often an inconsistent approach to interpreting Paul when he discusses the law and a confusion that hinders a confident Christian reading of the Law of Moses. My aim is to write something fresh and readable,

---

[13] In responding to my book on Paul's use of Scripture for ethics, published in 1994, Witherington (2010: 608) offers a four-point critique, culminating with the objection that my approach 'does not account for Paul's approach to the Mosaic law'. He is right that a high view of the importance of Torah for Pauline ethics does require some explanation as to how this fits with Paul's view of the law, especially Paul's negative critique of the law. The present study takes up the challenge.

which examines enough trees to sketch a reliable guide to the wood, along with a map of the broader lie of the land (for subjects related to the law, like justification and ethics).

Paul's apparent inconsistency

The crux of the problem of Paul and the law is the fact that his letters present both negative critique and positive approval of the law. James Dunn makes this observation with reference to Romans and Galatians: 'Paul does not hesitate to describe it [the law] as "holy, just and good" (Rom. 7.12), a very positive gift of God (Rom. 9.4). . . . On the other hand, he clearly speaks of the law as an enslaving power, increasing trespass and used by sin to bring about death (Gal. 4.1–10; Rom. 5.20; 7.5).'[14] Some specific examples in Ephesians and Romans underline the problem. (An apparent contradiction in a single verse appears in 1 Corinthians 7:19 and will be dealt with in detail in a following section of this chapter.)

Ephesians 2:15 is a clear example of negative critique of the law: Christ has 'abolished the law with its commandments and ordinances'.[15] The sheer redundancy of the expression 'the law with its commandments and ordinances', typical of the style of Ephesians, indicates that Paul intends to refer to the entire Law of Moses. The precise syntax is not the point so much as the impression left by the repetition: Christ has abolished every last bit of the law.

The words in question echo the introduction to the Shema in Deuteronomy 6:1: 'This is the command – the statutes and ordinances – the Lord your God has instructed me' (HCSB). 'Command' (Hebr. *miṣwâ*) in the singular is often interpreted as the law-covenant in its entirety, and the plural, 'statutes and ordinances', sums up the contents of the law-covenant.[16]

The verb 'to abolish', *katargeō*, is equally unambiguous. BDAG's (526a) glosses include 'abolish, wipe out, set aside'. A survey of Pauline usage confirms the strength of the term, along with frequent apocalyptic overtones. The following translations appear in the NRSV: 'nullify' (Rom. 3:3; 4:14; Gal. 3:17); 'discharge' (Rom. 7:2, 6); 'reduce to nothing' (1 Cor. 1:28); 'doom to perish' (1 Cor. 2:6); 'destroy' (1 Cor. 6:13; 15:24, 26); 'come to an end' (1 Cor. 13:8 [2×], 10–11); 'set aside' (2 Cor. 3:7, 11, 13–14); 'cut off' (Gal. 5:4); 'remove' (Gal.

---

[14] Dunn 1997: 328–329.

[15] See the section in chapter 2, 'Clarification and confirmation', for a full discussion.

[16] I am indebted to Dr Andrew Shead for this observation.

5:11); 'annihilate' (2 Thess. 2:8); and 'abolish' (Eph. 2:15; 2 Tim. 1:10). To paraphrase Ephesians, using Louw and Nida's definition of *katargeō* (13.100), 'Christ has put an end to the law in its entirety.'

Ephesians 2:15 stands in obvious tension with two other verses in Paul's letters, the first of which is in the same letter. If Ephesians 2:15 typifies negative critique, just a few chapters on, in Ephesians 6:1–2, we find positive approval of the law. Paul quotes one of the 'commandments' that Christ had presumably done away with and uses it as an instruction for Christian living: 'Children, obey your parents in the Lord, for this is right. "Honour your father and mother" – this is the first *commandment* with a promise.' The word 'commandment' in Ephesians 6:2, *entolē*, is the same word used in Ephesians 2:15 to describe what it is that Christ has abolished. Christ has abolished the law and yet the law is still of value for Christian conduct. It is genuinely puzzling how an author could write both things in the same letter.

If Ephesians 6:1–2 stands in tension with Ephesians 2:15, Romans 3:31 is its formal contradiction. There Paul asks whether his teaching about the critical nature of faith abolishes the law: 'Do we then *overthrow* the law by this faith?' Paul answers, 'By no means! On the contrary, we uphold the law.' The verb translated 'overthrow' is *katargeō*, the same word that appears in Ephesians 2:15. If in Romans Paul insists his teaching about Christ and faith by no means abolishes the law, in Ephesians he affirms that Christ has indeed abolished it.

Andrew Errington suggested the following apt and wry analogy:

> Discussing Paul and the Law is a bit like being watched while you carve a chicken: it's fairly easy to start well, but you quickly have to make some tricky decisions (about which everyone has an opinion), and it's very easy to end up in a sticky mess with lots of bits left over that no one knows what to do with.[17]

Studies of Paul and the law distinguish themselves by whether they face these unmistakable tensions in his letters and how they explain them.

Definition of terms: 'Paul', 'law' and 'believer'

Three terms call for definition before proceeding with our study of Paul and the law.

---

[17] Personal communication.

The apostle Paul

By *Paul* I mean both the Jew who was seized by Jesus Christ (Phil. 3:12) and became his apostle to the Gentiles and the letters he wrote that are collected in the New Testament. The extent of his corpus is of course a matter of dispute. While I am convinced of the authenticity of all thirteen letters traditionally attributed to Paul, little hangs on this decision for a study of the subject at hand. As already noted, Paul's most sustained discussions of Israel's law and the church's faith are in the undisputed letters. Nonetheless, significant evidence in Ephesians (see e.g. 2:15 and 6:1–2 above) and the Pastoral Epistles, for example, should not be ignored and sometimes offers support to one interpretation over another of texts in Romans and Galatians. Even those scholars who work with a truncated Pauline corpus should recognize that if the law is a central concern for Paul, the pseudo-Pauline epistles provide early reflections of, or on, his views. It is a mistake to disregard such evidence, even if it is not accorded primary status.

The meaning of 'the law'

What Paul meant by *law* is no less contentious and his use of the term *nomos* may not be univocal. When we study Paul *and the law*, what are we talking about? With respect to the sense of *nomos* in the New Testament, BDAG (677–678) is typical of most lexica in noting three general meanings of the word in the New Testament: 'rule, principle, norm', 'legal system' and 'collection of holy writings'. Most treatments of the subject of Paul and the law take 'law' in the second sense of 'legal system' as their primary, if not exclusive, focus. Westerholm is a clear example: '[T]he "law" in Paul's writings frequently (indeed, most frequently) refers to the sum of specific divine commandments given to Israel through Moses'.[18] This concentration often leads to a tight focus on the law's commandments: 'The law that can be kept, done, fulfilled, or transgressed is clearly "the legal parts" of the Pentateuch.'[19] Schreiner concurs: 'In the NT . . . the term *law* most often refers to what is commanded in the Mosaic law.'[20]

[18] Westerholm 2004a: 299.
[19] Ibid. Cf. Winger 1992: 104: *nomos* refers to '[t]hose words given to and possessed by the Jewish people, which guide and control those who accept them and according to which those who accept them are judged.'
[20] Schreiner 2010: 21, italics original.

In favour of this approach we note that on a few occasions Paul may use 'law' to refer to commandments or collections of commandments. Romans 7:7 is a candidate for such a reading, where Paul introduces one of the Ten Commandments as coming from the 'law': 'Yet, if it had not been for the law, I would not have known sin. I would not have known what it is to covet if the law had not said, "You shall not covet."' The phrase 'the giving of the law [to Israel]' (Rom. 9:4) also points to the law as a body of commandments, most commentators taking it as referring to the divine legislation delivered to Moses at Sinai. Galatians 3:17 is a comparable usage, in that it refers to 'the law, which came four hundred and thirty years later [after the promises to Abraham]'. Parts of the Pentateuch readily fit the description of 'laws', such as the Decalogue, the Covenant Code (Exod. 21 – 23) and the Holiness Code (Lev. 17 – 26). Similarly, the word 'law' is used frequently in Deuter-onomy (e.g. 1:5; 4:8, 44; 17:18; 27:3; etc.; cf. 28:61, 'the book of this law') to refer to itself, as 'the sovereign will of Yahweh, now coded into teaching that is palpably available in scrolls'.[21]

But to take 'law' exclusively to mean *legal material in the Pentateuch* poses problems. It is certainly true that the five books of Moses contain a lot more than just laws. Narrative dominates Genesis, the first half of Exodus and most of Numbers. And Sloane notes that when Deuteronomy intimates that Moses will 'expound this law [MT: *tôrâ* / LXX: *nomos*]' in a series of speeches to Israel, his first speech 'contains no rules or regulations; it consists entirely of a recitation of Israel's history, or, more properly, of Yahweh's great and gracious acts on their behalf and their past response'.[22]

It is more accurate to say that Torah or 'law' most commonly came to denote not just Deuteronomy, some collection of laws, or even the contents of the Sinai covenant, but rather the first five books of the Bible together.[23] According to John P. Meier, the notion of the law being treated as a 'literary whole' can be found throughout the so-called Deuteronomistic history (Joshua – 2 Kings), and it is continued in 1–2 Chronicles, Ezra and Nehemiah. In support he cites 2 Kings 23:2 ('the book of the covenant'), Joshua 24:26 ('the Law of God'), 2 Kings 10:31 ('the Law of the LORD') and Joshua 23:6 ('all that is written in the book of the law of Moses').[24] Even if the

---

[21] Brueggemann 2002: 218.
[22] Sloane 2008: 38.
[23] Cf. BDAG's (678d) third definition of *nomos*, noted above: 'collection of holy writings'.
[24] Meier 2009: 29.

references to the 'law' in Deuteronomy are limited to one book (which is predominantly laws, but not exclusively – see Sloane above), the other references point to a broader referent taking in all of the five books of Moses.

Correspondingly, Paul generally deals with the law as a unity, customarily referring to Mosaic 'law', not 'laws'. This means that, in the main, his responses to the law are not to its various parts, however we may wish to divide it, but to the law as a whole. And he can not only introduce 'laws' from the Pentateuch (see e.g. 'you shall not covet' in Rom. 7:7, noted above) as 'law', but also narrative as 'law', as in Galatians 4:21 (Hagar and Sarah, discussed below).

In terms of referent, both Hebrew *tôrâ* and Greek *nomos* in Jewish and Christian writings frequently denote the first five books of the sacred Scriptures attributed to Moses, often labelled the 'Pentateuch' or 'Torah'. Paul can write of 'the law [the Pentateuch] and the prophets', as in Romans 3:2. He can also introduce quotations from the Pentateuch as being found in the law, as in 1 Corinthians 9:8–9 where 'law' and 'law of Moses' are equivalent: 'Do I say this merely on human authority? Doesn't *the Law* say the same thing? For it is written in *the Law of Moses*: [quotation of Deut. 25:4].'[25] Watson is correct: 'When Paul speaks of "the law", he has in mind the text known as "the Law of Moses."'[26]

A test case for the meaning of *nomos* for Paul occurs in Galatians, where in a single verse Paul writes of the law in apparently different ways: 'Tell me, you who want to be under the law, are you not aware of what the law says?' (Gal. 4:21 TNIV).

If the first part of the verse sums up the dilemma facing the Galatian Christians, the second introduces Paul's allegorical interpretation of the Genesis story of Hagar and Sarah. F. F. Bruce's comments are instructive:

> [N]ote the transition in this sentence from *nomos* in the strict sense of 'law' – 'you who wish to be under the law' – to *nomos* in the general sense of the Pentateuch. The patriarchal narrative [of Hagar and Sarah] does not belong to any of the law-codes of the Torah, but it is part of the Torah, and it is doubtful if Paul and his contemporaries made the explicit distinction in their minds between

---

[25] NIV. For further examples where 'law' means the Pentateuch, see Matt. 12:5; Luke 2:23; 24:44; John 8:5, 17; Heb. 9:19.

[26] Watson 2004: 275.

the narrower and wider senses of the term that modern students readily make.[27]

Galatians 4:21 contains two references to 'the law', one negative and one positive. Many scholars seem to take Paul as saying, 'Tell me, you who want to be under [the legal parts of] the law, are you not aware of what [another bit of] the law says?' (TNIV). But the most straightforward interpretation is to understand Paul as simply referring to the Pentateuch in both cases. As Hays puts it, for Paul *nomos* 'is always the same collection of texts, but the import of those texts shifts dramatically in accordance with the hermeneutical perspective at each stage of the unfolding drama'.[28] It is better to read the two occurrences of *nomos* in the verse in question as referring to different functions or, better, construals of the Law of Moses. The following interpretative additions to the verse pre-empt some of my main findings in this book: 'Tell me, you who want to be under the law [as law-covenant], are you not aware of what the law [as prophecy] says?' (Gal. 4:21 TNIV).

The question is not *which bits* of the law Paul is referring to in a given instance of *nomos*, but the law *as what*. More attention should be paid to the point of view from which Paul is reading the law.

A few other scholars have pointed in this direction for understanding Paul and the law. I will mention these at appropriate points in the book. To cite a couple of examples here, D. A. Carson writes that Paul does not uphold the law for Christians 'as *lex*, as ongoing legal demand', but rather its continuity is sustained in that it points to and anticipates the 'new "righteousness from God" that has come in Christ Jesus'.[29] And Donald Hagner, confronted with the problem of negative and positive comments in Paul's letters about the law, recommends that we 'take the negative statements as referring to *nomos* understood *as commandments*, and the positive statements as referring to the broader meaning of *nomos*, namely *as Scripture*'.[30] I said much

[27] Bruce 1982: 215.

[28] Hays 1996b: 164.

[29] Carson 2004a: 139. In terms of this book's construal, Carson points to law as legal code and prophecy respectively.

[30] Hagner 2007: 108, italics added. As it turns out, Westerholm (2004a: 37) is close to this view when he comments, 'The law, *as* law, is meant to be observed' (italics original). Cf. Schreiner 2010: 22: 'the law is conceived as a body of commands summarized in the Mosaic covenant'. My point is that while this conception is the most common in Paul's letters, Paul also 'conceives' of the law as a testimony to the gospel (prophecy) and as instruction for living (wisdom).

the same thing in my 1994 study *Paul, Scripture and Ethics*: 'There is a sense in which the Law *as Mosaic covenant* is abolished, but the Law *as Scripture* has ongoing value for Christians.'[31]

My aim in this book is to sharpen this point and to develop it more comprehensively, constructing what might be called, to recall Hays's words quoted above, *a hermeneutical solution* to the puzzle of Paul and the law. Rather than studying 'the law's commandments', we are more in tune with Paul when we consider 'the law as commandments', as well as 'the law as prophecy' and 'the law as wisdom'. This is my approach in chapters 2–3, 5 and 6 respectively.[32]

As it turns out, John P. Meier detects the same three categories (legal, prophetic and wisdom) when he describes the dominant Old Testament conception of the Law of Moses:

> [T]he word *torah* has clearly come to mean a written document that comes from God to Israel by the hands of Moses, a scroll in which the foundational stories and ordinances of Israel are woven into a literary whole that retains traits of prophetic and sapiential [wisdom] as well as legal *torah*.[33]

Meier pinpoints the three attributes of law, prophecy and wisdom in the Pentateuch in Moses' depiction in Deuteronomy: 'In Deuteronomy, Moses is not only lawgiver but also prophet [and] wisdom teacher.'[34]

A final note on the meaning of *nomos* for Paul concerns a couple of exceptions to the rule that *nomos* for Paul refers to the five books of Moses. Perhaps surprisingly, on two occasions Paul uses *nomos* to refer to Jewish Scripture outside the Pentateuch. In Romans 3:19 he cites a catena of texts from Psalms and Isaiah (Rom. 3:10–18) as evidence of what 'the law says'. And in 1 Corinthians 14:21 he introduces a quotation of Isaiah 28:11–12 with the words 'in the law it is written'.

BDAG suggests (*nomos*, 3b) this 'wider sense' was employed 'on the principle that the most authoritative part gives its name to the whole'. Synecdoche, substituting a part for the whole, is common in many languages and cultures, including those of the Bible. The figure

---

[31] Rosner 1994: 182, italics added.

[32] The word 'as' here is meant in the sense of 'in the capacity of' or 'with the force of'.

[33] Meier 2009: 29.

[34] Ibid.

of speech is present for example in Romans 3:15, where 'feet' (swift to shed blood) stand for whole persons. The usage of 'law' for the whole Hebrew Bible suggests the latter part was considered to have the same authority as the first five books; but clearly the Pentateuch was foundational.

Paul's description of the Scriptures as 'law' is in fact explicable in both of the abovementioned apparent exceptions. The texts quoted in Romans 3 function as the verdict on all of humankind, climaxing Paul's indictment of the whole human race in 1:18 – 3:9, in which the Law of Moses played a prime role in the condemnation of the Jews. To say 'the law says' that no one is righteous and so on is to appeal both to the judgment of the psalter and Isaiah and also to the basis of the judgment in the Law of Moses.

In the citation of Isaiah 28:11–12 in 1 Corinthians 14:21 Paul may not only be identifying the text as a quotation from Scripture, but possibly also be hinting that he locates its primary significance within the dispensation of the Mosaic covenant. His argument depends on a contrast between the situation of the Israelites and Jews under the law (in need of the redemption that has come in Christ) and the situation that already holds for those who have now experienced the redemption that was especially associated with part of the prophetic message.

The meaning of 'believers in Christ'

A third term calls for comment when discussing Paul's teaching about the relationship between *believers in Christ* and the Law of Moses. Which believers are we talking about? Paul was a Jewish apostle to the Gentiles and both Acts and his own letters testify to his evangelism among both Jews and Gentiles.

Does Paul distinguish between Jewish believers and Gentile believers when it comes to how they relate to the Law of Moses? The answer is yes and no. The best way to answer the question is in reference to the phrase 'under the law', which I will take up in detail in chapter 2. For now it is worth noting that there is a sense in which all believers, both Jewish and Gentile, are not under the law, and a more limited sense in which Jewish believers may choose to live under the law.

This more limited sense is clearly demonstrated in Romans 14:1 – 15:6, a passage in which Paul addresses the observance or non-observance of certain laws from the Law of Moses in the Roman churches. Two topics are mentioned directly, namely the restriction of diet (see 14:2, 21) and observing certain days in preference to others (14:5). Barclay summarizes the consensus of commentators: 'In common with many others, I take these verses to refer to Jewish scruples concerning the consumption of meat considered unclean and the observance of the sabbath and other Jewish feasts or fasts.'[35] Whereas 'the weak' keep Jewish kosher laws and observe the sabbath, 'the strong' do not.[36]

Paul counts himself among the strong (see 15:1) and is convinced that the Christian believer may 'eat anything' (14:2); Christians are not under the law (6:14–15; 7:1–6). But while holding his own convictions, 'Paul accepts an element of subjectivity in the definition of proper conduct relating to diet and calendar.'[37] On such matters, individuals are to act in accordance with their own convictions (14:5–6). As Paul states in 14:22, 'The faith that you have, have as your own conviction before God.' In effect, he allows for the expression of Jewish cultural tradition, living under the law's direction, but not its dominion. Chapter 2 of this book, in exploring Paul's use of 'under the law', explains this distinction in greater detail.

As it turns out, the great bulk of Paul's teaching about the law concerns all believers regardless of their ethnic or religious background. Jews in the ancient world conceived of just two categories of people, setting the people of God off against the rest, namely the Gentiles. And at many points Paul's letters reflect a similar classification. However, Paul identifies believers in Christ, from whatever background, as the people of God, effectively dividing the human race into three groups rather than two. This is seen in 1 Corinthians 10:32, where Paul refers to 'the church of God', 'Jews' and 'Greeks'. It is this new grouping, 'the church of God', that is Paul's main and undifferentiated focus when it comes to his various interactions with the law.

Having dealt with some preliminaries and offered some preview, an investigation of 1 Corinthians 7:19, a text that gives the subtitle to

[35] Barclay 2011: 39. See his full treatment, 37–59, for an illuminating study that arrives at similar conclusions to my own.

[36] The two groups probably did not divide neatly into Jewish Christians and Gentile Christians: 'the weak' may have included some Gentile Christians and 'the strong' may have included some of Paul's Jewish-Christian friends in Rome, such as Prisca and Aquila.

[37] Barclay 2011: 51. Barclay (2011: 54) notes that Paul's response to the issue is echoed by Justin, in *Dial.* 46–47, who accepts that Jewish Christians may practise circumcision, keep the sabbath and observe other Jewish laws, but strongly opposes attempts to persuade Gentile Christians to follow suit.

this book, will serve to open our discussion of the subject. As Dunn has observed, 'the ways in which 1 Corinthians 7:19 is interpreted by different commentators is very instructive'.[38] Beginning inductively with one text will help us to identify the points of tension and to frame more sharply the questions that the study of Paul and the law must address.

An initial sounding: 1 Corinthians 7:19

Circumcision is nothing and uncircumcision is nothing, but keeping the commandments of God.[39]

This verse is properly described by E. P. Sanders as one of the most amazing sentences Paul ever wrote.[40] Indeed, it is hard to imagine a more un-Jewish statement than the opening words 'Circumcision is nothing and uncircumcision is nothing'.[41] Far from an ill-considered slip, Paul says the same thing in Galatians 5:6 and 6:15. His attitude to circumcision was also borne out in practice: in Galatians 5:2 he tells Gentile believers not to be circumcised.

Circumcision was a sign of membership of the covenant community and virtually all Jews considered it a principal command. When Antiochus Epiphanes wanted to eradicate Judaism, one of the things he did was have all those who circumcised their children killed (1 Macc. 1.60–61). Philo firmly criticizes some who argued that the Mosaic laws (including that regarding circumcision) had merely symbolic significance and thus did not need to be literally obeyed (*Migr.* 89–93). *Jubilees* 15.33–34 warns against 'children of Israel . . . [who] will not circumcise their children according to the law'. 1 Maccabees 1.15 denounces Jewish men who remove the marks of circumcision. For a Jew to be selective about the law was tantamount to disobeying it. To abandon circumcision was as good as annulling the law.

The story of Izates from Josephus provides the exception that proves the rule. When the Gentile King Izates pondered whether to get circumcised, the Jewish merchant Ananias advised him 'that he might worship God without being circumcised, even though he did

---

[38] Dunn 2009: 204.
[39] My tr.
[40] Sanders 1983: 161–162.
[41] Gk. *ouden estin*: 'means nothing, is unimportant' (BDAG 735c). Cf. Matt. 23:16, 18; John 8:54; Acts 21:24.

resolve to follow the Jewish law entirely' (*Ant.* 20.41b–42). However, the advice of another Jew, Eleazar, underscores Jewish scruples concerning circumcision:

> But afterward, as he had not quite abandoned his desire of doing this thing [getting circumcised], a certain other Jew that came out of Galilee, whose name was Eleazar, and who was esteemed very skilful in the learning of his country, persuaded him to do the thing; for as he entered into his palace to greet him, and found him reading the law of Moses, he said to him, 'You do not consider, O king! that you unjustly break the principal of those laws, and are injurious to God himself [by failing to get circumcised]; for you ought not only to read them, but chiefly to practice what they enjoin you. How long will you continue uncircumcised? but if you have not yet read the law about circumcision, and do not know how great impiety you are guilty of by neglecting it, read it now.' (*Ant.* 20.43–45)

How are we to understand Paul's extraordinary words in 1 Corinthians 7:19, 'Circumcision is nothing'? The context in 1 Corinthians 7 is worth reviewing. The paragraph of which it is a part, 1 Corinthians 7:17–24, is the central element in a ring composition or ABA pattern, with 7:1–16 and 7:25–40 being the A elements. The function of 7:17–24 is to reinforce Paul's advice to be content in one's life situation. Paul states repeatedly in the chapter not to seek a change in marital status (7:2, 8, 10–16, 26–27, 37, 40). Then in verses 17–24 he says three times to remain in the situation in which one is called, with reference to the two great social dividers of his day concerning the questions of race and social class (7:17, 20, 24). Whether a Christian is married or single, *circumcised or uncircumcised*, slave or free, makes no difference to God, or more accurately 'before God' (as v. 24 literally says), so there is no need to change.

That Paul chose circumcision and slavery to make his point takes on greater significance in the light of Galatians 3:26–28, where Paul lists the same three pairs relevant to 1 Corinthians 7 when he proclaims that 'in Christ Jesus . . . there is neither Jew nor Greek, neither slave nor free, neither male or female' (my tr.). The great divisions of the ancient world are redundant in the light of the new creation. What matters in Galatians 3 is being 'children of God through faith' (Gal. 3:26). The more we recognize the imminence of the final transition to the fullness of the new creation, the greater our indifference to the distinctions and distinctive concerns of life in this present age (cf. 1 Cor. 7:29–31). The tension and relationship between the 'already' and 'not-yet' aspects of Christian eschatology must inform the moral and ethical thinking and behaviour of the believer. Only in this light can Paul say that circumcision is nothing.

In one sense, Paul's sentiments in verses 18–19 concerning the relative irrelevance of circumcision, despite the obvious contradiction of Genesis 17:10–14, and other texts, finds some sympathy in passages like Deuteronomy 10:16 and Jeremiah 4:4, where membership in the covenant community is a matter of the heart, not an outward sign. Other figurative uses of circumcision (see Exod. 6:30, Jer. 6:10, 9:26, which speak of uncircumcised lips, ears and heart respectively) also point in Paul's direction. Nonetheless, 1 Corinthians 7:19a is radical by comparison with these Old Testament attitudes. It is one thing to say circumcision has a deeper significance, but quite another to say it has no significance. Paul's opinion here with respect to the Law of Moses could not be more negative. In Acts 21:21 refusing circumcision is equated with 'apostasy [*apostosia*] from the teaching of Moses' (my tr.).

However, Paul's next words (1 Cor. 7:19b) come as even more of a surprise and apparently create a confusing paradox: literally, 'but [or instead] keeping God's commands', an idiom well translated as, 'Keeping God's commands is what counts' (TNIV). Translations differ on whether the relationship between the clauses suggests simply that while (un)circumcision does not matter, keeping God's commandments does, or if opposites are implied, such that while (un)circumcision means nothing, keeping God's commandments means everything. Other translations say keeping God's commandments 'matters' (NAB, NASB) or is 'what counts' (NET, NIV), is 'what is important' (NJB, NLT) or 'is everything' (NRSV). Either way, if the first half of 1 Corinthians 7:19 assaults the law, the second half seems to contradict this, saying something strongly in its favour.

Both the main terms 'keeping' and 'commands' seem to point to Paul's saying that what is paramount is observing the Law of Moses. Apart from here in verse 19, the noun 'commandments' or 'command-ment'[42] is used thirteen times in Paul's letters. In the majority, ten times, it refers unambiguously to the Jewish Law (Rom. 13:9; Eph. 2:15; 6:2; Titus 1:14; and six times in Rom. 7). In the other three occurrences of the word (1 Cor. 14:37; Col. 4:10; 1 Tim. 6:14) it refers

---

[42] Gk. *entolē*.

to Paul's own instructions. The verb 'to keep'[43] can mean 'obey' in the New Testament and is used regularly with reference to keeping the Law of Moses, namely 'God's commandments' (Rev. 12:17; 14:12), the 'commandments' (of Moses; Matt. 19:17), 'the Law of Moses' (Acts 15:5), the sabbath commandment (John 9:16) and 'the whole [Jewish] law' (Jas 2:10).[44] In 1 Corinthians 7:19 the related noun is used,[45] which refers to 'persisting in obedience' (BDAG 1002d). Thielman is right to observe that 'keeping the commandments/laws' in Jewish and Christian literature regularly referred to obeying the Mosaic law (Sir. 29.1; 32.23; Wis. 6.18; Matt. 19:17; Josephus, *Ant.* 8.120, 395; 17.159).[46] Since circumcision was an essential part of the law (Gen. 17:10–14, 23–27), what could Paul possibly have meant when he said that 'circumcision is nothing' but the important thing was 'keeping God's commands'? How is this paradox to be resolved?[47]

A common way forward is to draw on the venerable distinction between different parts of the law (civil, ceremonial and moral), dating back, in part at least, to the time of Origen.[48] According to Thielman, for example, Paul distinguishes between parts of the law that count and parts that do not count. Circumcision falls squarely into the latter category.[49] But most of the rest of the law is still valid as 'the command-ments of God'.

The problem with this explanation is threefold. First, while the distinction between moral, ceremonial and civil law may be a useful heuristic in a limited sense, and it does acknowledge the salvation-historical distinctions between Israel as a theocracy in the land and the church, scholars rightly judge it to be anachronistic. Paul K. Jewett explains with reference to the Old Testament:

> It should always be remembered, however, that the distinctions Christians make between 'moral' and 'ceremonial' laws in the Old Testament, was hardly perspicuous to the Hebrew mind. In the Old Testament, cultic and ethical, moral and ceremonial, religious and civil enactments are all worked together, with no sense of

[43] Gk. *tereō*.

[44] The other 'commandments' to be 'kept' are those of Jesus in John 14:15, 21; 15:10; 1 John 2:3–4; 3:22, 24; 5:3.

[45] Gk. *terēsis*; cf. Wis. 6.18 and Sir. 32.23.

[46] Thielman 1992: 237–240.

[47] N. T. Wright 1996: 137: 'Paul is expressing a sharp paradox.'

[48] See C. J. H. Wright 1992a: 102; 1992b: 205.

[49] Thielman 1992: 237–240.

impropriety, since they all express the will of Yahweh for his covenant people Israel.[50]

Hermann N. Ridderbos makes the related point in relation to Paul's letters: 'In the epistles that have been preserved to us, nowhere is a distinction made explicitly between the moral and ceremonial, particularistic parts of the law.'[51] Paul, Jews contemporary with him, and early Christians make no such distinctions.

Secondly, the distinction is also impractical, with many laws defying classification. Schreiner writes, 'Many of the so-called ceremonial laws have a moral dimension that cannot be jettisoned.'[52] The same goes for the civil laws, such as in Deuteronomy 25:4, which speaks of not muzzling an ox while treading out the grain, a law from which Paul (in 1 Cor. 9:9 and 1 Tim. 5:18) and many Jews contemporary with Paul derive a moral lesson.[53]

The third problem for the resort to moral, ceremonial and civil categories of law is that such a strategy ultimately proves unsuccessful in explaining the tensions in Paul's thought on the law. It fails to do justice to the absolute nature of Paul's negative statements about the law (see chapter 2) and misses the rhetorical function of the other statements.

Two parallel texts in Galatians undermine further treating 1 Corinthians 7:19 as a paradox expressing both negative and positive assessments of the Law of Moses. In both cases the thing contrasted with the irrelevance of circumcision is not part of the law that remains (contra Thielman et al.) but something that replaces the law entirely:

For in Christ Jesus neither circumcision nor uncircumcision counts for anything; the only thing that counts is *faith working through love*. (Gal. 5:6)

For neither circumcision nor uncircumcision is anything; but *a new creation* is everything! (Gal. 6:15)

The complement to the repudiation of circumcision in both Galatians 5:6 and 6:15 is a substitute for the law. Since 'faith through love' and 'a new creation' cannot be understood as the Law of Moses in part

[50] P. K. Jewett 1971: 118.
[51] Ridderbos 1975: 284.
[52] Schreiner 2010: 94.
[53] See Ciampa and Rosner 2010: 403–408.

or in any sense,[54] it seems only reasonable that neither should 'keeping the commandments of God' in 1 Corinthians 7:19 be taken that way.

A fourth example of Paul's contrasting law observance with something far more important appears in Romans 14:17. There, in the context of discussing Jewish laws of diet and sabbath, he concludes that such laws are not determinative of Christian community or character: 'For the kingdom of God is not food and drink but righteousness and peace and joy in the Holy Spirit.' Paul regularly puts something in the place of the law (see further chapter 4).

In this light 1 Corinthians 7:19 thus turns out to be not a paradox, marking off one part of the law from another, but polemic. Instead of obeying the law, Paul says the important thing is to obey 'the commandments of God', which, I believe, the Corinthians would have understood as Paul's own instructions in the letter. The only other place where 'command' appears in 1 Corinthians is in 14:37: 'what I am writing to you is a *command* of the Lord'.[55] Furthermore, if 'God's commands' in 1 Corinthians 7:19 refer to the Law of Moses, in whole or in part, this would be the only place in his letters where Christians are instructed to 'keep' them. Christians do not 'keep' the commands of the Law of Moses, but instead 'keep' some other commands (that are nonetheless from God). When Paul speaks of Christians positively vis-à-vis the law, he does not say that they 'keep' or 'obey' it but rather that they 'fulfil' it.[56] Paul's words in 7:19 are formulated in a deliberately polemical fashion.

What, then, is the precise referent of the divine *commandments* Paul expects the Corinthians to *keep* in 1 Corinthians 7:19b? Barrett suggests Paul has in mind 'an obedience to the will of God as disclosed in his Son [which is] far more radical than the observance of any code, whether ceremonial or moral, could be'.[57] Can we be more specific than saying Paul is referring to God's will? Furnish looks for a more contextual definition of 'God's commands' in this text, taking the phrase to mean 'leading one's life in accordance with God's call (v 17a), as one who belongs to Christ (v 22)'.[58] Without developing the thought, Garland suggests that verse 19b might be a reference to avoiding *porneia*: 'What matters is keeping the commandments of

---

[54] On the meaning of these phrases see the section in chapter 4, '"Circumcision is nothing" complements'.

[55] Cf. Col. 4:10 and 1 Tim. 6:14, where 'command' likewise refers to apostolic instruction.

[56] See further chapter 3 in this book.

[57] Barrett 1968: 169.

[58] Furnish 1999: 62.

God (7:19), in particular, avoiding fornication (7:2) . . . Paul implies that the important distinction is not between those who are married and those who are celibate but between those who avoid fornication and those who fall prey to it.'[59] The context supports Garland's reading of the text.[60]

As I have argued elsewhere (with Roy Ciampa), the commands to 'flee sexual immorality' (NET) in 6:18 and 'glorify God with your body' (NET) in 6:20 dominate chapters 5–7 and are never far from view.[61] As it turns out, from 6:12 to 7:16 Paul uses ten imperative mood verbs. Interestingly, six of these refer either directly or indirectly to keeping away from sexual immorality: 6:18, 20; 7:2–3, 5, 9.[62] And it would certainly not be unlike Paul to give this command prominence, as 1 Thessalonians 4:3, penned by Paul in Corinth, demonstrates: 'It is God's will that you should be sanctified: that you avoid sexual immorality [*porneia*]' (my tr.). In its broader context, then, 1 Corinthians 7:19 resonates with Paul's argument in chapter 7 and its significance would not have been lost on the Corinthians. The better readers would have seen its relevance to the main message in the chapter and 'connected the dots' to conclude that not only is circumcision nothing, but marriage and singleness are also nothing, and keeping God's commandments is what counts, especially avoiding sexual immorality.

Three moves

In my view Paul does three things with the law and each one must be fully heard without prejudicing the others: (1) polemical repudiation; (2) radical replacement; and (3) whole-hearted reappropriation (in two ways). These respectively correspond to treating the law as *legal code*, *theological motif* and *source for expounding the gospel and for doing ethics*. When describing Paul's view of the law, too often scholars notice only one or at best two of these impulses and minimize, ignore or deny the other(s).[63] All three moves occupy a vital place in what Paul says about and does with the law.

---

[59] Garland 2003: 299, 306.

[60] In the broader context of the whole letter, perhaps a second basic command of God that Paul would have the Corinthians think of is the avoidance of idolatry (cf. 10:14 and 10:31).

[61] Ciampa and Rosner 2006, 2010.

[62] The other four consist of commands concerning divorce: 7:11–13, 15.

[63] Davies (1982: 4) was right when he noted in 1982 that 'Paul's view of *Torah* [the law] has led interpreters, concentrating on one aspect to the exclusion of others, to oversimplify his response to it' (italics original).

The three moves are evident in 1 Corinthians.

1. The first move, of repudiation, can be seen in the negation of circumcision in 1 Corinthians 7:19a. Another instance is in 1 Corinthians 9:20, where Paul says simply 'I myself am not under the law'.

2. The second, replacement, is evident in 7:19b with the call to keep God's commandments, that is, apostolic instructions. Elsewhere in 1 Corinthians replacement of the Law of Moses can be seen clearly in 9:21, where Paul says, 'but am under Christ's law'.[64]

3a. The first form of the third move, the reappropriation of the law as prophecy, as a witness to the gospel of Jesus Christ, can be seen in 8:5–6, where the language of Deuteronomy 6:4 governs Paul's wording and argument.[65] Alluding to Israel's Shema, Paul reaffirms strict Jewish monotheism along with finding Christ embedded within the very definition of that one God/Lord of Israel.[66] It is also evident in 15:45, where Paul uses Genesis 2:7, 'the first man, Adam, became a living being', to point to the significance of Jesus Christ, who is of equally universal bearing as our first ancestor.[67]

3b. The second form of the reappropriation of the law, using the law for questions of conduct, can be seen at various points. For example, Paul closes 1 Corinthians 5 and his call to exclude the incestuous man with the words 'Expel the wicked person from among you' (5:13b NIV), a quotation of a frequent expression of the LXX of Deuteronomy, where it is used on six occasions to signal the execution of a variety of offenders (13:5; 17:7; 19:19; 21:21; 22:21; 24:7; cf. Judg. 20:13).[68] In 9:24 Paul asserts that Deuteronomy 25:4, the call not to 'muzzle the ox', 'was written for us', helping to establish that ministers of the gospel deserve to be supported financially. And in 10:11 Paul asserts that the events of the exodus and wilderness wanderings 'were written down as warnings for us', supporting his warning against sexual immorality and idolatry.

Evidently, Paul does not think his utter repudiation and radical replacement of the Law of Moses entail its complete redundancy. The question to ask in these cases is not *which bits* of the law are still useful,

---

[64] The interpretation of not being 'under the law' and 'the law of Christ' receives more detailed attention in chapters 2 and 4 respectively.

[65] Chapters 5 and 6 take up these and many other examples from Paul's letters of law as prophecy and wisdom respectively.

[66] See Ciampa and Rosner 2007: 717–718; and Rosner 2007: 127–128.

[67] See Ciampa and Rosner 2007: 746–777.

[68] The Greek word for 'expel', *exairō*, occurs only here in the NT, suggesting Paul's intentional and explicit use of the formula from Deuteronomy. See Ciampa and Rosner 2007: 709–710.

but *in what sense* is the law valuable for Christians. In short, Christians are instructed by the law, but not as Jewish law. Instead, Paul models reading the Law of Moses as prophecy and as wisdom.

The subtle influence of Scripture in 1 Corinthians 7:17–24 itself points indirectly to a rejuvenated role for the law in determining Christian conduct. Paul conceives of conduct as 'walking' (in v. 17) 'before God' (v. 24), appeals to a saving event as forming the identity of the people of God in verse 23a (reminiscent of the exodus), possibly alludes to Leviticus 25:42 in verse 23b and gives the 'call of God' a key place in everyday life throughout the paragraph. All these show that Paul continues to draw on the Hebrew Bible, including the law, when he formulates moral teaching and seeks moral guidance.

To summarize, the table overleaf suggests Paul's approach to the law in 1 Corinthians consists of three moves. As we will see in the following chapters, the same pattern can be observed in most of Paul's other letters (see chapter 7 for seven more summary tables).

The way forward

In terms of method, three guidelines steer the solution to the puzzle of Paul and the law that I am defending and expounding in this book.

Look at all of the evidence

As already mentioned, in my view too many studies of the subject limit the investigation to the undisputed Pauline epistles and concentrate on texts using the word *nomos*. Along with widening the net to the traditional Pauline corpus, we need to take into account four classes of evidence: (1) what Paul says about the law; (2) what he does with the law; (3) what he does not say about the law (that one might have expected him to say); and (4) what he says about other things (that one might have expected him to say about the law).

The Jewish context of Paul's interactions with the law must also be kept in mind. The question of Paul and the law is a subset of the larger question of the relationship between Paul and Judaism. Critical evidence in this connection includes Paul's use of certain Old Testament texts, such as Leviticus 18:5 (see chapter 2), the character of the Pentateuch itself and the use of the law in the Psalms. And intertestamental Jewish texts that bear on the subject of the Law of Moses supply critical background to Paul's teaching on the law and often set it in sharp relief.

Table 1.1 Paul and the law in 1 Corinthians

Text	Repudiation	Replacement	Reappropriation as Prophecy	Reappropriation as Wisdom
7:19	'circumcision is nothing'	'Keeping God's commands is what counts' (my tr.)		
9:20–21	'I am not under the law' (my tr.)	'I am under the law of Christ' (my tr.)		
8:5–6			Allusion to Deut. 6:4 – 'there is but one Lord' (my tr.), establishing Christ as Lord	
15:45			Use of Gen. 2:7, 'the first Adam became a living being' (my tr.), to underscore the universal signifi-cance of Christ	
5:13b				Words from Deuteronomy quoted to enforce the expulsion of the incestuous man
9:9				Deut. 25:4, 'do not muzzle the ox . . .' (my tr.), quoted to support the argument for paying ministers
10:11				The exodus and wilderness wanderings 'were written down for our moral instruc-tion' (my tr.)

Use the biblical-theological method

The subject of Paul and the law can be investigated from many angles. It is, for example, a topic in New Testament exegesis, Christian ethics, church history and systematic theology. While not disputing the legitimacy of such work, the present study is a biblical-theological investigation. This means that as far as possible I seek to adopt the terms and categories Paul himself uses and take seriously the way in which he frames the question in terms of salvation history. Many studies impose categories of thought and terminology that are alien to Paul's historical context and consequently skew the results of the investigation. The best biblical theology comes from patient, inductive enquiry. To signal my intention, Paul's own words form the chapter titles of this book and each chapter closes with a section 'In Paul's own words (a summary and paraphrase)'.

In connection with Paul and the law, impatience leads, for example, to not allowing Paul to say just one thing (or at most two things) at a time. According to my understanding, in 1 Corinthians 7:19 Paul says something negative about the law, effectively rejecting and replacing it. Keen to find a synthesis in Paul's thought that allows for a positive view of the law, many scholars seem unwilling to consider this possibility. Paul's full understanding of this complex subject is not in view in any single text or even chapter. The genre of Paul's letters and his forceful style of communication mean that his discussions of the law, which usually appear as a supporting point in a larger discussion, supply only part of the picture.

Treat the law as a unity

As noted in my discussion of the meaning of 'law' earlier in this chapter, Paul generally deals with the law as a unity. If his letters are marked by negative and positive statements about the law, the question to ask is not 'which bits' of the law he refers to in each case, but the hermeneutical question of 'in what sense', or 'as what'? In my view asking the question of 'the capacity in which' or 'the force with which' the law meets the Christian resolves the tension between the negative and positive material.

In developing a hermeneutical solution to the puzzle of Paul and the law I am seeking to apply the widely held view that early Jews and Christians treat the law as a unity. I am also following the lead of a number of scholars who have on occasion responded to the question of Paul and the law in this light, even if in most cases only in passing. These include F. F. Bruce, D. A. Carson, Roy E. Ciampa, Donald Hagner, Richard B. Hays, Markus Bockmuehl, P. T. O'Brien and, at points, Thomas Schreiner and Stephen Westerholm.

A hermeneutical solution

In his letters Paul undertakes a polemical rereading of the Law of Moses, which involves not only a repudiation and rejection of the law as 'law-covenant' (chapters 2 and 3) and its replacement by other things (chapter 4), but also a reappropriation of the law 'as prophecy' (with reference to the gospel; chapter 5) and 'as wisdom' (for Christian living; chapter 6). This construal finds support not only in what Paul says about the law, but also in what he does not say and in what he does with the law. And it highlights the value of the law for preaching the gospel and for Christian ethics.

Chapter Two

'Not under the law'
Explicit repudiation of the law as law-covenant

The Law of the Decalogue has no right to accuse and
terrify the conscience in which Christ reigns through grace,
for Christ has made this right obsolete.

(Martin Luther)[1]

The law, *as* law, is meant to be observed: only so can the
life and blessings that it promises be enjoyed.

(Stephen Westerholm)[2]

The Law originally had the primary function of *defining
the identity of God's elect people*, the Jews. Within that
hermeneutical perspective, the Law was understood
primarily as *commandment*.

(Richard B. Hays)[3]

If the crux of the problem of understanding Paul and the law is the
tension between Paul's negative critique and positive approval of the
law, the task of this and the next chapter is to look squarely at Paul's
negative stance towards the Law of Moses. Chapters 5 and 6 will
consider the positive things he says about (and does with) the law. As
it turns out, 'circumcision is nothing' is nothing out of the ordinary
in Paul's thought. The apostle to the Gentiles makes negative remarks
about the Jewish law at a number of points in eight of his letters. This
material raises critical questions: What is the nature and extent of
Paul's opposition to the law? Does Paul abolish only parts of the law?
Does he just take issue with a legalistic misunderstanding of the
law or a nationalistic abuse of the law? Or is his critique more radical?

[1] Luther 1962: 4.
[2] Westerholm 2004b: 37, italics original.
[3] Hays 1996b: 163, italics original.

These questions have not only theological and ethical import, but are also of historical interest. Paul and the law must be seen as a subset of the bigger question of the apostle's relationship with Judaism. If Paul opposed keeping the Law of Moses, did he cease being a Jew? When Paul arrived at Jerusalem after his second missionary journey, he was accused by zealous Jews of teaching 'all the Jews who live among the Gentiles to commit apostasy [*apostasia*] with respect to the teaching of Moses, telling them not to circumcise their children, or live according to our customs' (Acts 21:21, my tr.). Eusebius in the fourth century reports that Ebionites regarded Paul to be an apostate from Judaism.[4]

It is no accident that two of Paul's earliest letters, Galatians and 1 Thessalonians, renounce the Law of Moses and the Jewish opponents of the gospel respectively. Compare his assertion in Galatians 2:16 and elsewhere, that 'by observing the law no one will be justified' (my tr.), with 1 Thessalonians 2:14–16, where he charges that the Jews 'displease God'. In both places Paul appears to have departed from his heritage. Paul's responses to the Jewish law and to Judaism are obviously related.

Scholarly opinion is divided as to whether Paul the Jew is guilty of the charge of apostasy. Alan F. Segal, for example, argues in his book *Paul the Convert* that Paul would have been judged to be a renegade by both Jews and Jewish Christians.[5] And it is true that Paul apparently abandoned some Jewish practices when he lived among Gentiles (1 Cor. 9:22; Gal. 1:13–14). Dunn, on the other hand, argues that 'Paul could never have accepted that his apostleship to the Gentiles constituted apostasy from Israel. Quite the contrary, he was apostle to the Gentiles precisely as apostle *for* Israel, apostle *of* Israel.'[6] The question comes down to the interpretation of Paul's own claims over against the reactions he provoked. Either way, the issue places Paul's relationship to the Law of Moses in a sharply polemical setting.

In assessing the nature and degree of Paul's negative stance towards the law we need to consider three types of evidence: (1) what he says about the law; (2) what he does not say in connection with the law; and (3) what he does with the law. All three support the view that Paul repudiates the law as commandments and law-covenant. What I mean by this will become apparent as we proceed. This chapter surveys the first type of evidence, that is, the apostle's explicit repudiation of

[4] Eusebius, *Hist. eccl.* 3.27.4.
[5] Segal 1990.
[6] Dunn 1998: 269, italics original.

the law. Chapter 3 examines more indirect and implicit repudiation. The third, what Paul does with the law, will be examined in chapters 5 and 6.

Statements against the law can be found in Romans, 1 and 2 Corinthians, Galatians, Ephesians, Philippians, Colossians and 1 Timothy. I will treat related material together, rather than letter by letter, to avoid repetition. This strategy in no way denies that contingent circumstances have given rise to the expression of Paul's views. Nonetheless, a synthesis that respects the varied historical and literary contexts is both possible and necessary. Failing to observe usage across Paul's letters diminishes our understanding no less than ignoring context within a letter. As it turns out, many of these texts are saying roughly the same thing in different ways. The variety of expression and its wide distribution across eight of Paul's letters is testimony to the strength of conviction with which Paul held his views and the basic consistency with which he expressed them.

To examine all of the relevant terms and texts in Paul's letters on the law in detail would subvert my aim of presenting a comprehensive view of the subject of a readable length. Instead, we will look at what I consider two of the most critical pieces of evidence, both of which shed ample light on the extent and nature of Paul's opposition to the law. First, Paul's assertion that believers are 'not under the law'; and secondly, his use of Leviticus 18:5, which promises life to those who do the law. A third section will offer a brief survey of further evidence to check and clarify the main findings, and a fourth will consider the question of the origin of Paul's view.

Not under the law

Paul uses the phrase 'under the law', *hypo nomon*, eleven times (in eight verses) in Galatians, Romans and 1 Corinthians. A common mistake in determining what it means is to assume a technical sense across the board, committing the fallacy of 'totality transfer', where the various meanings are gathered from diverse contexts and read into every occurrence. Although the meaning of 'under the law' is disputed, context, usage and syntax make clear what Paul meant each time it is used. An initial survey of usage shows that Paul employs the phrase

- six times to indicate that Jews are 'under the law' (1 Cor. 9:20 [3×]; Gal. 3:23; 4:4–5);

- three times to affirm that believers are not 'under the law' (Rom. 6:14–15; Gal. 5:18);
- once to affirm that he himself is not 'under the law' (1 Cor. 9:20); and
- once to address believers who want to be 'under the law' (Gal. 4:21).

In the following analysis of Paul's letters I seek to establish three points.

1. Jews are those who are 'under the law', meaning that they are 'bound by the demands of the Mosaic law code and subject to its sanctions'.[7]

2. Gentiles are not and were never 'under the law'. Even though the second point follows logically from the first (if Jews are those who are 'under the law', then Gentiles are not), certain texts are widely seen as contradicting it. Part of my discussion below is thus a defence of Paul's consistency of usage with respect to the phrase.

3. If for Paul being 'under the law' can have a neutral sense, simply referring to Jewish identity (as in point one above), it can also carry more ominous and negative connotations: 'under the law' can be equivalent to being 'under the penalty and power of sin', and is thus something from which Jews need to be released (and something to which being under grace can be favourably contrasted). The semantic range of 'under the law' is analogous to Paul's use of 'flesh'. Just as *sarx* in Paul's letters refers simply to the human body[8] but at other points denotes the 'sinful nature',[9] so too 'under the law' can point to either neutral or negative statuses depending on the context.

Jews are 'under the law'

In terms of defining 'under the law' 1 Corinthians 9:20, where the phrase occurs four times, is a good place to start. The verse indicates that Jews are 'under the law', but Christians, represented by Paul, are not: 'To the Jews I became like a Jew, to win the Jews. To those *under the law* I became like one *under the law* (though I myself am not *under the law*), so as to win those *under the law*' (TNIV).

In 1 Corinthians 9:19–23 Paul explains his strategy of adapting his behaviour according to the context in which he worked: 'Though I

[7] Westerholm 2004a: 300.

[8] Cf. 1 Tim. 3:16: 'he appeared in a *body*' (TNIV); lit. 'God was manifest in the *flesh*' (AV).

[9] E.g. Gal. 5:16 in many English translations.

48

am free and belong to no one, I have made myself a slave to everyone, to win as many as possible' (NIV). Jews and Gentiles appear as the first two examples of Paul's flexible approach in verses 20 and 21 respectively. In terms of defining 'under the law', the phrase appears here as a virtual synonym for 'Jew'. By 'Jews' in verse 20 Paul means the same thing as he does in the same verse by those 'under the law'. Although technically 'under the law' may include Jewish proselytes (cf. the other group in Gal. 2:15, 'Jews by birth'), the first two sentences of verse 20 are parallel and should be understood synonymously: 'To the Jews I became as a Jew, in order to win Jews' and 'To those *under the law* I became as one *under the law* . . . so that I might win those *under the law.*'

Galatians 4:4–5 fits this pattern of usage. In Galatians 4:4 God's Son is 'born of a woman, born under the law', by which Paul simply means that Jesus was a Jew. In Galatians 4:5 Paul writes of Christ coming 'to redeem those under the law' (NIV), again meaning Jews. Coming from the other side, as BDAG (478c) observes, the word 'Jew(s)' [in the New Testament] often has a 'focus on adherence to Mosaic tradition', suggesting 'conformity to Israel's ancestral belief and practice'. Psalm 147:19–20 makes the same point with synonymous parallelism:

> [God] declares his word to Jacob,
>> his statutes and ordinances to Israel.
> He has not dealt thus with any other nation;
>> they do not know his ordinances.

Although Paul is a Jew in terms of his ethnicity and heritage, according to 1 Corinthians 9:20 he apparently no longer understands himself to be a full member of Judaism, and does not consider himself a Jew in the sense that such a person understands his or her relationship with God to be based on adherence to the Mosaic covenant. In Acts Luke has Paul twice call himself a Jew (21:39; 22:3), but significantly Paul prefers to call himself an 'Israelite' in his letters (Rom. 9:3–4; 11:1; 2 Cor. 11:22; Phil. 3:5).[10]

To become like a Jew in order to win Jews would entail adapting his language and lifestyle to better communicate the gospel message in a way that would not seem foreign to one who (like Paul) was raised

---

[10] Bird 2012: 27: 'The designations "Israel" and "Israelite" were evidently positive for Paul as they denoted continuity with God's purposes and plan first announced to the Patriarchs and fulfilled in the economy of God's action in Jesus Christ.'

in a Jewish household. Acts 16:1–3 (where Paul circumcises Timothy) and 21:20–26 (where Paul purifies himself and goes to the temple) are suggestive of Luke's understanding of how Paul would become like a Jew for the sake of the Jews. Romans 14:1 – 15:6, where Paul is tolerant of Jewish Christians who wished to continue traditional observances, may also be comparable.[11] For Paul there is nothing inappropriate about keeping the law as a matter of tradition or preference, as long as such law-keeping is not imposed on Gentiles and does not undermine the fellowship of brothers and sisters in Christ (cf. Gal. 2:11–14).

As Conzelmann points out, Paul 'does not have to deliver the Jews from their practice of the Law, but from their "confidence" in the Law as a way of salvation'.[12] Although Paul understood himself to live under the conditions of the new covenant in Christ rather than under the Law of Moses, he was happy enough to observe the law when living among those who might have stumbled if he had not. Paul probably has in mind issues like the observance of food and sabbath laws, as well as the halachic standards of the communities where he ministered. As Fee puts it,

> [t]he difference [between Paul's behaviour] and that of his social companions is not in the behavior itself, which will be identical to the observer, but in the reasons for it. The latter abstain because they are 'under the law'; it is a matter of religious obligation. Paul abstains because he loves those under the law and wants to win them to Christ. Despite appearances, the differences are as night and day.[13]

Whereas Paul did not qualify his statement that to the Jews he became like a Jew (since he was a Jew, in the most basic sense), he does qualify his statement that he became like someone under the law when working among those under the law, by pointing out that he himself was 'not under the law'. On this score Paul is like all believers in Christ, whom he affirms in Romans 6:14–15 and Galatians 5:18 are 'not under the law'.

The Jews are not only those who are 'under the law', *hypo nomon*; they are also 'in the law', *en nomō* (Rom. 2:12),[14] and 'from the law',

---

[11] See the discussion of this text in chapter 1, 'Definition of terms: "Paul", "law" and "believer"'.

[12] Conzelmann 1975: 160.

[13] Fee 1987: 429.

[14] Most English versions translate Rom. 2:12 as 'under the law'.

ek nomou (Rom. 4:14).[15] They are, so to speak, both possessed by the law as well as possessors of the law (cf. Rom. 9:4: 'to the [Israelites] belong . . . the giving of the law' [*nomothesia*]). The law defines Jewish identity – according to both Paul and the Old Testament, Jews are law-people, those who read and hear the law (2 Cor. 3:15; cf. Exod. 24:7).

It is clear that for Paul 'under the law' can simply mean under the jurisdiction of the Law of Moses, non-pejoratively, the natural state of every Jew, which is a key element of their identity that distinguishes them from Gentiles.

Gentiles are not 'under the law'

If in 1 Corinthians 9:20 'under the law' is equivalent to 'Jew' in verse 21, 'those not having the law', *anomos*, is a reference to Gentiles. As Paul says in Romans 2:14, Gentiles 'do not have the law'. Paul moves from those who were under the law to those who were not. The same word for 'without law', *anomos*, is used four times in 1 Corinthians 9:21, with two different referents in mind: 'To those *outside the law* I became as one *outside the law* (though I am not *outside God's law* but am under Christ's law) so that I might win those *outside the law*.'

As BDAG (85c) affirms, in the first part of verse 21 *anomos* refers 'to the Mosaic law, used of gentiles as persons who do not know it' and 'those without (Mosaic) law (= "gentiles")'. The implied contrast with the previous reference to those 'under the law' indicates 'those not having the law' refers to Gentiles as people who are 'not under the [Mosaic] law'. Paul's statement that he became like one of them suggests he adapted to the ways and customs of the Gentiles among whom he worked. Of course, under those circumstances halachic concerns would not have been an issue.

Even though in 1 Corinthians 9:20 and Galatians 4:4–5 'under the law' means 'Jew' and 'not under the law' means 'Gentile', according to many scholars Paul's writing in Romans 6:14–15 and Galatians 3:23, 4:21 and 5:18 fails to observe this distinction. At first blush Paul's argument that Gentile believers in Christ are 'not under the law, but under grace' (Rom. 6:14–15 NIV; cf. Gal. 5:18) seems to contradict his definition in 1 Corinthians 9:21 of Gentiles not being under the law.

Why do Gentiles need to be freed from the dominion of the law if they were never under the law in the first place? This problem is

[15] NRSV: 'the adherents of the law'.

51

frequently cited in the secondary literature as an example of Paul's imprecision at best, and at worst, his muddle-headedness.[16] Westerholm is a good example:

> In Romans 6:14–15 Paul declares that the Roman believers (Gentiles presumably included!) are not 'under law but under grace'; the implication would seem to be that prior to their experience of grace, they were in bondage to the law. Still clearer is [Rom.] 7:4–6: those to whom Paul writes have 'died to the law'; in the process they were discharged from it.[17]

Paul's apparent inconsistent use of 'under the law' has been explained in three ways.[18] All three proposals raise difficulties. First, it may be that Paul is writing of the law from an exclusively Jewish-Christian perspective in Romans 6 – 7, or even 5 – 8, and therefore does not have Gentile believers in mind when he speaks of being under the law or the need to be released from the law. This view is difficult to sustain given that Romans 6 in particular gives no indication that Paul is addressing only Jewish Christians and not Christians in general; the statements about union with Christ in his death and resurrection are too embracing (e.g. 6:3: 'all of us who have been baptized into Christ Jesus') to be restricted to Jewish Christians.

Secondly, perhaps Paul can legitimately speak of Gentiles being under the law by analogy, in that according to Paul being led by their consciences Gentiles are a 'law to themselves' (Rom. 2:14). The problem with this view is that the argument in Romans 1 – 2 does not pave the way for seeing Gentiles as 'under the law', a phrase Paul elsewhere uses only with reference to the Law of Moses,[19] since in 2:17–24 and 4:14, 16 the law is clearly the possession of Jews. Romans 2:12 and 3:19 contain an equivalent phrase, often translated as 'under the law', employing the preposition *en* plus the dative of *nomos*. Romans 3:19 reads, 'Now we know that whatever the law says, *it says to those who are under the law* [*tois en tō nomō lalei*]' (TNIV). In context this refers to Jews, those existing 'in the realm of' the Law of Moses.

---

[16] See Westerholm 2004a: 415–417.

[17] Ibid. 415.

[18] See ibid. 415–417. He lists Donaldson as a proponent of the first two, and Sanders and himself as supporters of the third.

[19] Schreiner (1998: 325) contends, 'the word *nomos* [in Rom. 6:14–15, 'not under the law'] refers to the Mosaic law (most commentators), not to religion'. The absence of the article in the phrase *hypo nomon* is not significant, since prepositional phrases often include an anarthrous noun.

Attempts to include Gentiles in this orbit are unconvincing.[20] Schreiner explains, 'the parallel phrase (*hosoi en nomō*, "as many as in the law") in [Rom.] 2:12 specifically distinguishes Jews from Gentiles'.[21] Indeed, Romans 2:12 makes it clear that only Jews are under the law: 'All who sin apart from the law [Gentiles] will also perish apart from the law, and all who sin under the law [Jews] will be judged by the law', NIV). Before we get to 6:14–15 in Romans we learn that only Jews are 'under the law'.

Thirdly, Paul may be generalizing unconsciously from what he perceives as the plight of Jews, treating it as though it were universal. This view, while only explicitly accusing Paul of 'imprecise usage',[22] certainly weakens his overall argument by introducing an inconsistency at a basic level. If Paul does not consistently distinguish Jews and Gentiles vis-à-vis the Law of Moses, and mistakenly (or at best sloppily) conceives of Gentiles in the situation of Jews, this clashes with a patent distinction between them that he observes in Romans 1:18 – 3:8. If Paul is unclear about the plight of the Gentiles, his solution is less compelling. In my view the evidence for Paul's inconsistency on the matter of whether Gentiles are or were under the law needs to be reconsidered.

As it turns out, the relevant texts in Romans and Galatians do not say that Gentiles are or were under the law. For starters, Paul says that believers are 'not under the law, but under grace', not believers are 'no longer [*mēketi*] under the law, but under grace'. While the temporal indication that all believers are *no longer* under the law may be a valid implication, it is also possible that it is not a logically necessary entailment. Logically, to say that someone is not under something does not necessarily mean that they ever were. This is not special pleading but rather a plea to read the verses in the broader contexts of the books in which they appear. Many seem to miss this basic point.

A tongue-in-cheek analogy, which could easily be reversed, may help. Imagine you are addressing a mixed audience of Australians and people from England in Australia and that you wish to argue that living in Australia offers a better lifestyle. Prior to drawing your conclusion, you marshal arguments to support your case, such as the fact that in Australia the weather and food are better and the people friendlier. You conclude with the exhortation 'Enjoy your life, for you

[20] E.g. Murray 1959: 106–107.
[21] Schreiner 1998: 168.
[22] Westerholm 2004a: 416.

are not in England, but in Australia.' This does not mean that all of the hearers were previously in England; just that in your opinion Australia is a better place in which to live. The statement is intended to extol Australia, by proclaiming its superiority over the alternative, without necessarily saying that all of the audience had ever lived in the less preferred place. Your words would make sense if the option of being in that place is on the table, some of the group are from the place being used as a negative contrast and its relative demerits have just been discussed.

Each of the elements of our analogy holds for Paul's statement in Romans 6:14–15 that believers are 'not under law but under grace'. Paul is addressing a mixed audience of Jewish and Gentile believers in Christ. In chapter 6 his aim is to convince them that genuine obedience to God that leads to holiness and eternal life (6:22–23) results from being united with Christ in his death and resurrection. As a Jew Paul feels obliged to answer a legitimate Jewish objection to his teaching, as he does customarily throughout the letter. In this case it is that the Law of Moses was given by God to Israel to lead to holiness and life. His repudiation of the law in 6:14–15 builds on what he has already said about the law in earlier chapters that contradict this claim: 'through the law comes the knowledge of sin' (3:20); 'law brings wrath' (4:15); when 'law came in . . . the trespass multiplied' (5:20). In 6:16 Paul assumes the close association of law and sin, asserting that to be 'under law' is to be a 'slave of sin, which leads to death'. In this context, for Jewish believers, 'not under law but under grace' is a reference to their transference from one realm to another, but for Gentile believers it is simply a preferring of one realm (under grace / in Christ) over the main alternative (under the law).

The train of thought in Romans 5 and 6 reveals the purpose of the contrast in 6:14. At the end of chapter 5 Paul traces two impressive domino effects: law increased sin, which brought death; but sin increased grace, which leads to life (5:20–21). In chapter 6 Paul confronts the objection that if sin increases grace, 'why not go on sinning so that grace might increase even more?' (my tr.). His answer is that our union with Christ in his death and resurrection has broken the dominion of sin. This indicative is expounded in verses 1–10, followed by the imperative in verses 11–14 not to go on sinning. Thus the words 'you are not under law but under grace' recall the assertion in 5:20 that law increases sin. They are introduced with an explanatory *gar*: the reason that 'sin shall no longer be your master' (6:14a NIV) is that 'you are not under law but under grace' (6:14b). Paul is not reminding all of his readers of their transference but rather reassuring them all that faith in Jesus breaks the power of sin to which law is an accomplice.

But what of Romans 7, which Westerholm describes as 'still clearer' evidence that Paul taught that Gentiles were under the law?[23] There Paul appears to go a step further than saying that believers are not under the law, and explains how they are released from the law. The question is whether Paul is speaking of both Jewish and Gentile believers, or only Jewish ones? Careful attention to context is critical. Romans 6 and 7 are closely related. According to Moo, '7:1–6 repeats with respect to the law many of the same points that were made in Rom. 6 with respect to sin'.[24] Similarly, Dunn thinks 7:1–6 gathers up 'the main thrust of chap. 6, but now with reference to the law'.[25] In Romans 7 Paul makes clear that the law does not lead to obedience, holiness and life, but rather, by increasing sin (cf. Rom. 5:20), it leads to death.

Romans 6 and 7 function respectively as exposition of Paul's gospel to both Jews and Gentiles and defence of that law-free gospel in the light of Jewish objections.[26] In the latter, as Paul makes clear in the first verse, he is not addressing all believers but rather 'brothers and sisters . . . who know the law' (7:1), that is, Jewish believers. The contents of the chapter confirm this address, especially in verses 7–25 where Paul speaks of his own experience as a Jew under the law. The second appearance of the vocative *adelphoi* in the chapter is in verse 4 where Paul assures those who were under the law that 'you also died to the law through the body of Christ' (NIV). This information is not directly applicable to Gentile believers, who are set free from sin through Jesus Christ (see ch. 6), but not from the law, since they were never under it in the first place. As noted above, Romans 2:17–24 and

---

[23] Ibid. 415.

[24] Moo 1996: 409. Tobin (2004: 222) argues, 'One can begin to understand this rather complex passage only by realizing the extent to which Paul draws on and develops the vocabulary and viewpoints of Romans 6. Much of the vocabulary he uses in 7:4–6 he already used in Romans 6.' He notes 'risen from the dead' (6:4, 8; 7:4); 'newness' (6:4, 8; 7:4); 'old', 'oldness' (6:6; 7:6); 'death' (6:3–5, 8–9; 7:5); 'die' (6:2, 7–8, 10); 'serve' (6:6; 7:6); 'members' (6:13; 7:5); 'sin' (6:1–2, 5, 7, 10; 7:5).

[25] Cf. Dunn (1988a: 358), who lists the various ways in which Rom. 7:1–4 recalls Rom. 6.

[26] Thanks are due to Dr Richard Gibson for pointing this out to me. Tobin and Gibson argue that this pattern can be observed throughout the letter. Cf. Tobin 2004: 86: 'each of the livelier, more argumentative sections takes off from some aspect of the preceding expository section . . . Each of the argumentative sections turns to issues raised by the expository sections of the letter.'

4:14, 16 make it clear that Jews are under the Law of Moses, and Romans 2:12 says that Gentiles are not. Being under law and under sin are of course not unrelated. The latter is a consequence of the former, but the two groups (those under the law and those under sin) are not coterminous. Paul creatively brings law, sin and death together in 8:2 where he affirms of all believers, both Jewish and Gentile, that Christ Jesus has 'set you free from the law of sin and of death'.

When we come to Galatians, the phrase 'under the law' appears five times. In the first three (3:23 and 4:4–5) it designates the Mosaic era in which Jews were subject to a legal code, just as 'under grace' in Romans 6:14–15 describes the new age inaugurated by the death and resurrection of Christ in which the distinction between Jew and Gentile is redundant.[27] The order of the next two occurrences of 'under the law' in Galatians is significant. In 4:21 Paul writes of the Gentile Christians 'who want to be *under the law*' (NIV). Clearly, part of Paul's purpose in Galatians is to persuade them not to take this step. Then in chapter 5 Paul demonstrates that not being under the law does not lead to moral licence; walking by the Spirit takes the place of walking by the law. Climactically, in 5:18 Paul concludes that 'if you are led by the Spirit, you are not under the law' (TNIV). The prior reference to wanting to be under the law in 4:21 makes it clear that those to whom Paul writes in 5:18 are not already under the law and needing to be released, but instead are those who are tempted to be under the law and need convincing not to be. Being 'led by the Spirit' is the Galatians 5 equivalent of being 'under grace' in Romans 6. It represents a new era in salvation history, one that, as Galatians 5:16 asserts, leads to moral transformation: 'walk by the Spirit, and you will not gratify the desires of the sinful nature' (TNIV).

While Paul nowhere says that Gentiles are 'not under the law', *ouk hypo nomon*, in 1 Corinthians 9:21 he says as much in different language, describing them as 'those outside the law' (NRSV) or 'those not having the law' (TNIV), *tois anomois*. In my view Romans and Galatians do not contradict this assertion.

'Under the law' is sometimes equivalent to being 'under sin'

Having seen that for Paul Jews are those who are 'under the law' and Gentiles are not, we are left to probe the semantic range of the phrase in its various contexts. By way of review, in the context of 1 Corinthians 9 Paul uses 'under the law' as a way of referring to the

---

[27] Dunn 1988a: 339; Moo 1996: 406.

ordinances of the Law of Moses that mark off Jews from other nations as God's people. As noted above, Paul claims that when he lives among Jews he conducts himself as 'under the law', referring to his willingness to conform his conduct to 'demands whose observance or non-observance is for Paul a matter of effective missionary strategy rather than moral right or wrong: food laws and the observance of Sabbaths and festivals must be in mind'.[28] This is consistent with the strife in the church in Galatia, where those to whom Paul writes are apparently eager to be 'under the law' (4:21) by observing 'days, months, seasonal festivals, and years' (4:10, my tr.), effectively wanting to 'live as Jews' (2:14, my tr.). In such contexts 'under the law' is to be understood as 'under the law as commandments marking out the people of God from the nations'.

Elsewhere in Galatians, however, and in Romans Paul uses 'under the law' more negatively and his response to such a condition is far from neutral. Even if the Galatian believers sought to live 'under the law' in the above sense, Paul warns them that such a move entails something far more worrying if it is seen as additional to faith in and union with Christ. Paul uses the phrase to mark a distinction in terms of salvation history, depicting the law as an enslaving power:

> Now before faith came, we were imprisoned and guarded *under the law* until faith would be revealed. Therefore the law was our disciplinarian until Christ came, so that we might be justified by faith. But now that faith has come, we are no longer subject to a disciplinarian. (Gal. 3:23–25)

The same usage is found in Galatians 4:5, where those 'under the law' are in need of redemption and adoption as God's children now that God's Son has come. Likewise, as noted in the previous section, Galatians 5:18 draws a contrast between under law and under grace in salvation-historical terms: 'But if you are led by the Spirit, you are not under the law' (TNIV; cf. Rom. 6:14–15).

The syntax of *hypo nomon*, 'under the law', leaves open both the neutral and negative connotations. Louw and Nida (37.7b) take the preposition *hypo* with the accusative as 'a marker of a controlling person, institution, or power – "under, under the control of, under obligation to"'. BDAG (1036c) concurs, locating the sense 'in ref. to power, rule, sovereignty, command', and translating Galatians 4:5 as

---

[28] Westerholm 2004a: 417.

'those who are under (the power of, obligation to) the law'. The construction takes on more or less oppressive overtones (or better, 'undertones'), depending on who or what it is that one is subject to. A married woman in Romans 7:2 is *hypandros*, literally 'under a man', reflecting without any negative implications a patriarchal world view. On the other hand, several of the other uses of *hypo* with the accusative show how ominous the construction can become.

In 1 Corinthians, outside 1 Corinthians 9:20 instances of 'under the law', Paul uses *hypo* with the accusative three times. Whereas the first is neutral ('all under the cloud' [10:1]), the second and third are positive references to the lordship of Christ ('he must reign until he has put all his enemies under his feet' [15:25; cf. 15:27]). Such usage does not move the reader to take 'under the law' in a negative way. However, Galatians and Romans are a different story.

Outside the 'under the law' references, Paul uses *hypo* with the accusative seven times in Galatians and Romans in ways that move the reader to take 'under the law' quite negatively, through 'guilt by association'. As well as being 'under the law' people are 'under the control of' or 'under obligation to' a number of things to their distinct disadvantage:

- 'all who rely on the works of the law are *under a curse*' (Gal. 3:10)
- 'the scripture has imprisoned all things *under the power of sin*' (Gal. 3:22)
- 'now that faith has come, we are no longer *under a disciplinarian*' (Gal. 3:25, my tr.)
- 'but they remain *under guardians and trustees* until the date set by the father. So with us; while we were minors, we were *under the elemental spirits of the world*' (Gal. 4:2–3, my tr.)
- 'we have already charged that all, both Jews and Greeks, are *under sin*' (Rom. 3:9 ESV)
- 'we know that the law is spiritual; but I am of the flesh, sold into slavery *under sin*' (Rom. 7:14)

The only time in Romans Paul uses *hypo* with the accusative not in reference to what humans are subject to is in Romans 16:20, where the connotation is still that of an oppressive (if more advantageous) control: 'The God of peace will shortly crush Satan *under your feet*.'

Such considerations lead translations like the NRSV legitimately to translate 'under the law' in Galatians 4:21 and 5:18 in more sinister terms as '*subject to* the law',[29] and 'under sin' in Galatians 3:22 and Romans 3:9 as '*under the power of* sin', 'under a disciplinarian' in Galatians 3:25 as '*subject to* a disciplinarian', and 'under the elemental spirits of the world' in Galatians 4:3 as '*enslaved to* the elemental spirits of the world'. Clearly, the syntax of being 'under' something or someone may carry negative connotations. Where such a sense is uniform, as it is in Galatians and Romans, this predisposes a similarly negative understanding of 'under the law'.

Summary of 'under the law'

What have we learned then about Paul and the law from his use of the phrase 'under the law'? An investigation of this theme raises a number of themes we will revisit in connection with other material in Paul's letters. Distinctive here is the conclusion that if Paul himself is willing to live under the *direction* of the law as marking out the historic people of God from the nations for the sake of the progress of the gospel (in 1 Corinthians), he is not willing to live under the *dominion* of the law as law-covenant or legal code (in Galatians and Romans). Paul's opposition to the law as a master has to do with its alliance with sin and its obsolescence in the light of the new era of grace and the Spirit. These reasons are clarified and amplified in the following section.

The law as a failed path to life

The association of the Law of Moses with life is clear from Sirach 17.11:

> He bestowed knowledge upon them [the Jews],
>   and allotted to them the law of life [*nomon zōēs*].

Paul, on the other hand, did not believe that the law could give life. As he reasons in Galatians 3:21, 'if a law had been given that could impart life, then righteousness would certainly have come by the law' (NIV). In Paul's view neither life nor righteousness comes through the law.[30]

---

[29] Cf. Moo 1996: 389, commenting on Rom. 6:14–15: 'under the law' means 'subject to the rule of Mosaic law'.

[30] Cf. Westerholm 2004a: 419: 'For Adamic human beings the law cannot serve as a path to righteousness and life.' Watson (2004) argues that Paul saw a conflict between the law's promise to give life to those who obey it and the accounts in the law of what actually happened to the generation that received the laws of Torah – they were condemned to die in the desert! For a summary of Watson 2004 see the section in chapter 5, 'The "prophetic" character of the law'.

If 'not under the law' (Rom. 6:14–15; Gal. 3:23; 4:21; 5:18) is Paul's most compact and comprehensive rejection of the law, Paul's clearest explanation for his opposition to the law emerges from his use of Leviticus 18:5: 'the one who does these things will live by them' (Gal. 3:12; Rom. 10:5).

The interpretation of Leviticus 18:5

Paul cites Leviticus 18:5 on two occasions in discussions of the relationship of the law to salvation in Christ (Gal. 3:10–14; Rom. 9:30 – 10:10). Solving 'the puzzle of Paul's use of Lev. 18:5'[31] goes a long way towards clarifying Paul's response to the law and, in terms of recent scholarship, also serves as a litmus test for perspectives old and new. The importance of this Old Testament text for Paul's view of the law and justification (along with Hab. 2:4 and Gen. 15:6) can scarcely be overstated. Paul takes Leviticus 18:5 to be a summary of the law *as law*.

In its original literary context Leviticus 18:5 is a call to obey the Law of Moses with a promise of the reward of life. The 'these things' a person is meant to 'do' are explained in the first half of the verse as 'keep my decrees and laws' (NIV). This is a description of the Mosaic laws in general, with a possible focus on the purity laws that are so prominent in Leviticus 18 – 20 (the so-called Holiness Code). While grammatically it is possible to understand the Hebrew as 'the one who does these things will live *in them*', in the sense of 'according to them', it is better to take the preposition instrumentally: 'the one who does these things will live *by them*'.

Sprinkle gives five arguments in the verse in favour of life being the result of obedience.[32] First, Leviticus 18:29 is parallel to Leviticus 18:5 in reverse; there, being 'cut off' is the result of 'doing' certain 'abominations', suggesting that in 18:5 life is the result of 'doing' the commandments. Secondly, several passages describe the blessing of dwelling in the land as dependent on obeying the statues, judgments or commandments (Lev. 18:26, 28; 2:22; 25:18–19; 26:3–4, 5b). Thirdly, 'life' in Deuteronomy is a covenantal blessing contingent on obedience to the law (e.g. Deut. 4:1; 5:32–33; 8:1; 16:20; 30:6, 15–20). Fourthly, the LXX, which Paul quotes, takes the verse to be promising 'life' as a result of 'doing'. And fifthly, the book of Ezekiel, in allusions to Leviticus 18:5 (Ezek. 20:11, 13, 21) and in the restoration

---

[31] Dunn 1998: 153.
[32] Sprinkle 2007: 31–34.

oracle (37:1–14; note life-language), renders life as a result of keeping the law.

The promise of 'life' to those who obey probably refers to the covenantal blessings of Leviticus 26:3–13: 'If you follow my decrees and are careful to obey my commands . . . [you] will live in safety in your land' (Lev. 26:3, 5 NIV). The opposite outcome is also evident, with Leviticus 26:14–39 warning of covenant curses for disobedience: '[I]f you reject my decrees and abhor my laws . . . and so violate my covenant . . . I will bring the sword upon you to avenge the breaking of the covenant' (Lev. 26:14, 25, my tr.). Failing to 'do these things' (Lev. 18:5) will result in expulsion from the land and ultimately death.

With this context in mind J. D. G. Dunn is representative of the New Perspective in concluding that when Paul quotes Leviticus 18:5, he is in dialogue with Deuteronomic covenant theology and opposes the view that the life of believers in Christ should be regulated by the law. According to Dunn, Paul does not have the reward of eternal life in view, but rather the promise of 'lengthening of days' in the land:[33] 'Keeping the statutes and ordinances of the law was the way of living appropriate to the covenant.'[34] The focus of Leviticus 18:5 for N. T. Wright is likewise the doing of the law as a way of marking off Jews from Gentiles (circumcision, food laws, special days), something that has been overturned by the new covenant. Galatians 3:11–12 'simply asserts that the Torah as it stands is not the means of faith, since it speaks of "doing", which is best taken in the sense of doing the things that mark Israel out'.[35] In my view this reading of Leviticus 18:5 and its meaning for Paul does not do justice to Galatians 3 and Romans 10, nor does it take into account the crucial history of interpretation of the text.

The only literary influence of Leviticus 18:5 outside Paul in the New Testament is an allusion in Luke 10:28, a part of the narrative introduction to the parable of the good Samaritan. The episode in question is introduced in Luke 10:25 with a lawyer asking Jesus a question: 'What must I do to inherit eternal life?' Jesus asks him, 'What is written in the law?' (v. 26). He replies, correctly reciting the two great commandments of love of God and neighbour. Jesus responds with the words 'you have answered right; *do this and you will live*' (v. 28, my tr.). Jesus' answer indicates 'a deferral of promises [in

[33] Dunn 1998: 152–153.
[34] Dunn 1988b: 612.
[35] N. T. Wright 1991: 150.

Lev.] to a future eschatology'.[36] Gathercole draws the telling conclusion:

> Luke 10 is usually omitted from discussions of the relation between Torah observance and 'life.' The emphasis among most 'new perspective' scholars is to see Torah as regulating life and not so much in terms of leading to future life. . . . Luke 10 contributes evidence to the contrary understanding of Lev. 18:5.[37]

The way Jews contemporary with Paul understood Leviticus 18:5 is also instructive for an investigation of Paul's use. This is especially the case for two reasons.[38] First, Paul uses the Leviticus text to sum up the theology of the Mosaic covenant, which is the theology of his opponents. And secondly, the phrase Paul uses in Romans 10:5 to introduce Leviticus 18:5, 'the righteousness that comes from the law', is the same phrase he uses in Philippians 3:9 to describe his own stance prior to his conversion. We should expect Paul to follow an understanding of Leviticus 18:5 that mirrors the interpretation of (at least some of) his contemporaries.

A number of authors have considered the influence of the text in early Judaism, including Sanders, Dunn and N. T. Wright, and (in response) Gathercole, Watson and Sprinkle.[39] Sprinkle's monograph is the most thorough examination and makes a good case for the *Damascus Document* and the *Psalms of Solomon* as the best candidates for a comparison and contrast with the apostle's use.[40] Leviticus 18:5 is critical for the understanding of the law in both of these Jewish texts, just as it is for Paul. However, if Paul understands the words 'the one who does these things will live by them' in a negative way, and cites them to show that the law does not lead to life because of human disobedience, the *Damascus Document* and the *Psalms of Solomon* take them much more positively. Sprinkle explains:

> [T]he *Damascus Document* alludes to Leviticus [18:5] to signify the life-giving power of the 'hidden' halachic laws revealed to the founders of the Qumran community. The *Psalms of Solomon* allude

---

[36] Gathercole 2004: 140.
[37] Ibid.
[38] See ibid. 142.
[39] See Sprinkle 2007 for references.
[40] Ibid. 195: 'Lev 18:5 attracts its most noteworthy reflection in Paul, Qumran (esp. the *Damascus Document*), and the *Psalms of Solomon*.'

to Lev 18:5 to show that the remnant of Israel, who truly 'love the Lord' and 'walk in his commandments' (14:1–2a), have eternal life through their obedience to the Mosaic law.'[41]

The two texts interpret Leviticus 18:5 as promising eschatological life to those who keep the commandments of God. In short, Leviticus 18:5 undergoes a transformation in later Jewish interpretation (in line with what we saw in Luke 10), whereby 'lengthening of days' turns into 'eternal life'.[42] The eternal life the community enjoys and looks forward to is dependent on their 'doing these things' (4Q266 11 1–2). For the *Damascus Document* (see CD 2.14 – 3.20), Leviticus 18:5 offers an explanation for the plight of Israel and for their own sectarian response: the nation has surrendered to the 'evil inclination' by disobeying the law, and the new community possesses life because it obeys the life-giving instructions referred to in Leviticus 18:5:

> But when those of them who were left held firm to the command-ments of God he instituted his covenant with Israel forever, revealing to them things hidden, in which all Israel had gone astray: his holy Sabbaths, his glorious festivals, his righteous laws, his reliable ways, and the desires of his will, *which if a man does he will live by them.* He disclosed to them and they 'dug a well,' yielding much water; and *whoever spurns them shall not live.* (CD 3.12b–17a)

Throughout the *Damascus Document* 2 – 3 God preserves those who 'remain steadfast in God's commandments' (CD 3.13; cf. 2.18, 21; 3.5–6). These good deeds are 'a precondition of God's eschatological revelation'.[43]

Likewise in the *Psalms of Solomon* 14.1–5 as a precondition for life there is an emphasis on 'doing' the commandments of the law. In the *Psalms of Solomon* 4.3, which alludes to Leviticus 18:5, eschatological life is also a blessing conditional on 'doing these things', understood to be the Law of Moses:

> The Lord is faithful to the ones who love him in truth, to the ones who endure his discipline, to the ones who walk in the righteousness

---

[41] Ibid.
[42] For further evidence that Jews increasingly took Lev. 18:5 as referring to eternal life see Avemarie 1996: 104–116; Gathercole 2004.
[43] Sprinkle 2007: 198.

of his commandments, in the law, which he commanded us for our life. The righteous of the Lord *will live by it forever*; the paradise of the Lord, the trees of life, are his pious ones. Their planting will never be uprooted, they will not be plucked out all the days of heaven; for the portion and inheritance of God is Israel. (*Pss Sol.* 14.1–5)

The *Damascus Document* forges a specific connection between escaping the curse of the covenant and this obedience. In its use of Leviticus 18:5 the text builds on the theology of Leviticus 27 and Deuteronomy 27 – 30, where blessing is contingent on obedience to the law and a curse comes from disobedience. The community at Qumran has received the blessings of life and escaped the curse by 'doing these things'. Leviticus 18:5 is understood in this narrative context to refer to the covenantal blessing of life.

If Jews contemporary with Paul understood Leviticus 18:5 positively as promising eternal life to those who do the law, the contrast with Paul's approach to the text could hardly be more stark. For Paul, the emphasis on obedience to the law for the attainment of eschatological life is the very antithesis of the gospel; 'doing these things', that is, keeping the law, is not the solution. The failure to observe the law and the forfeiting of life is in fact the problem from which those under the law need to be rescued. Reading Paul's quotations of Leviticus 18:5 in context is essential.

The law and life in Galatians and Romans

If a key issue is the question of what Paul means by 'life' in his quotations of Leviticus 18:5 in Galatians 3:12 and Romans 10:5, it is worth considering how 'life' is used elsewhere in the two letters. The issue in Galatians 3:10–14 is quite explicitly one of life and death: failure to do the law leads to a curse and death; paradoxically, faith in Christ's death leads to life. The verb *zaō*, 'to live', turns up in two other places in Galatians with reference to Paul or believers. In both cases there is an implicit contrast between eternal life in Christ or the Spirit and the life that the law failed to deliver. Leviticus 18:5, and its negation by human sinfulness, is the rationale for such contrasts:

For through the law I died to the law, so that I might *live* to God. I have been crucified with Christ; and it is no longer I who *live*, but it is Christ who *lives* in me. And the life I now *live* in the flesh I *live*

> by faith in the Son of God, who loved me and gave himself for me.
> (Gal. 2:19–20)[44]

> There is no law against such things. And those who belong to Christ
> Jesus have crucified the flesh with its passions and desires. If we
> *live* by the Spirit [and not by doing the law], let us also be guided
> by the Spirit. (Gal. 5:23b–25)

The noun *zōē*, 'life', occurs just once in Galatians: 'If you sow to
your own flesh, you will reap corruption [*phthora*[45]] from the flesh;
but if you sow to the Spirit, you will reap eternal life from the Spirit'
(Gal. 6:8). Once again, a connection with Leviticus 18:5 is noticeable.
In Galatians 5 Paul had associated the law with the flesh, a connection made clear also in Romans 7:5: 'While we were living in the
flesh, our sinful passions, aroused by the law, were at work in our
members to bear fruit for death.' If the law, weakened by the flesh,
leads to death, by contrast walking according to the Spirit leads to
eternal life.

'Life' in Romans tells the same story. Leading up to chapter 10 Paul
associates the law with death in 7:10 ('the very commandment that
promised life proved to be death to me') and 8:2 ('For the law of the
Spirit of life in Christ Jesus has set you free from the law of sin and
of death').[46] On the other hand, eternal life is repeatedly associated
with Christ and/or the Spirit (see 5:17–18, 21; 6:4, 22–23; 8:10).[47] The
verb 'to live' is especially common in Romans, occurring twenty-three
times. It is announced as a key theme in the seminal quotation of
Habakkuk 2:4 in Romans 1:17 ('The one who is righteous *will live* by
faith'). As with the noun 'life' Paul uses the verb 'to live' to signify
the eternal life associated with Christ Jesus (6:8, 13), and living
according to the flesh and the law leads to death (7:1–3, 9). Romans
8:13 contains both threads: '[I]f you live according to the flesh, you
will die; but if by the Spirit you put to death the deeds of the body,
you will live'.

To sum up, the broader contexts of both Galatians and Romans
support 'life' in the quotations of Leviticus 18:5 to mean 'eternal life'.

[44] Gk. *zaō* occurs five times; see italics.
[45] The term is a synonym for death; cf. its use in 2 Pet. 2:12.
[46] Rom. 8:6 connects the flesh with death: 'To set the mind on the flesh is death, but
to set the mind on the Spirit is life and peace.'
[47] Cf. also Rom. 11:15, which speaks of eternal life in relation to the Jews accepting
the gospel.

In terms of the argument of Romans, both 5:12–21 and 7:1–25 consider the efficacy of the Law of Moses as a remedy for sin and a source of life. According to Paul, Jews expected that through the law Israel would undo Adam's sin and the consequence of death, so that the law would expel sin, achieve righteousness and bring life. Paul judges the law to have failed on all counts and finds the solution in the death of Christ. Both chapters are replete with the vocabulary of sin, law, death and life.[48] In 5:12–21, rather than solving the problem of sin and death, the law multiplied Adam's transgression and increased sin (see 5:21).

In 7:1–25 Paul effectively revisits the narrative of Genesis 2 – 3. Cranfield notes Paul's intentions with reference to the focus on coveting:

> It was perhaps with that narrative [of Gen. 2 – 3] in mind that Paul chose the tenth commandment as his example; for there is a specially close relationship between the tenth commandment, understood in the generalized way we have noted . . . and the prohibition of Gen 2.17, and between the *epithymia* which the commandment forbids and what is described in Gen 3.6.[49]

Paul's conclusion in Romans 7:10 has obvious relevance to Leviticus 18:5: 'the very commandment that promised life proved to be death to me'.

Thus the theme of life and death in Galatians and Romans has three facets, all of which are reinforced by Paul's use of Leviticus 18:5 (in Gal. 3 and Rom. 10): (1) although it was meant to lead to life, (2) the law led to death, and (3) the gift of eternal life is found in Christ Jesus. This is the broader context in which Paul's treatment of the Levitical formula should be read.

Leviticus 18:5 in Galatians 3

Having set the scene by tracing the theme of 'life' in the two letters, Paul's actual quotations of Leviticus 18:5 in Galatians and then in

[48] *Hamartia*: 5:12 (2×), 13 (2×), 20–21; 7:5, 7 (2×), 8 (2×), 9, 11, 13 (3×), 14, 17, 20, 23, 25; *nomos*: 5:13 (2×), 20; 7:1 (2×), 2 (2×), 3–6, 7 (3×); 8–9, 12, 14, 16, 21–23 (3×), 25 (2×); *thanatos*: 5:12 (2×); 14, 17, 21; 7:5, 10 (2×), 13, 24; *zōē*: 5:10, 17–18, 21; 7:10; *zaō*: 7:1–3, 9. For my understanding of the connection between Rom. 5 and 7 I am indebted to my colleague Dr Richard Gibson.

[49] Cranfield 1975: 350–351. Cf. Dunn 1988a: 399: 'Paul's first answer to the question ("Is the law sin?") [in Rom. 7:7] is to refer in effect once again to Adam and the story of Gen 2–3: the relation between the law on the one hand and sin and death on the other as depicted in Gen 2–3 is the vital clue.'

Romans may now be considered. In Galatians 3:10–14 Paul engages in a dialogue between no fewer than four scriptural texts: Deuteronomy 27:26; Habakkuk 2:4; Leviticus 18:5; and Deuteronomy 21:23. The passage is worth quoting in full:

> For all who rely on the works of the law are under a curse; for it is written, 'Cursed is everyone who does not observe and obey all the things written in the book of the law' [Deut. 27:26]. Now it is evident that no one is justified before God by the law; for 'The one who is righteous will live by faith' [Hab. 2:4]. But the law does not rest on faith; on the contrary, 'Whoever does these things will live by them' [Lev. 18:5, my tr.]. Christ redeemed us from the curse of the law by becoming a curse for us – for it is written, 'Cursed is everyone who hangs on a tree' [Deut. 21:23] – in order that in Christ Jesus the blessing of Abraham might come to the Gentiles, so that we might receive the promise of the Spirit through faith. (Gal. 3:10–14)

Michael Bird and Andrew Das summarize the logic of Paul's argument in nine steps.[50] By my presenting their views slightly differently, Paul's exposition of the three main texts may be summarized as three syllogisms:

FIRST SYLLOGISM
Major Premise: Deuteronomy 27:26 threatens a curse to all who do not keep the law.
Minor Premise: It is evident that no one keeps the law perfectly.
Conclusion: Hence everyone related to the law is under a curse.

SECOND SYLLOGISM
Major Premise: Habakkuk 2:4 states that the righteous will live by faith.
Minor Premise: Yet the law is not of faith, because it requires dutiful performance of its commands.
Conclusion: Hence no one is justified before God by the law.

THIRD SYLLOGISM
Major Premise: Leviticus 18:5 promises life to those who keep the law.

---

50 Das 2001: 145–146; Bird 2011: 137.

Minor Premise: It is evident that no one keeps the law perfectly.
Conclusion: Hence no one receives life through the law.

Some would suggest the fundamental issue was not a failure to keep the law perfectly but that Israel's history had revealed an even more radical problem – the inability of the law to keep people and the nation as a whole from adopting a posture of wholesale rebellion, idolatry and apostasy. The law never created the kind of people God had intended, the kind that is brought about for the first time through the life given to those who have faith in Christ Jesus.[51]

According to this understanding, Leviticus 18:5 had promised life for doing those things commanded in the Mosaic law, and Deuteronomy 27:26 threatened curses on those who rebelled against the law. History had shown that Israel had never been able to 'cash in' on the promise of Leviticus 18:5 but had rebelled grievously against the law and brought the curse of the law in their exile and continuing experience of judgment. The law had turned into a dead end rather than a way of life. That was all in contrast to faith in Christ. Habakkuk 2:4 stated that the righteous would live by faith (understood as faith in Christ), which was resulting in blessing (rather than a curse) for Jews and Gentiles alike.

The exact nature of 'the curse of the law' in Galatians 3:10 is also hotly debated. Does the curse refer to the failure of the covenant and subsequent exile of corporate Israel (e.g. N. T. Wright)? Or is the curse more individualistic in focus (e.g. Schreiner)? Perhaps there is a sense in which Paul has both in mind, with both redemptive history and an emphasis on human inadequacy and divine agency in view.[52]

Either way, it is clear that Paul is contrasting two paths to life: one of 'doing what the Mosaic law commands', the other of 'believing in Jesus Christ'; based on two Old Testament proof texts, Leviticus 18:5 and Habakkuk 2:4; leading to two opposing outcomes, the curse of the law and the blessing of Abraham.

Typical of the letter's apocalyptic theology, Paul conceptualizes the achievements of Christ's work in terms of a radical dualism, drawing a sharp distinction between the times before and after the coming of Christ. The letter opens with the dichotomy of the source of Paul's apostleship: it has either a divine or a human origin. Such distinctions are then developed throughout the letter, especially in

---

[51] Thanks are due to Roy Ciampa for alerting me to this alternative.
[52] Suggested by Preston Sprinkle in an unpublished 2010 Evangelical Theological Society paper.

chapters 3–6. Ciampa notes ten,[53] all of which relate to Paul's theology of the law:

Table 2.1 The law and Paul's apocalyptic perspective

Receiving the Spirit	By works of the law	By faith
Two outcomes	The curse of the law	The blessing of Abraham
Walk	Not according to the gospel	According to the gospel
Justified	By works of the law	By faith
Status as	Slaves	Children
Children of	The slave woman	The free woman
Two cities	The present Jerusalem	The Jerusalem above
Realm of	The flesh	The Spirit
Two dominions	Under the law	Led by the Spirit
Two ethical orientations	Vanity	Love

Clearly, Paul's rejection of the law has to do with the arrival of a new economy, dispensation or stage of salvation history, one that replaces the Mosaic law and covenant. Galatians 3:13–14 makes this abundantly clear. Redemption in Christ Jesus involves the blessing of Abraham and the promise of the Spirit, who is the harbinger of the new age, being extended to Gentiles: 'Christ redeemed us from the curse of the law . . . in order that in Christ Jesus the blessing of Abraham might come to the Gentiles, so that we might receive the promise of the Spirit through faith.'

The same point is made in other ways elsewhere in Galatians. The law was an impermanent parenthesis in God's purposes, coming 430 years after the Abrahamic Covenant and lasting only 'until faith would be revealed . . . until Christ came' (3:23–24). Christ 'has set us free . . . [from the] yoke of slavery' (Gal. 5:1), a well-known metaphor for the law (cf. Acts 15:10). The New Perspective answer to the question of what is wrong with the law for Paul is in line with this evidence: in the new age adherence to the Law of Moses, with the identity badges of circumcision and food laws, no longer defines the people of God. While the end of the law in terms of its sociological function of demarcating the people of God is a critical point for Paul, not least in his role as apostle to the Gentiles and his commitment to a universal gospel for both Jews and Gentiles, it is not the whole story and does not exhaust his negation of the law.

---

[53] Ciampa 2000: 312.

Paul's rejection of the law in Galatians 3:10–14 is not just about a new phase in salvation history. Paul's quotation of Leviticus 18:5 in Galatians 3:12 indicates that his polemic against the law is concerned with a contrast between 'doing' and 'faith' as alternate paths to life. In Galatians Paul deploys both a positive and a negative argument in his efforts to persuade Gentile Christians not to put themselves 'under the law': they are already children of Abraham without the law and, in Galatians 3:10–14, 'all who rely on the works of the law [*erga nomou*] are under a curse' (Gal. 3:10a). This is the fourth time Paul has used the phrase 'works of the law' in the letter (cf. 2:16; 3:2, 5). It also turns up in Romans 3:20, 28. 'Works of the law' is Paul's shorthand for 'doing what the law requires'.[54]

Why are all who rely on observing the law under a curse? Paul quotes Deuteronomy 27:26 in Galatians 3:10b to make clear that the problem is that no one does what the law requires: 'for it is written: "Cursed is everyone who does not observe and obey all the things written in the book of the law"' (Deut. 27:26). The law pronounces a curse on all those who fail to keep it. It is not that attempting to do the law is flawed, but rather Paul's point is a simple one that he makes elsewhere in the letter: no one keeps everything that the law requires.[55]

Further confirmation that no one keeps the law is that 'no one is justified before God by the law'. These words sum up what Paul has just said in verse 10. If not doing the law is the problem, verse 11b quotes Habakkuk 2:4 to show that a righteous standing before God is obtained not by way of doing but by faith: 'The righteous will live by faith.' Verse 12a explains why the law is to no avail if the righteous live by faith: 'the law is not of faith' (NASB). The law here is the Law of Moses as a legal code to be obeyed, 'a system of "doing" whereby "works" become prominent and end up defining an individual's status before God'.[56] Those who seek righteousness and life cannot turn to the law since faith is the path to life and the law is of doing, not of faith.

---

[54] See Schreiner 2008: 526–527 for a recent survey of the interpretation of 'works of law'. Cf. Bird 2006: 98, who defines the phrase as 'a metonym for the stipulations of the entire Mosaic code' and notes that such works are 'just as much *ethical* as they are *ethnic*' (italics original). Bird (2006: 96–99) offers a convincing critique of Dunn's and N. T. Wright's attempt to limit the phrase to those laws that functioned as boundary markers between Jews and Gentiles (i.e. circumcision, sabbath-keeping and dietary regulations).

[55] Thielman 1994: 124–125: 'Paul argues clearly in [Gal.] 2:15–16 and 3:10–14 that no one can keep the law and seems to assume that position in more concise and obscure statements in 2:19, 5:3 and 6:13.'

[56] Silva 2004: 243.

Final confirmation that faith in Christ and not doing the law is the way to life is supplied by the quotation from Leviticus 18:5 in verse 12b: 'the one who does these things [the works of the law] will live by them' (HCSB). The verb 'to do' echoes 'works of the law' in verse 10, its semantic equivalent, where it was associated with a curse. The verb 'to live' also sets this verse up as a contrast to 'the righteous live by their faith' (Hab. 2:4). As noted above, some Jews understood this verse to mean that life was conditional upon doing the law. Thus Paul quotes Leviticus 18:5 polemically and we are meant to hear the verse conversely: since no one does the law, the one who fails to do the law will not find life. The law gives life only to those who do it, and as the quotation from Deuteronomy 27:26 says, everyone who does not do everything that the law requires, the 'works of the law', is under a curse, the sentence of death.

Paul presents the Leviticus 18:5 path to life as it was understood by his Jewish contemporaries. The problem is that this path is a 'dead end'. As Habakkuk 2:4 proves, only faith gives life. Universal human sinfulness requires a path that does not involve 'doing'. As verses 13–14 indicate, the alternate path of faith has come in the work of Christ, who redeems us from the curse of the law by his vicarious death, by becoming a curse for us.

Leviticus 18:5 in Romans 10

This picture of the law as a failed path is confirmed by Paul's use of Leviticus 18:5 in Romans 10, with the emphasis shifting from the goal of life to the related goal of righteousness. Righteousness made an appearance in Galatians 3:11 (where Hab. 2:4 was quoted) and is closely associated with life in several Pauline texts (e.g. Rom. 5:18: 'one man's act of righteousness leads to justification and life for all').[57] In Romans 10:5 Paul contrasts the righteousness of the Law of Moses with the righteousness that comes by faith:

> Brothers and sisters, my heart's desire and prayer to God for them [the Jews] is that they may be saved. I can testify that they have a zeal for God, but it is not enlightened. For, being ignorant of the right-eousness that comes from God, and seeking to establish their own, they have not submitted to God's righteousness. For Christ is the end of the law so that there may be righteousness for everyone who

[57] See also Rom. 5:17; 6:13; 8:10. Cf. Ps. 119:40: 'I have longed for your precepts; / in your righteousness give me life'; and Prov. 12:28: 'In the path of righteousness there is life.'

believes. Moses writes concerning the righteousness that comes from the law, that 'the person who does these things will live by them.' But the righteousness that comes from faith says . . . (Rom. 10:1–6a)[58]

If in Galatians 3 Paul contrasts two paths to life, in Romans 10 we see two paths to righteousness. One comes from faith, the other from obedience to the law and is based on doing. One prevails; the other will fail, 'for Christ is the end of the law so that there may be righteousness for everyone who believes'. The assumption that righteousness from the law is a failed path due to human sinfulness is not so much implicit here, as it is in Galatians 3, as it is argued at length earlier in the letter. Paul established in Romans 1:18 – 3:20 that all without distinction or exception are in need of righteousness before God. Specifically, Jews are condemned in 2:17 – 3:8 (see esp. 2:21–23) for their failure to keep the law. If those who do the law can expect life and righteousness, in the context of the argument of Romans, no one fits this category, which means that that law is a failed path to righteousness.

Summary of Paul's use of Leviticus 18:5

Paul concludes in both Galatians 3 and Romans 10, in connection with Leviticus 18:5, that as a result of sin the Law of Moses has failed to bring righteousness and life. Here we come to the heart of Paul's opposition to the law. It is not just that the law is obsolete and a new phase of salvation history has arrived. Nor is it that the law marked off the Jewish people and not the new people of God, which now includes Gentile believers too. It is also not simply that Paul's opposition to the law is that it is not Christ. Sprinkle is right that 'whatever Paul found wrong with the law is contained *in nuce* in his understanding of Lev 18:5',[59] and 'Paul understands the Leviticus formula to be a summary of the law.'[60]

For Paul, the essence of the law as law-covenant or legal code is its call for something to be done in order to find life, and this path has failed, due to the universal sinfulness of humanity, and instead the law has led to death. As Westerholm observes, 'Paul regards the mark of the old covenant as its demand for obedience and sees the reason for its failure in human transgressions.'[61]

---

[58] On Rom. 10:6–9 and its use of Deut. 9:4 and 30:11–14 see the section 'Deuteronomy 9:4 and 30:11–14 in Romans 10:6–9' in chapter 5.
[59] Sprinkle 2007: 1.
[60] Ibid. 193.
[61] Westerholm 1988: 165.

Hence it is no surprise that Paul says that the alternative to being under the law is to be *under grace* (Rom. 6:14–15). Believers in Christ stand in grace (Rom. 5:2; cf. Gal. 1:6). In Galatians 2:21 to put yourself under the law is to 'set aside the grace of God' and to render the death of Christ 'to be without purpose' (*dōrean*; BDAG 266b). It is to 'fall from grace' (Gal. 5:4). As Westerholm puts it, 'Paul believes the coming of the new covenant implies the inadequacy of the old. . . . He characterizes the one as resting on divine grace, the other on human works.'[62]

Clarification and confirmation

Along with 'not under the law' and Paul's use of Leviticus 18:5, two further texts may be examined briefly as key instances of Paul's negative critique of the law: 1 Timothy 1:8–10 and Ephesians 2:15. In part perhaps because they appear in epistles whose authorship is disputed, neither receives much attention in studies of Paul and the law. However, both help clarify the sense in which Paul repudiates and rejects the Law of Moses.

The law used as law is for the lawless

When it comes to the law, 1 Timothy 1:8–10 is among the most intriguing texts in the New Testament. Although obscured in the more recent English translations, the passage contains a memorable play on words involving three 'law' words: 'the *law* [*nomos*] is good, if any one uses it *lawfully* [*nomimōs*], . . . the *law* [*nomos*] is not laid down for the just but for the *lawless* [*anomos*]' (1 Tim. 1:8–9 RSV).

The passage affirms that the law is 'good', but somewhat surprisingly it also asserts that the law is not intended for believers; most take 'the just' or 'the righteous', *dikaioi*, as referring to Christians. Commentators struggle, with some, like Hanson, even judging its sentiments to be un-Pauline.[63]

The context concerns the false teachers in 1 Timothy 1:3–7 who seem to be using the law as a source of speculative thinking involving myths and genealogies. 1 Timothy 1:8–10 functions as indirect polemic against

---

[62] Ibid. 163. Cf. Marshall 1996: 358: 'If works are explicitly put in antithesis to faith in the *Hauptbriefe* [Romans, 1 and 2 Corinthians and Galatians], the later epistles emphasise the more fundamental implicit opposition between grace and works which is the ultimate basis of the antithesis between faith and works. . . . Paul was opposed to any view that regards works as something on which people may depend for salvation rather than purely on divine grace.' The evidence that Marshall cites from 'the later epistles' includes texts from Ephesians and the Pastoral Epistles.

[63] Hanson 1968: 58–59.

these opponents and appeals to commonly accepted tradition ('we know . . . understanding this') concerning the proper use of the law. As Marshall notes, the *nomos* in verse 9 'must surely refer in the context of the preceding verse primarily to the Jewish law'.[64] This is confirmed by impressive correspondence between the Decalogue and the activities listed in verses 9–10 that the law prohibits.[65] To describe this law as 'good' (*kalos*) probably refers to its moral usefulness in restraining evil, but the usage of *kalos* elsewhere in the Pastorals (e.g. 1:18; 2:3; 2 Tim. 4:7) suggests that Paul may also have the divine origin of the law in mind.

What does it mean to use the law 'lawfully'? The NRSV and HCSB translate the adverb as 'legitimately' and the TNIV as 'properly'. This rightly implies a contrast with the way the false teachers were using the law in verse 7, that is, illegitimately and improperly. The word *nomimōs* occurs only twice in the New Testament, here and in 2 Timothy 2:5, with reference to an athlete's being crowned only if he competes 'according to the rules' (NRSV, TNIV, HCSB). That some legal connotations might be present in the word is suggested by the definitions in some of the lexica: BDAG (676a): 'in accordance with rule(s)/law'; Louw and Nida (72.18): 'pertaining to being correct according to rules and regulations'.

Jewish usage clarifies how the 'lawful' use of the law might be understood. In early Jewish texts *nomimōs* is consistently used for observance of the legal requirements of the Law of Moses. Josephus uses the word four times: in *Antiquities of the Jews* 7.151 David is 'justly and *legally* married'; in *Antiquities of the Jews* 11.202, 'he [King Ahasuerus] made her [Esther] his *lawful* wife'; in *Against Apion* 2.152 the ancient Jews 'delivered a *lawful* way of living [contained in the Law of Moses; see 2.149] to others after them'; and *Against Apion* 2.217, in the context of disobedience to the Decalogue, speaks of 'the reward for such as live exactly *according to the laws*'. Philo uses *nomimōs* just once, in *Hypothetica* 7.8, in a discussion of various Mosaic laws, with reference to 'lawful' marriage. And in *Sibylline Oracles* 11.81–82 'a mighty king' speaks of 'pleasing things, which God ordained *according to the law* [of Moses]'.

---

[64] Marshall 1999: 375.

[65] See ibid. 378–379. Dishonouring God in v. 9 (NRSV: 'the lawless and disobedient, for the godless and sinful, for the unholy and profane') is an echo of the so-called first table, the first four commandments. And 'those who kill their father or mother, for murderers, fornicators, sodomites, slave-traders, liars, perjurers' (vv. 9–10) lines up in the same sequence to commandments five to nine.

The following context of 1 Timothy 1:9–10, with its list of sinners and sins, supports taking *nomimōs* in 1:8 as pointing to using the law *as a legal code to punish sin*. With this in mind, a number of commentators, without exploring Jewish usage of the word, come to similar conclusions concerning the meaning of using the law *lawfully* in 1 Timothy 1:8. Kelly translates, 'the law is excellent, provided one treats it *as law*'.[66] Lock argues that the passage teaches that the law must be used 'in accordance with its true spirit, "*as a law*"'.[67] Fee explains that the goodness of the law 'relates to its being used properly, that is, treated *as law*'.[68] And Marshall sees the word as expressing a concern to 'use it [the law] *as law*'.[69]

What is most important for our purposes in this chapter is to notice that the Law of Moses, *as law*, or as a legal code or law-covenant, is not 'laid down for the just', that is, for believers. As Marshall puts it, 'viewed from the perspective of its condemnatory purpose, the law was not "set up" to bind the righteous'.[70] The 'righteous' here are those who do not need the law to tell them what not to do. In context they are those who follow 'sound teaching based on the glorious gospel' (1:10–11). According to Titus 2:11–12, believers in Christ are those taught to live righteously (*dikaiōs*) by the grace of God that has appeared and brought salvation to all.

1 Timothy 1:8–10 teaches that the law used lawfully, as a law code, is not for Christians, but for the lawless. Does this contradict other Pauline teaching on the law? It does not say that the law restrains sin, which would contradict teaching in Romans where the law stirs up sin. Rather, it teaches that the law condemns sinners, which Romans also asserts.

The central assertion of this chapter is that Paul does not believe that believers in Christ read the law with the force of law, or if you like, as law. 1 Timothy 1:8–10 supplies striking confirmation of this position at the lexical level: the law used lawfully, *nomimōs*, is not for the righteous.[71]

Does this text teach that the law is of no use to believers? It does not. The question is not addressed here. 1 Timothy 1:8–10 is a case study in allowing Paul to say one thing at a time. The rest of the

---

[66] Kelly 1963: 205.

[67] Lock 1924: 11.

[68] Fee 1988: 45, italics original.

[69] Marshall 1999: 376, italics added.

[70] Ibid. 377.

[71] In chapter 3 I discuss four terms for the law that function in Paul's letters as descriptions of the law as law: 'book', 'decrees', 'commandments' and 'letter'.

Pastoral Epistles make clear that the law is indeed useful for Christians, as in 1 Timothy 5:18, which quotes Deuteronomy 25:4, and in 2 Timothy 3:15–17, which declares that 'all Scripture is profitable for training in righteousness' (my tr.). That 'all Scripture' includes the law is clear in that the only time 'Scripture' is referred to is in introducing the quotation from the law in 1 Timothy 5:18.[72]

The abolition of the law-covenant

In chapter 1 we noted the tension between Ephesians 2:15a ('[Christ] has abolished the law with its commandments and ordinances') and Ephesians 6:1–2 (where he quotes a commandment for Christian conduct) as well as Romans 3:31 (where he denies that the law is abolished) as a glaring example of Pauline inconsistency with respect to the law. My understanding as to how to resolve this tension will become clear in later chapters of the book (and will be revisited in chapter 7). At this point Ephesians 2:15 repays closer inspection for us to grasp the sense in which the law is abolished for Paul.

If in Ephesians 2:1–10 Paul reveals how the mercy and grace of God solve the plight of every human being, in 2:11–22 he focuses on the plight of the Gentiles as a people estranged from God because of their alienation from Israel. In the former passage all those who believe are 'made alive together with' Christ (v. 5), 'raised together with' Christ (v. 6) and 'seated together with' him (v. 6). In the latter passage Gentile believers are 'citizens together with' the saints (v. 19), 'joined together' into a holy temple (v. 21) and 'built together' into a dwelling place for God (v. 22).[73] God in Christ has achieved peace both between Jews and Gentiles and with himself. As Thielman puts it, Ephesians 2:14–18 'explores precisely how Christ's death brought "peace" (vv. 14,15,17) to a divided humanity and to a humanity divided from God'.[74] It is in this context that Paul's comments about the abolition of the law appear:

> For he is our peace; in his flesh he has made both groups into one and has broken down the dividing wall, that is, the hostility between us. *He has abolished the law with its commandments and ordinances,*

[72] The way in which the law is still of value for Christian ethics is explored in chapter 6.

[73] Each of the six verbs in question has a *syn-* prefix in Greek, underscoring the corporate focus of the whole chapter.

[74] Thielman 2010: 149.

so that he might create in himself one new humanity in place of the two, thus making peace, and might reconcile both groups to God in one body through the cross, thus putting to death that hostility through it. So he came and proclaimed peace to you who were far off and peace to those who were near; for through him both of us have access in one Spirit to the Father.

The clause of most interest for our purposes is verse 15a, which affirms that Christ has abolished the law (see italics above). Although translated as a full sentence in most English versions, in the Greek 'abolished' is a participle that modifies the breaking down (*lysas*) of the dividing wall between Jews and Gentiles in the previous verse: 'Christ tore down the dividing wall *by abolishing the law*' (my tr.) He did this in order to (*hina*) 'create in himself one new humanity' (v. 15b), achieving peace and reconciliation (vv. 16–17).

The verb 'to abolish', *katargeō*, is in fact a favourite word for Paul to describe what Christ does to the law. Its strength in this context can hardly be missed, as it sits in company with 'tearing down' and 'putting to death'. In 2 Corinthians 3:7 Paul uses it in the passive voice to say that the Law of Moses has been 'set aside', with its 'ministry of death, chiselled in letters on stone tablets'. Similarly, in Romans 7:6 believers have been 'discharged from the law', just as a wife is 'discharged from the law concerning the husband' when her husband dies (7:2). In each of these uses someone is released from the obligations to obey certain laws and is free from the sanctions of disobedience to those laws.

But is it only certain elements of the Law of Moses that Christ has abolished in Ephesians 2:15? John Calvin held that Paul intends that only certain ceremonies in the law are abolished.[75] Proponents of the New Perspective hold to a similar position in taking the phrase 'commandments and ordinances' to refer only to those Mosaic laws that marked off Jews from Gentiles, thereby excluding them. While this position does fit with Paul's main idea in the second half of Ephesians 2,[76] the usage of *entolē* and *dogma* does not support a reference to such specific laws, and the categorizing of the law in such

---

[75] Cited in ibid. 169.

[76] See the two purposes of the abolishing of the law in 2:15b–16: making peace between Jewish and Gentile believers and reconciling all humanity in Christ to God. While the first may have required only the removal of laws excluding Gentiles, the latter needed a radical change involving an entirely new era of salvation in which keeping 'the law with its commandments and ordinances' was replaced.

a manner is anachronistic.[77] 'Commandments and ordinances' is better understood as a reference to the content and promulgation of the Law of Moses; 'Paul clearly intends the phrase to refer to the entire Mosaic law.'[78] As Meyer put it, 'the dictatorial character of the legal institute (as a whole, not merely partially) is exhibited'.[79]

In what sense then is the law abolished? Paul's positive reference to the law in Ephesians 6:1–2 suggests that it is not in every sense. F. F. Bruce writes that what has been done away with in Christ is not the law 'as a revelation of the character and will of God' but the law 'as a written code, threatening death instead of imparting life'.[80] Schreiner draws a similar conclusion, arguing that the abolition of the law concerns 'the commanding focus of the law . . . the law in terms of its requirements'.[81]

O'Brien's explanation, building on the suggestion of Carson, points to another perspective on Paul's critique of the law:

> What is abolished is the 'law-covenant,' that is, the law as a whole conceived as a covenant. It is then replaced by a new covenant for Jews *and* Gentiles. . . . Because the old *Torah* as such, that is, the law-covenant, has gone, it can no longer serve as the great barrier between Jews and Gentiles.[82]

The Law of Moses has at its heart the Mosaic covenant, and this covenant is about keeping commandments. Furthermore, that which replaces the Mosaic covenant is the new covenant. The view that the law *as law-covenant* is that which Paul sets aside complements Paul's negative take on the *law as commandments* and represents the most comprehensive (and least ambiguous) way of expressing the capacity in which the law has been abolished by Christ. It is for this reason

---

[77] Cf. Schlatter 1999: 243, who anticipates the emphasis of the New Perspective: 'Done away with through Christ is the restriction of the community to Israel and thus all those ordinances of the Law that established Israel's peculiar separated existence.' Schlatter (222), however, also refuses to restrict Paul's opposition to the law to this matter: 'When giving his final answer to the question of the Law, [Paul] did not address ritual issues such as the value of the Sabbath or washings. Rather, he dealt with the commandment proscribing covetousness (Rom. 7:7).' From Paul's repudiation of the law we learn that justification is on the basis of neither ethnicity nor effort, but rather rests wholly on divine grace through faith.

[78] O'Brien 1999: 197; cf. Thielman 2010: 169.

[79] Meyer 1880: 130.

[80] Bruce 1984: 298.

[81] Schreiner 1993: 39.

[82] O'Brien 1999: 199, italics original.

that the phrase 'law as law-covenant' appears as the subheading of this chapter.

The origin of Paul's view

According to Paul the law is a failed path to life and righteousness because of human transgression, to which God has responded with a tsunami of grace. Paul was not the first to come to this conclusion. Teaching in a range of Old Testament prophetic texts has much in common with Paul's response to the law.

To varying degrees Jeremiah, Ezekiel and Daniel each lament that the Mosaic covenant and law have failed due to human sinfulness and declare that the time has come, or will come, when people must look to God's mercy and grace alone apart from the law. For Paul these prophetic hopes come to fruition in Christ, in the new covenant and in giving of the Spirit.

Jeremiah writes concerning the new covenant:

> The days are surely coming, says the LORD, when I will make a new covenant with the house of Israel and the house of Judah. It will not be like the covenant that I made with their ancestors when I took them by the hand to bring them out of the land of Egypt – a covenant that they broke, though I was their husband, says the LORD. But this is the covenant that I will make with the house of Israel after those days, says the LORD: I will put my law within them, and I will write it on their hearts; and I will be their God, and they shall be my people. (Jer. 31:31–33)

The new era Jeremiah describes is unlike the old one in that, instead of laws on tablets of stone God will graciously put his law 'within them' and 'write it on their hearts'. A new covenant will supersede the old. The reason he gives for this radical change is because Israel 'broke [God's] covenant'. The Mosaic covenant will be supplanted precisely because the nation had failed to keep its laws and statutes.

Ezekiel's version of new-covenant expectation (Ezek. 36:22–32) makes the same point. The Lord will act to restore his people to the land for the sake of his holy name, cleansing them from their idols and impurities, and promises to give them a new heart and new spirit. Verse 27 makes it clear that not keeping the Law of Moses is the problem and the Spirit of God's enablement will be part of the solution: 'I will put my spirit within you, and make you follow my statutes and be careful to observe my ordinances.'

In Daniel 9 the prophet prays that the nation's transgression of the law and disobedience had occasioned a disaster on the nation, which was itself foretold in the law ('just as it is written in the Law of Moses, all this disaster has come on us') – the only hope is that God might turn in mercy:

> The Lord our God is merciful and forgiving, even though we have rebelled against him; we have not obeyed the LORD our God or kept the laws he gave us through his servants the prophets. All Israel has transgressed your law and turned away, refusing to obey you.
>
> Therefore the curses and sworn judgments written in the Law of Moses, the servant of God, have been poured out on us, because we have sinned against you. You have fulfilled the words spoken against us and against our rulers by bringing on us great disaster. Under the whole heaven nothing has ever been done like what has been done to Jerusalem. Just as it is written in the Law of Moses, all this disaster has come on us, yet we have not sought the favour of the LORD our God by turning from our sins and giving attention to your truth. The LORD did not hesitate to bring the disaster on us, for the LORD our God is righteous in everything he does; yet we have not obeyed him.
>
> Now, Lord our God, who brought your people out of Egypt with a mighty hand and who made for yourself a name that endures to this day, we have sinned, we have done wrong. Lord, in keeping with all your righteous acts, turn away your anger and your wrath from Jerusalem, your city, your holy hill. (Dan. 9:9–16a TNIV)

In language that Paul echoes, the prophet Daniel prays, 'We do not make requests of you because we are righteous, but because of your great mercy' (Dan. 9:18b TNIV).

Stephen Westerholm, quoting Jeremiah 31 and Daniel 9, labels such parallels to Paul's treatment of the law 'a postscript' to the discussion in his 1988 *Israel's Law and the Church's Faith*,[83] and in the 2004 edition, *Perspectives Old and New*, he omits them altogether. To my mind the Old Testament background is not illustrative of or tangential to Paul's views, but rather critical and formative. The Old Testament prophets predict that a failure to do the law will result in an

---

[83] Westerholm 1988: 163.

unprecedented intervention of God's mercy and grace. Paul declares that this has come to fulfilment in Christ, which goes a long way to understanding his insistence that believers in Christ are not under the law.

In Paul's own words (a summary and paraphrase)

Unlike Jews, believers in Christ are not under the law, nor are they in the law or from the law. They are not imprisoned and guarded under the law, nor are they subject to the law as to a disciplinarian. Those who are under the law are under a curse and under sin. Even though the law promises life to those who keep it, it is evident that no one keeps the law. Consequently, no one receives life through the law. The law used as law is for the lawless. Christ has abolished the law with its commandments and ordinances.

Chapter Three

Not 'walking according to the law'
Implicit repudiation of the law as law-covenant

[T]he Jew is obliged to *do* the Torah (cf. [Gal.] 3:10, 12; 5:3;
also 6:13), while the Christian *fulfills* the Torah. . . . [Paul]
carefully distinguishes between the 'doing' and the
'fulfilling' of the Torah – the 'doing' of the Jewish Torah
is not required of Christians, but the 'fulfilling' is.

(Hans Dieter Betz)[1]

What authors do not say, especially when they are expected to say it,
can be just as significant as what they do say. For example, the
Galatians got the message when Paul's letter to them went straight
from the opening greetings to the body of the letter, leaving out the
customary thanksgiving![2]

On this score Paul's Jewish roots invite a comparison of his
teaching with contemporary Jewish teaching on matters of faith and
conduct. While considerable continuity is clearly discernible,
sometimes against this backdrop the apostle's teaching stands out as
distinctive, simply because Paul does not say what is commonly said
by his Jewish contemporaries. Of course the argument from absence
can easily be hijacked and ought not to be given too much weight.
Observing omission, however, can be a powerful confirmation if
used in conjunction with more explicit evidence (see chapter 2).
While each example should be judged on its own merits, the cumu-
lative weight of expectation and corresponding silence is what
counts.

---

[1] Betz 1979: 275, italics added.
[2] Cf. the boy whose letters from his girlfriend usually address him with affectionate
nicknames, who gets a clear signal from a missive headed 'Dear John'.

When it comes to what Paul does not say about the relationship of believers in Christ to the Law of Moses, there are three versions of the argument from silence that can be observed: omission, reversal and substitution. *Omission* is the simple observation of the absence of something one would have expected to be present. An example was noted in chapter 1 in connection with my discussion of 1 Corinthians 7:19, that when Paul speaks of Christians positively with respect to the law he does not say we 'keep', 'observe' or 'obey' it. *Reversal* is a stronger form of the argument, where not only does Paul not say something, but he says the very opposite. In Romans 7, for instance, whereas we would expect a Jew like Paul to associate bearing *fruit for God* with observing the law, instead he says, that 'the sinful passions aroused by the law were at work in our bodies, so that we bore *fruit for death*' (v. 5). Finally, an equally strong version of the argument from absence, *substitution*, occurs when Paul puts something in the place that is normally associated with the law. Substitution is the focus of chapter 4.

This chapter considers Paul's failure or refusal to say certain things in connection with the law. Such omissions are what we would expect if Paul believes that Christians are not under the law as law-covenant.

What does Paul not say? By way of preview:

1. Paul does not say that believers in Christ walk according to the law.
2. Paul does not say, as he does of Jews, that Christians 'rely on' the law, 'boast' in the law, know God's will through the law, are educated in the law, have light, knowledge and truth because of the law, are to 'do', 'observe' and 'keep' the law, on occasions 'transgress' the law, or possess the law as a 'written code'.
3. Paul does not say that believers learn the law, follow the way of the law, are fruitful from obedience to the law or do good works by observing the commandments.
4. When quoting Deuteronomy, Paul does not quote parts of the texts that urge obedience to the law.
5. Paul does not call the law 'letter', 'book', 'decrees' or 'command-ments' when referring to it as a positive possession of Christians, but keeps these labels for the law when Jews possess it.

The absence of 'walk according to the law' in Paul's ethics

'How to walk and please God' (1 Thess. 4:1, my tr.) was a question asked and debated in every quarter of Judaism in the first century. The standard Jewish answer, based firmly on Scripture, was to walk 'according to the law'. The Old Testament regularly calls Israel to 'walk in God's law/statutes/ordinances' (Exod. 16:4; Lev. 18:4; 26:3; 1 Kgs 6:12; 2 Kgs 10:31; 2 Chr. 6:16; Neh. 10:29–30; Jer. 44:23; Ezek. 5:6–7; 11:12; Pss 77:10; 89:30; 119:1). Leviticus 26:3 is typical: '*Walk* in my statutes, and keep my commandments and do them' (my tr.).[3] Although such texts often attach a number of qualifications to 'walking' as a metaphor for conduct, these are all consistently related to living 'according to the Law of Moses'. For example, to 'walk in God's ways' is to 'keep his commandments' (Deut. 8:6, my tr.; cf. 10:12–13). The same is true of walking with 'truth', 'uprightness', 'integrity' and 'wholeness of heart', and walking 'with', 'for', 'before' and 'after' God.[4]

A wide range of Second Temple Jewish texts stands in the same tradition of commending walking in a manner pleasing to God, which is taken to mean conduct according to the law:

- *Damascus Document* 7.1 and 9.1: 'walk according to the law' (cf. *T. Jos.* 4.5; *T. Jud.* 23.5).
- *Community Rule* 1.8; 2.2; 3.9; 8.18; 9.6, 8–9, 19: 'walk perfectly in all his ways' (a reference to conduct according to the community's interpretation of the Law of Moses).
- *Testament of Judah* 24.3: 'walk according to the commandments of the Lord'.
- Philo, *De congressu eruditionis gratia* 87: 'walk in the judgements and ordinances of the Lord'.
- 1 Maccabees 10.37: 'let them live by their own laws, just as the king has commanded in the land of Judah'.
- Baruch 1.18 (cf. 2:10): 'We have disobeyed him, and have not heeded the voice of the Lord our God, to walk in the statutes of the Lord that he set before us.'

---

[3] The words 'keep' and 'do' in this verse translate *phylassō* and *poieō* respectively in the LXX. As noted below, Paul uses both these verbs to describe how Jews are meant to respond to the law, but does not do so in relation to believers in Christ.

[4] Holloway 1992: 4–8.

Thus it comes as no surprise that Jews gave the name *hĕlāḥâ*, from the verb 'to walk', *hālak*, to guidance concerning conduct according to the law. Whether or not the term had currency in Paul's day, its coinage confirms the very Jewish nature of the metaphor of walking for everyday conduct. Mark 7:5 and Acts 21:21 supply evidence from the New Testament of *peripateō*, 'to walk', being used in connection with Jewish customs:

And the Pharisees and the scribes asked him, 'Why do your disciples not walk [*peripatousin*] according to the tradition of the elders, but eat with defiled hands?' (ESV)

But they have been told about you that you teach all the Jews who are among the Gentiles to abandon Moses, by telling them not to circumcise their children or to walk [*peripatein*] in our customs. (HCSB)

It is significant that pagan moral philosophy around the time of the first century does not use 'walk' as a term for conduct. As Dunn notes, 'the metaphor "walk" = conduct oneself was typically Jewish and atypical of Greek thought'.[5]

In agreement with this Jewish idiom, 'teaching Christians how to walk' is a good description of Paul's pastoral work. He uses the metaphor no fewer than thirty-two times in this letters. Banks notes that it 'is present in every one of the letters ascribed to him [Paul] except Philemon, the briefest, and the Pastorals, the most disputed'.[6] Holloway's comprehensive study of Paul's use of the metaphor of walking as a metaphor concludes correctly that 'themes introduced by the verb [to walk] in Paul's letters are fundamental . . . *peripateō* acts as a thematic marker for pauline ethics'.[7]

A point of difference for Paul's figurative use of the verb 'to walk' is his choice of terms. While the Philo reference above and 2 Kings 20:3 ('Remember Lord that I have walked before you faithfully and loyally', my tr.) and LXX Proverbs 8:20 ('I walk in the way of righteousness') use *peripateō*, the vast majority of Jewish texts in Greek, including the numerous examples from the LXX, use *poreuomai*. Paul prefers *peripateō* in every case except Galatians 2:14, where *orthopodeō* appears, a hapax legomenon in the New Testament and never used

---

[5] Dunn 1993a: 462.
[6] Banks 1987: 304.
[7] Holloway 1992: vi.

in the LXX. Paul's preference for *peripateō* is difficult to explain. Holloway makes the plausible suggestion that Paul may have avoided *poreuomai* since in the Greco-Roman period the word had become associated with heavenly journeys experienced in states of ecstasy.[8] Either way, Paul's penchant for 'pedestrian' imagery is thoroughly Jewish.[9] However, as it turns out, the same cannot be said for the use to which he put it.

The striking thing about Paul's use of the walking theme is that he never once says that believers should walk according to the law. Given his capacious knowledge and prodigious use of Scripture, this can hardly be accidental. Every one of his letters offers moral teaching,[10] and yet Paul avoids the standard Jewish answer to the question of how to walk and please God. In commenting on Galatians 2:14 ('walk in line with the truth of the gospel', my tr.), Dunn draws the same conclusion:

> The characteristic Jewish use [of the walking metaphor] was commendation of a 'walk in the law / statutes / ordinances / ways of God' (hence 'halakah'). In no doubt deliberate contrast, Paul speaks of a walk toward the truth of the gospel. Evidently he was implying *with polemical intent* that 'the truth of the gospel' provided a different and superior beacon for conduct [than the Law of Moses].[11]

Ciampa agrees: 'A key focus of Paul's strategy [in Galatians] is to associate what Judaism would call "halakha" with the Mosaic regime and to argue that we have moved beyond that epoch and have a new standard of conduct in the eschatological message of salvation in Christ.'[12] In the next chapter we will explore in more detail what Paul

---

[8] Ibid. 21, 24. Acts 1:10 uses *poreuomai* to describe Jesus' ascension (cf. also 1 Pet. 3:19, 22). The verb is also used in John 14:2–3, 12, 28 and 16:7, 28 of Jesus' return to the Father. John is the only other NT author to use the walking metaphor extensively, and like Paul he makes the lexical choice of *peripateō* over *poreuomai*.

[9] The tradition is conceptually based and not tied exclusively to one particular term.

[10] Without exception, Paul's letters were motivated in large measure by concerns about conduct: how to walk and please God. All thirteen letters traditionally attributed to Paul bear this out. Galatians, 1 and 2 Corinthians and Romans were written in order to heal potential or real divisions in the churches. 1 and 2 Thessalonians clarify matters of conduct in anticipation of Christ's return. Ephesians and Colossians endeavour to foster a lifestyle consistent with salvation in Christ. Philippians discusses the support of ministry and seeks to calm quarrels in the church. Philemon considers a case of slavery. And the Pastoral Epistles deal with false teaching by commending not only sound doctrine but godliness and church order.

[11] Dunn 1993a: 462, italics added.

[12] Ciampa 1998: 170.

puts in the place of the Law of Moses in expressions using the Jewish metaphor of walking: If believers do not walk according to the law, how do we walk? At this stage, suffice it to say that the walking theme provides clear evidence that when it comes to living a holy life, Paul does not turn to Jewish nomism.

Jewish identity and the law in Romans 2:17–29

It is commonly noted in discussions of Paul and the law that when Paul speaks of Christians positively vis-à-vis the law he does not say they 'keep' or 'obey' it, but rather 'fulfil' it. Hans Dieter Betz's 1975 Galatians commentary is an early and prominent example that is cited at the beginning of this chapter. In this section I wish to extend this kind of observation to other terms that we might have expected Paul to use in connection with the law.

There are three places to look for controls for this experiment: (1) where the Old Testament describes Jews and the law; (2) where inter-testamental Jewish literature describes Jews and the law; and (3) where Paul describes Jews and the law. For each of these we may simply ask the question 'Does Paul follow suit when he speaks of Christians and the law?'

More evidence that Paul's silence in such cases demonstrates a change in how he views the Law of Moses is the fact that he often puts something else in its place. For example, whereas we might expect Paul to say that believers obey the law, he says instead that we obey the gospel. Noting such transferences will lead into chapter 4 where the replacement motif is discussed in full.

In Romans 1:18 – 3:8 Paul indicts the whole world and brings down the verdict that everyone needs the righteousness of God (Rom. 3:9–20). Even the Jews are not exempt from judgment and the wrath of God. In Romans 2:17 – 3:8 the apostle turns his sights on the Jews: 'Now you, if you call yourself a Jew [*Ioudaios*] and rely on the law . . . ' (Rom. 2:17a, my tr.). This unit is the most extended reflection on Jewish identity in Paul's letters. Significantly, verses 17–29 contain no fewer than ten explicit references to the law (*nomos*). The first two verbs in verse 17, *eponomazē* ('call' yourself a Jew) and *epanapauē* ('rely upon' the law), contain 'an alliterative wordplay'.[13] With this device Paul makes it clear that to *take* the name of Jew is to *trust* in the Law of Moses.

[13] R. Jewett 2007: 219.

What do we learn about Jews and the law in Romans 2? Paul says that Jews rely on the law (v. 17a); boast about the law (v. 23; cf. v. 17b); know God's will through the law (v. 18); are educated in the law (v. 18); have light, knowledge and truth because of the law (vv. 19–20); do the law (v. 25); observe the righteous requirements of the law (v. 26); transgress the law (vv. 23, 25 and 27); and possess the (law as) written code (v. 27).

The question I wish to pose is a simple one: Does Paul say the same things of believers in Christ in relation to the law? As it turns out, every one of these ways in which Paul says Jews relate to the law (which are often reflected in writings by other Jews) is conspicuously absent when he describes how Christians relate to the law.

Jews rely on the law

The first feature of the Jew to which Paul draws attention is that they 'rely on the law'. This is not something any Jew would have disputed. *2 Baruch* 48.22 indicates how this sentiment can relate to Paul's next point in verse 17 of 'boasting in God': 'In you we have put our trust, because, behold, your law is with us, and we know that we do not fall as long as we keep your statutes' (my tr.). This text also shows that to trust in God and the law is not necessarily a negative thing. Paul is not censuring these Jewish characteristics. As verses 21–29 show, Paul's criticism is the Jews' failure to observe the law, not their possession of or high regard for the law.

The verb translated 'to rely upon', *epanapauomai*, occurs only twice in the New Testament. The other occurrence (Luke 10:6) carries the more literal sense of something ('peace') resting upon someone. About nine times in the LXX it also carries this more literal sense. The figurative meaning, evident in Romans 2:17, of 'find well-being or inner security . . . in the sense of rely on' (BDAG 358b) occurs in Micah 3:11 ('they lean upon the LORD'). As Louw and Nida note (31:83), 'The concept of dependence or reliance upon something may be expressed in a number of different ways.' Paul nowhere says that believers in Christ 'rely upon the law'. Although he does not use *epanapauomai* with reference to anything else Christians rely upon, conceptually they rely upon, or, more commonly in Paul, have faith in Christ.

Jews boast about the law

The second thing Paul lists in his profile of average Jews is that they 'boast in God' (v. 17b, my tr.). The other thing the Jew boasts in according to Paul is 'in the law' (v. 23). Although 'boasting' in English is usually a pejorative term (cf. Jas 4:16: 'You boast and brag. All such boasting is evil', my tr.), Paul can use it both negatively and positively, and both senses are evident in Romans. Both 'taking pride in' God and the law are positives in Romans 2.

Paul uses the verb *kauchaomai* five times in Romans. If in chapter 2 Jews boast in God and the law, in chapter 5 believers in Christ boast in hope, hardship and 'in God through our Lord Jesus Christ, through whom we have received reconciliation' (v. 11).[14] To fill out the picture of boasting in Romans, along with the verb 'to boast' Paul uses two cognate nouns. Romans 15:17 connects Christian 'boasting' directly to Jesus Christ via Paul's personal example: 'Therefore I glory [*kauchēsis*] in Christ Jesus in my service to God' (NIV). And Romans 3:27 and 4:2 pit faith against the law as ways of obtaining the righteousness of God.

According to Paul, if Jews boast in God and the law, Christians boast in God through Jesus Christ.

Jews know God's will through the law

In Romans 2:18 Paul affirms that Jews 'know his [God's] will[15] . . . because [they] are instructed by the law'.[16] The connection between the will of God and the Law of Moses is well established in biblical and Jewish tradition. The psalmist prays:

> I delight to do your will, O my God;
> your law is within my heart.
> (Ps. 40:8)

In *Community Rule* 'the Instructor . . . should fulfill the will of God in compliance with all revelation for every period' (9.13); 'he should perform (God's) will. . . . wish for nothing that he [God] has not commanded and be ever alert to the precept of God' (9.23–25).

Two senses of 'the will of God' are evident in Paul's letters (and in biblical idiom generally): his immutable will (his eternal purposes) and his moral will (the holiness of life that he desires for his people).

[14] Most English versions translate *kauchaomai* in Romans 5:2–3 and 11 as 'rejoice', obscuring the connection with 2:17 and 23.

[15] Gk. *to thelēma*. According to R. Jewett (2007: 223) the absolute use of the noun (lit. 'you know the will') 'follows a Jewish idiom'. See 1QS 8.6 and other Qumran references to the will of God.

[16] The adverbial participle 'instructed' modifies both 'know' and 'approve'. Cf. Moo 1996: 161.

Roughly speaking, the former is what God does sovereignly (Rom. 9:19: 'who resists his will?' NASB), and the latter, what God wants ethically (1 Thess. 4:3: 'It is God's will that you should be sanctified' NIV).

Reference to God's immutable will appears in seven letters in the Pauline corpus. Paul's plans are dependent on the will of God (in Rom 1:10 and 15:32), his apostleship is by the will of God (in epistolary prescripts: 1 Cor. 1:1; 2 Cor. 1:1; Eph. 1:1; Col. 1:1; 2 Tim. 1:1) and the plan of salvation is according to the will of God (Gal. 1:4; Eph. 1:9, 11).

The parallel clause in Romans 2:18, 'and approve what is superior', indicates that 'knowing the will of God' there refers to God's moral will (my tr.). Both clauses describe in a general way that, through the law, Jews know how to live a life pleasing to God. 'God's will' is attested at seven other points in Paul's letters: twice each in 1 Thessalonians, Ephesians and Colossians, and once more in Romans. All of these instances refer to Christians in relation to God's moral will. The point to note is that none of them indicates that Christians know God's will through the law.

Paul says that believers know God's will through other means. Of the seven passages, two supply no clues as to where Paul believes Christians find God's will (Eph. 6:6: 'doing the will of God from the heart'; and Col. 4:12: 'stand firm in all the will of God' NIV). Two passages give concrete guidance concerning some specific aspect of God's will (1 Thess. 4:3: 'It is God's will that you should be sanctified: that you should avoid sexual immorality' NIV; and 1 Thess. 5:18: 'give thanks in all circumstances, for this is God's will for you in Christ Jesus'). The only source indicated for this knowledge is that it is Paul's own instruction. Evidently, the Thessalonian believers know God's will through the authority of God's appointed messenger. Two passages forge a connection between wisdom and knowing the will of God: 'So do not be foolish, but understand what the will of the Lord is' (Eph. 5:17); and 'asking that you may be filled with the knowledge of God's will in all spiritual wisdom and understanding' (Col. 1:9, my tr.). We will return to the critical place of wisdom in Paul's thinking in chapter 6.

The seventh passage, Romans 12:2, which is the most significant for Paul, omits to mention the law in relation to God's will: 'Do not be conformed to this world, but be transformed by the renewing of your minds, so that you may discern what is the will of God – what is good and acceptable and perfect.'

Romans 12:1–2 signals the beginning of explicit exhortation in Romans, following a long theological exposition in chapters 1–11. Yet the switch to ethics is hardly abrupt, as it picks up thoughts from earlier parts of the letter. Total dedication to God is not some after-thought, but the climax to which Paul has been building. Paul bases his appeal on the mercies of God, which are ringing in the hearers' ears from chapters 9 to 11, where 'mercy' is a key term.[17] His call for reasonable worship and mind renewal brings to mind chapter 1 with its false and foolish worship and corrupted minds. The presentation of the believers' bodies reiterates and expands the same call in Romans 6:13 and 19.

Finally, with reference to our interests, Romans 12:2 invites readers to compare and contrast the experience of Jews and believers in Christ on the question of knowing God's will. The will of God which believers test and *approve* in response to the gospel (Rom. 12:12b) recalls and surpasses the experience of the Jews who know God's will and *approve* what is superior because they are instructed by the law (Rom. 2:18). This connection is rendered likely not simply because chapters 2 and 12 mention the moral 'will of God', but because of the repetition of the term *dokimazō*, a reference to the process of discerning approval. Jews discern in Romans 1:18 what is superior; believers in Christ discern in Romans 12:2 the good, pleasing and perfect nature of God's will. The term occurs only four times in Romans, the other two occurrences bearing no connection to God's will (Rom. 1:28; 14:22). Further, in Baruch 4.1–4, in a passage celebrating 'the book of the precepts of God, the law that endures forever', Jews can claim that 'what pleases God is known to us'.

Rather than linking knowledge of what pleases God to the law, Paul ties it to the gospel and an appropriate response of total dedi-cation to God. In the unfolding argument of Romans, if Jews know God's will and can approve of what is superior through the law (as Paul observed in 2:18) and believers in Christ are not under the law (as Paul so firmly insists in chapters 6 and 7), how do Christians know God's will and approve the good, that which is pleasing to him? Romans 12:1–2 supplies the answer.

According to Paul, if Jews know God's will through the law, Chris-tians find God's will in apostolic instruction, wisdom and in response to the gospel.

---

[17] Gk. *eleos* and *eleeō*.

Jews are educated in the law

According to Romans 2:18b Jews are '*instructed* by the law'. As Robert Jewett suggests, 'Paul selects the verb *katēcheō* because it was already being used as in-group jargon for religious schooling, instruction or catechizing of Christian converts.'[18] It is certainly true that Jews were taught the law. The normal first-century Jewish experience included considerable instruction in the Scriptures in the context of both home and synagogue (see Josephus, *Ag. Ap.* 2.178, 204). Philo wrote that the Jews 'consider their laws to be divine revelation and are instructed in them from their youth' (*Embassy* 210; cf. 115). According to *'Abot* 5.21, 'at five years old one is fit for the Scripture'. In *4 Maccabees* 18.10 there is intimation that the model Jewish father gave much instruction in the Scriptures to his sons. The educational character of the synagogue service is stressed by Josephus (*Ag. Ap.* 2.175): Jews 'gather together to listen to the law and learn it accurately'.

Outside Romans 2:18 *katēcheō* is used on six other occasions in the New Testament. Twice it carries the less technical sense of 'report'. The four texts that use it in the sense of 'instruction' make it clear that believers are 'instructed' by specifically Christian teaching: things about Jesus (Luke 1:4); 'the way of the Lord' (Acts 18:25); prophecy in a Christian gathering (1 Cor. 14:19); and 'the word' of the gospel (Gal. 6:6). Nowhere does Paul say that Christians are 'instructed by the law'; instead, throughout his letters they are instructed by the gospel.

Jews have light, knowledge and truth because of the law

In verses 19–20 Paul affirms that Jews possess much that is good in the law, specifically light, knowledge and truth. As Jewett notes, 'that knowledge and truth were revealed in the Torah was widely assumed [by Jews]'.[19] *2 Baruch* 44.14 claims that Jews 'have prepared for themselves treasures of wisdom and stores of insight . . . [and have] preserved the truth of the law'. Sirach 17.11 asserts that 'God gave them [the Jews] knowledge and the law of life.' A connection of the law with light was also a commonplace. In Isaiah 51:4 the prophet declares that '[t]he law will go out from me; / my justice will become a light to the nations' (cf. Isa. 8:20, my tr.).

---

[18] R. Jewett 2007: 224.
[19] Ibid. 227.

Paul makes no such claims in relation to Christians and the law. As Romans 13:12 intimates, he transposes light and darkness imagery onto an eschatological plane, a development anticipated by texts in Isaiah 59 – 60, to which Paul alludes in connection with his idea of walking *in the light* (examined in the next chapter). Following Romans 2:20, the word 'knowledge' is used twice more in Romans. Both are with reference to Christians. Romans likewise does not connect knowledge to the law, but rather intimates that Christians find knowledge in connection with the mercy of God revealed in the gospel (11:33). In Romans 15:14 Paul assures the Christians that even though the law embodied knowledge (2:20), because he has instructed them concerning the gospel, they are 'complete in *knowledge* and competent to instruct one another' (my tr.). In Romans 15:8 Paul lays claim to the third abstract noun associated with the law in 2:20 for Christians: 'Christ has become a servant of the Jews on behalf of God's *truth*, to confirm the promises made to the patriarchs.'

According to Paul, if Jews have light, knowledge and truth because of the law, Christians have these in even greater measure because of the gospel.

Jews do, observe and keep the law

In verses 25–27 Paul notes the response to the law required of Jews: they must '*do* [or 'practise'; *prassō*] the law' (v. 25), '*observe* [or 'keep'; *phylassō*] the righteous requirements of the law' (v. 26) and '*keep* [or 'complete'; *teleō*] the law' (v. 27). A highly debated passage, these verses not only describe what Jews are meant to do with the law, but also speak of 'those who are uncircumcised' observing and keeping the law (2:26–27, my tr.). Whether Paul is referring to Christian Gentiles or non-Christian Gentiles, or speaking hypothetically,[20] must not derail us here. What is clear is that the apostle's description of Gentiles obeying the law is couched in highly rhetorical terms; the tone is polemical.[21] Paul supports the charge of Israel's breaking of the law (see vv. 25, 27) by 'showing how an unrepentant and stiff-necked (Rom. 2:5) Israel actually compares unfavourably with a law-abiding Gentile

---

[20] See a full discussion in Gathercole 2002, who defends the view that these verses, along with Rom. 2:14–15, refer to Gentile Christians.

[21] Cf. Byrne 1996: 88: 'In the present connection, however, where Jews and Gentiles are being played off against each other, its formulation is sharply polemical.'

group'.[22] The irony is delicious, even if some of the details of interpretation are hard to digest. As demonstrated in what follows,
outside such an exceptional setting Paul nowhere says that Gentile
believers in Christ 'do/observe/keep' the law. In more sober contexts,
where Paul is not shaming Jews but instructing Christians, he avoids
such language.

Looking for distinctions among the three verbs is to indulge in
overinterpretation. In Romans 2:25–27 Paul uses them in close
proximity, suggesting that the change of verbs may be put down to
stylistic variation. As Moo notes,

> most of the phrases [Paul uses for Jewish obligations in relation
> to the law] were already being used by Jews to denote obedience to
> the law; and most have close equivalents in the Hebrew of later
> rabbinic literature. They are all different ways of expressing the
> general idea of obedience to the Law of Moses.[23]

Paul uses all three verbs not infrequently. Sometimes these are in
relation to the responsibilities of Christians, but the law is not the
thing that Christians do, observe or keep.

The verb 'to do', *prassō*, appears eighteen times in Paul's
letters. Frequently it refers to 'doing' something sinful, as in Romans
2:1: 'You, therefore, have no excuse, you who pass judgment on
someone else, for at whatever point you judge another, you are
condemning yourself, because you who pass judgment *do* the same
things' (NIV; cf. Rom. 1:32; 2:2–3; 13:4; 1 Cor. 5:2; 2 Cor. 12:21;
Gal. 5:21). In Romans 7 Paul the Jew is unable to 'do' the requirements of the law (Rom. 7:15, 19). He 'does' his preaching voluntarily
in 1 Corinthians 9:17. People are said to 'do' things, whether good
or bad, in Romans 9:11 and 2 Corinthians 5:10. 'Doing' as a
neutral description of behaviour appears in Ephesians 6:21 and
1 Thessalonians 4:11. The only thing that Christians are instructed
to 'do' in a more general sense is in Philippians 4:9, where Paul

---

[22] Gathercole 2002: 48. Cf. the quotation of Isa. 52:5 in Rom. 2:24 and also Rom.
9:30–32, 'where it is precisely the Gentiles who believe who are contrasted with unbeliev-
ing Israel' (ibid. 32). Stuhlmacher (1994: 49–50) points out that whereas '[a]ccording to
early Jewish expectation, the righteous will one day execute judgment over sinners (and
the Gentile nations) (cf. Dan. 7:22, 27; Wis. 3:7f.; *1 Enoch* 90:19; 95:3) . . . [here] the
Gentiles who are obedient to God will sit in judgment over those Jews who, in spite of
their knowledge of the Law, which has been written and entrusted to them, and in spite
of their circumcision, are transgressors of the Law.'

[23] Moo 1996: 170.

instructs believers in Christ, not to do the law, but rather to '*do* . . . whatever you have learned or received or heard from me, or seen in me' (my tr.).

A similar picture emerges with Paul's observation that Jews 'keep [*phylassō*] the righteous requirements of the law' (Rom. 2:26, my tr.). As in Romans 2:26, in Galatians 6:13 Jews are to 'keep' the law. The two words *phylassō* (keep) and *dikaiōmata* (righteous requirements) appear together more than seventy times in the LXX. Almost uniformly these verses refer to keeping the *dikaiōmata* of the Lord (see e.g. Deut. 4:40; 6:2; 17:19; 28:45; 30:10, 16; Pss 104:45; 118:5, 8; Prov. 2:8; Mic. 8:16; Ezek. 11:20; 18:9; 20:13, 18–19, 21; 43:11), meaning doing the Law of Moses.[24] In Paul's letters most of the occurrences of *phylassō* refer to 'keeping' in the sense of 'guarding' (2 Thess. 3:3; 1 Tim. 6:20; 2 Tim. 1:12, 14; 4:15). Like Philippians 4:9, which issues a call to 'do' (*prassō*) what believers have seen Paul do, 1 Timothy 5:21 contains a more general call to 'keep' (*phylassō*) something. Once again, it is not the Law of Moses that Christians are called to heed. Rather, in 1 Timothy 5:21 Paul tells Timothy to 'keep' not the law but his own apostolic directions: 'In the presence of God and of Christ Jesus and of the elect angels, I warn you to *keep* these instructions'.

The third verb, *teleō*, 'to keep' or 'complete', appears only five times in Paul's letters. The other occurrences (Rom. 13:6; 2 Cor. 12:9; Gal. 5:16) bear no relation to the law. Paul does not say that Christians 'keep' the law. On the other hand, to continue our theme of substitution, 2 Timothy 4:7 does say that Paul has 'completed [not the law, but] the race [or course]' (my tr.) set out for him in connection with the mission given him by the risen Christ.[25]

Put simply, according to Paul, if Jews are obliged to obey the Law of Moses, believers in Christ are not.[26] Instead, they are to obey apostolic instructions. The Christian does, however, have a positive

---

[24] R. Jewett (2007: 233) is right to call it 'technical terminology of legal conformity from the LXX'. As Dunn (1988a: 121–122) observes, 'The full phrase, "keep the (God's) ordinances" occurs regularly in Deuteronomy (4:40; 6:2; 7:11; etc.) and Ezekiel (11:20; 18:9; 20:18; etc.).'

[25] Two other (basically synonymous) verbs Paul uses for 'obeying' the Law of Moses, not found in Rom. 2, are worth mentioning. He links both to Jewish observance of the law, but does not use them to connect Christians to the law: 'to do', *poieō*, in Rom. 2:14; 10:5; Gal. 3:10, 12; 5:3 (cf. *poiētēs* in Rom. 2:13); and 'to remain in', *emmenō*, in Gal. 3:10, quoting Deut. 27:26.

[26] The only possible exception, Rom. 2:26–27, as noted above, which may refer to Gentile Christians, occurs in a polemical context, the purpose of which is not to define a Christian's relationship to the law but to condemn Jews as lawbreakers.

response to the law: to 'fulfil' the law (*plēroō* and cognates; Rom. 8:4; 13:8; Gal. 5:14; cf. Gal. 6:2).[27]

Jews transgress the law

Three times in Romans 2 Paul warns of the danger of Jews *transgressing* the law (v. 23: *parabasis*; 'transgression'; and vv. 25, 27: *parabatēs*; 'transgressor'). That this language is standard Jewish parlance is evident in Josephus, who refers repeatedly to 'transgressing the law' (*Ant.* 3.218; 8.129; 9.243; 14.167; 18.81; 18.268[28]).

Paul has a potent arsenal of words for sin and deploys them fearlessly when targeting the shortcomings of individual believers and churches. Yet he never condemns the sins of believers as *transgressions*. Outside Romans 2 he uses the language of transgression on only five other occasions.[29] In each case he is talking about either failing to observe the Law of Moses, or Adam's or Eve's breaking a command from God (which Paul thinks of as a prototype of the Mosaic law): (1) 'where there is no law there is no transgression' (Rom. 4:15 NIV); (2) 'the transgression of Adam' (Rom. 5:14); (3) 'Why then the law? It was added because of transgressions' (Gal. 3:19); (4) 'and Adam was not deceived, but the woman was deceived and became a transgressor' (1 Tim. 2:14); and (5) 'If I rebuild what I destroyed [i.e. the law – see v. 19], I prove that I am a transgressor' (Gal. 2:18, my tr.).

In the last case (Gal. 2:18) *parabatēs* is translated interpretatively, but uncontroversially, as 'lawbreaker' by NIV 1984, TNIV and HCSB. In support, it is worth noticing that all three occurrences of transgression terminology in Romans 2 are found in genitive expressions involving 'the law' (lit. 'transgression of the law' once and 'transgressor of the law' twice).[30] It does seem that Paul uses the two words in question not for sin in general but as technical terms for 'breaking the law'.[31] He never names the sins of Christians as such, which is consistent with the view that Paul thinks Christians are not under the law as law. If you are not under the law, you cannot transgress it. According to Paul, while Jews *transgress* the law, Christians do not.

---

[27] The sense in which Christians fulfil the law is debated. For our purposes, however Paul is to be understood, as Betz observed (noted above), fulfilling the law is different from keeping it.

[28] Cited in R. Jewett 2007: 230.

[29] The first four are *parabasis*; the last is *parabatēs*.

[30] Cf. Jas 2:11.

[31] Louw and Nida (36.29) define *parabatēs* as to 'disobey, break the law'.

Jews possess the law as a written code

The last element in Paul's reflections on Jewish identity in Romans
2:17–29 that I wish to comment on is Jewish possession of 'the written
code', or, more literally, their possession of the 'letter' (v. 27; cf. 29).
The next step in Paul's indictment of Jews as guilty before God and
in need of his righteousness is that Paul inverts the usual Jewish
expectation of the righteous judging the unrighteous, which Jews took
to mean their own condemnation of Gentiles, to have Gentiles judging
and condemning Jews: 'the one who is not circumcised physically and
yet obeys the law will condemn you!' (NIV). Paul charges that Jews
have broken the law they were obliged to keep.

Commentators and translators disagree over how to understand the
next phrase in verse 27, *dia grammatos kai peritomēs*.[32] Are Jews
condemned '*through* the letter and circumcision' or '*even though* they
have the letter and circumcision'? In the former case the preposition is
taken in its common instrumental sense and the law and circumcision
are somehow at fault; AV translates, 'who by the letter and circumcision dost transgress the law'. The preposition may also be taken as
signifying attendant circumstance ('with the letter') or concession ('even
though they have the letter'). Most modern English versions prefer this
option, which absolves the law of any blame (see NASB, NIV, TNIV, TEV,
RSV, NRSV). It is argued that Paul does not hold the law responsible for
the condemnation of the Jews, since he continues to esteem both the
law and circumcision highly (see 7:12: 'the law is good' NIV; and 3:1–2,
where circumcision is affirmed as valuable). The problem is not with
some incomplete grasp of the law but with disobedience to the law, the
very charge Paul has been laying since verse 21.

While this is true, the way Paul refers to the law in Romans 2:27
and 29 as 'letter' inclines us towards the view that the law, if not
to blame, is at least complicit in the condemnation of the Jews. In
2 Corinthians 3:6 Paul charges that 'the letter kills', a thought not too
far from saying that Jews are transgressors 'by the law', and Romans
7:6 speaks of the need to 'die to what once bound us' (my tr.), namely
the law. Even more telling for the interpretation of *dia grammatos kai
peritomēs* in Romans 2:27 is the phrase *dia tou nomou* in Romans 7:5,
which is usually understood instrumentally: 'For when we were con-
trolled by the sinful nature, the sinful passions aroused *by the law* were

---

[32] Cf. R. Jewett 2007: 234: 'the precise meaning of the phrase . . . remains a matter
of debate'.

at work in our bodies, so that we bore fruit for death' (NIV 1984). While it is not critical for the point I wish to make about Romans 2:27 and 29, the evidence does seem to point to the law's direct involvement, as 'letter', in the condemnation of Jews.

In Romans 2:29 Paul sets up a contrast between 'letter' and 'Spirit': 'circumcision is circumcision of the heart, by the Spirit, not by the letter' (Rom. 2:29, my tr.).

The same contrast also appears in two other Pauline texts:

But now, by dying to what once bound us, we have been released from the law so that we serve in the new way of the Spirit, and not in the old way of the letter. (Rom. 7:6, my tr.)

He has made us competent as ministers of a new covenant – not of the letter but of the Spirit; for the letter kills, but the Spirit gives life. (2 Cor. 3:6, my tr.)

Romans 2, 7 and 2 Corinthians 3 are the only three places in Paul's letters where he refers to the law as 'letter'. While 'letter' is not the standard Jewish epithet for the law, Jews did refer to the law as 'letters' in the plural, as in the phrase 'the holy writings', or, more literally, 'the holy letters', *ta hiera grammata*. The phrase was common and 2 Timothy 3:15 uses it to refer to the 'Holy Scriptures' (NIV) or 'sacred writings' (NRSV).

Most commentators agree that Paul uses 'letter', *gramma*, to refer to the Law of Moses as a written document. Although in English the most common meaning of 'letter' is 'a unit of an alphabet' (cf. Gal. 6:11), in Greek it can mean 'a set of written characters forming a document or piece of writing' (BDAG 205d). Given this basic sense, can we specify more accurately what law as 'letter' denotes for Paul? A clue to its meaning is found in 2 Corinthians 3:7–8, where 'letters' refer to the Decalogue written on tablets of stone:

Now if the ministry of death, chiselled in letters on stone tablets, came in glory so that the people of Israel could not gaze at Moses' face because of the glory of his face, a glory now set aside, how much more will the ministry of the Spirit come in glory?

Another pointer is the fact that 'letter' is contrasted with 'Spirit' in Romans 2, 7 and 2 Corinthians 3, and in Romans 2:27 is linked *heart vs external*

with circumcision. This has led many to suggest that 'letter' refers to 'the externality of the law'.[33] When Paul critiques circumcision, he frequently conceives of it as an external action. And the 'letter–Spirit' contrast is often taken to point to a distinction between an external versus a condition of the heart.

Taking matters a step further, several English versions translate 'letter' in Romans 2 and 7 as 'written code' (e.g. TNIV, NIV, NRSV, ESV; cf. HCSB: 'letter of the law').[34] The context of Romans 7 supports this decision. In Romans 7:7–12, following 7:6, the last word of which is 'letter', Paul refers interchangeably to the law as *nomos* (six times) and as *entolē* ('commandment', five times). He directly associates the two as virtual synonyms in verse 12: 'So then, the law is holy, and the commandment is holy and just and good' (HCSB).

Paul uses 'letter' as a way of referring to the law as a set of commandments to be obeyed, as a written 'legal code'. As such, it is significant that he confines his references to the law as 'letter' and 'commandment' to contexts in which he is discussing Jewish adherence (or more accurately, non-adherence) to the law. When writing of the law positively in connection with Christians, he can refer to it as *grammata* ('letters'; 2 Tim. 3:15), *nomos* ('law'; e.g. 1 Cor. 9:8–9), *graphē* ('Scripture'; e.g. Rom. 4:3; Gal. 3:8; 1 Tim. 5:18; 2 Tim. 3:16) and *graphai* ('Scriptures'; e.g. Rom. 15:4); he never refers to the law as *gramma*, 'letter', as 'legal code', when describing how Christians read the Law of Moses.

Paul, it seems, uses *gramma* as a technical term for the law as an obsolete Jewish legal code, from which Christians are exempt. Romans 2 and 7, and 2 Corinthians 3 all contain a contrast in terms of salvation history. As Moo contends, 'letter describes the past era in which God's law through Moses played a central role and "Spirit" summing up the new era in which God's Spirit is poured out in eschatological fullness and power'.[35] The Holy Spirit as the gift characterizing the new age is prophesied in texts such as Joel 2:28–29; Isaiah 44:3; and Ezekiel 11:19; 36:26–27.

In short, according to Paul, if Jews have the law as 'letter', legal code and a written collection of commandments, Christians do not.

[33] Schreiner 1998: 142.
[34] 'Letter' is preferred in 2 Cor. 3, perhaps to retain the play on words with 'letters on stone' in v. 7.
[35] Moo 1996: 175.

The omission of other terms in connection with the law

Four further subtle indications point unobtrusively to a change in the way Paul the Jew relates to the Law of Moses, in addition to the eight we discovered in Romans 2: learning the law; the way of the law; the fruit of the law; and good works and the law.

Learning the law

The verb 'to learn', *manthanō*, not surprisingly appears in the LXX in connection with the law. Five times in Deuteronomy Israel are told to *learn* the law: 'Moses summoned all Israel and said: Hear, Israel, the decrees and laws I declare in your hearing today. *Learn* them and be sure to follow them' (Deut. 5:1 NIV; cf. 4:10; 17:19; 31:12–13). In Psalm 119 the psalmist prays three times, 'give me understanding to *learn* your commands' (119:73b NIV; cf. vv. 7 and 71).

Paul is also fond of the verb, but never says that believers are to 'learn' the law. Instead, he speaks of 'learning' the Christian 'way of life' (Eph. 4:20 NIV), 'learning' from Christian teaching (Rom. 16:17; 2 Tim. 3:14), from his own instruction (1 Cor. 4:6) and example (Phil. 4:9), from Christian prophecy (1 Cor. 14:31), from Epaphras (Col. 1:7), and 'learning' 'to put their religion into practice' (1 Tim. 5:4), by 'doing what is good' (Titus 3:14, my tr.). Most succinctly, Christians 'learn Christ' (Eph. 4:20 NASB). According to Paul, if Jews learn the law, Christian 'education' has a different syllabus.

The way of the law

Without developing the thought, W. D. Davies noted that in Paul's letters 'the way of the Law gives place to the law or way of Christ'.[36] Frequently in the Pentateuch, historical books and in the psalter the phrase 'his ways', especially in connection with the verb 'to walk', is a reference to the law; Israel believed that God has 'made known his ways to Moses' (Ps. 103:7). As noted above, to 'walk in God's ways' is to 'keep the commandments' (Deut. 8:6; cf. 10:12–13).

The 'way', *hodos*, understood in the figurative sense of 'course of behavior, way of life' (BDAG 691b), is used in Acts as a name for the early Christian movement (see Acts 9:2; 19:9, 23; 22:4; 24:22). In Acts 18 Apollos knew basic Christian teaching, 'the Way of the Lord'

---

[36] Davies 1982b: 10.

(v. 25), and has 'the way of God [more Christian teaching, including baptism, explained to him] more adequately' by Priscilla and Aquila (v. 26 NIV). Before Felix, Paul testifies, 'I worship the God of our ancestors as a follower of the Way, which they [the Jews] call a sect. I believe everything that is in accordance with the Law and that is written in the Prophets' (Acts 24:14 NIV).

That Paul in Acts 24:14 confesses both his allegiance to 'the Way' *and* to 'the law' and 'the prophets' is significant, since across the Hebrew Scriptures 'the way' or 'ways' (*hodos, hodoi* in the LXX) are frequent descriptions of the life of obedience to the Law of Moses. In Exodus 18:20 Jethro tells Moses, 'Teach them his [God's] decrees and instructions, and show them the *way* they are to live and how they are to behave' (NIV). And Moses instructs the Israelites in Deuteronomy 8:6, 'Observe the commands of the Lord, walk in his *ways* [*en tais hodois autou*] and fear him' (my tr.). According to Paul, if for Jews following the ways of God involved keeping the Law of Moses, for Christians Christ is the way.

The fruit of the law

The figurative use of 'fruit' to mean 'the product or outcome of something in the spiritual realm' (BDAG 1b) can be found in five of Paul's letters.[37] Both good and bad fruit, and bearing fruit for death and for God, are evident.

The background to the figure suggests that Jews used the metaphor of fruitfulness in relation to the negative consequences of not obeying the Law of Moses. Jeremiah 6:19 connects harmful fruit with disobedience to the law:

> Hear, you earth: I am bringing disaster [*kakos*] on this people,
> the *fruit* [*karpos*] of their schemes,
> because they have not listened to my words
> and have rejected my law. (NIV)

Two texts in *4 Ezra* forge the same link: *4 Ezra* 1.34: 'Your children shall not be fruitful; for they have despised my commandment, and done the thing that is an evil before me'; and *4 Ezra* 3.33, which is especially striking, since it is the Gentiles who are judged to be lacking in fruit because of their ignorance of the law: 'And yet their reward does not appear, and their labour has no fruit (*karpos*): for I have gone

---

[37] This is true for both the noun *karpos*, 'fruit', and the verb *karpophoreō*, 'bear fruit'.

here and there through the heathen, and I see that they flow in wealth, and don't think about your commandments.'

Jews also expected to be 'fruitful' if they obeyed the law. Psalm 1:2–3 is typical: 'but their delight is in the law of the LORD . . . '

> They are like trees planted by streams of water,
>   which yield their fruit [LXX: *karpos*] in its season,
> and their leaves do not wither.
> In all that they do, they prosper.

In this light some of Paul's use of figurative 'fruit' forms a contrast to Jewish teaching on the 'fruit of the law'. In Romans 6:20–21 bad and good fruit in relation to the reign of sin and submission to God are presented as two ways to live in a typically Jewish fashion. However, in terms of bearing fruit, Paul departs markedly from a positive view of the law. In fact, in Romans 7:4 it is those who have 'died to the law . . . [who] bear fruit [*karpophoreō*] for God'. And in Romans 7:5 'our sinful passions, aroused by the law, were at work in our members to bear fruit [*karpophoreō*] for death'. Jews connected fruit for God to obeying the Law of Moses. In a striking piece of polemical inversion, for Paul the law is a bad thing that bears fruit for death rather than life.

Paul also does not connect positive fruitfulness to observing or delighting in the law. In Colossians 1:10 the apostle prays that the believers 'may lead lives worthy of the Lord, fully pleasing to him, as you bear fruit [*karpophoreō*] in every good work and as you grow in the knowledge of God'. In Philippians 1:11 'the fruit of right-eousness . . . comes through Jesus Christ' (NIV). In Ephesians 5:9 'the fruit of the light is found in all that is good and right and true'. Most telling is Galatians 5, where 'the fruit of the Spirit' (Gal. 5:22) actually replaces a commitment to circumcision and the law (see Gal. 5:3, 23b).

According to Paul, if Jews expect the Law of Moses to bear good fruit, Paul thinks the opposite and looks for fruitfulness elsewhere.

Good works and the law

The concept of 'good works' played a major role in both ancient Judaism and early Christianity. Whereas in chapter 6 I will focus on the broader question of conduct that pleases God, here it is worth comparing briefly the usage of the specific terminology of 'good works' in Paul's letters with Jewish usage.[38] This includes both *agathon ergon* and *kalon ergon*, and verbal constructions of 'doing good' involving a form of *poieō* or *ergazomai*,[39] which are virtually synonymous.

In Jewish thought the notion of 'good' is inextricably tied to God. In Luke 18:19 Jesus affirms the Old Testament truth that 'no one is good but God alone'. Psalm 52:9 praises God with the words 'your name is good' (NIV). In the Hebrew Scriptures God's nature (e.g. Pss 100:5; 118:1) and conduct (e.g. 1 Chr. 16:34; 2 Chr. 5:13) are good. His goodness is evident in his works of creation (Gen. 1:10, 12, 18, etc.) and history (Exod. 18:9; Num. 10:29–32) and in the fulfilment of his promises (1 Kgs 8:56; Jer. 29:10). His commands are also good, especially the Law of Moses (Deut. 30:15; Prov. 28:10). In rabbinic Judaism the Torah is labelled as good: 'The wise shall inherit honour, and the perfect shall inherit good . . . The Good only means Torah' (*'Abot* 6.3). This is something Paul is also able to affirm: 'So the law is holy, and the commandment is holy and just and *good*' (Rom. 7:12; cf. v. 13 and 1 Tim. 1:8: 'the law is good').

Not surprisingly then, for Jews, obeying the law is 'good', since it contained 'the good' and was given by the One who alone is 'good'. The Psalms teach that to 'do good' is to observe the commands of the law (cf. Pss 34:14–15; 37:3, 27). Thus in Judaism generally 'good works' refers to 'obeying Torah'.[40] The Dead Sea Scrolls provide clear evidence that 'doing good' is in response to the law. In the *Community Rule* the 'Instructor' was to teach the community to 'do that which is good and upright' (1QS 1.2) and 'hold fast to all good deeds' (1QS 1.5). Significantly, such teaching is set in the context of the foundational call to 'live by the Laws of God' (1QS 1.7) and 'walk faultless in all his ways [the law]' (1QS 2.2).

Although Paul has much to say about 'good works', he never connects them to obeying the law. While the plural 'good works' is found frequently in the Pastoral Epistles, and turns up in the famous summary of Paul's gospel in Ephesians 2:8–10, the related notion of 'doing good' is found throughout the undisputed Pauline letters, where believers are urged to 'do good' (Rom. 13:3; Gal. 6:9–10; 1 Thess. 5:15; 2 Cor. 5:10). The singular 'good work' occurs in Romans

[38] Both the Old and New Testaments agree that 'good works' are that which is pleasing to God (eg. Pss 34:14–15; 37:27; Matt. 5:16; 1 Pet. 2:12).

[39] That *kalos* and *agathos* are roughly synonymous in this connection is reflected in the Pastoral Epistles, with an equal occurrence of both to denote 'good works'; see respectively 1 Tim. 3:1; 5:10, 25; 6:18; Titus 2:7, 14; 3:8, 14; and 1 Tim. 2:10; 5:10; 2 Tim. 2:21; 3:17; Titus 1:16; 3:1.

[40] Lincoln 1990: 114. See e.g. Pss 34:14–15; 37:27; 2 Chr. 19:11.

2:7[41] and the phrase 'every good work' also appears (2 Cor. 9:8; Col. 1:10; 2 Thess. 2:17). If Paul does not speak of good works in connection with the law, how does he characterize them?

Having excluded adherence to the Law of Moses for believers in Christ in Galatians 1 – 5, in 6:9–10 Paul urges them nonetheless 'not to become weary in doing good. . . . [to] do good to all people, especially to the household of faith' (my tr.). Betz understands the nature of these deeds as 'everything the Christian is responsible for doing'.[42] Longenecker argues that Galatians 5:13 – 6:10 are a unit, with 'serve one another in love' (5:13, my tr.) and 'doing good' (6:9–10 NIV) forming an inclusio. In the context of Galatians 5 – 6, 'doing good' is the outworking of 'the fruit of the Spirit' (5:22), the result of 'crucifying the flesh' in union with Christ Jesus (5:24, my tr.) and 'guided by the Spirit' (5:25). In other words, 'doing good' becomes a general way of referring to the believer's ongoing response to the gospel. The other references to 'good works' in Paul's letters also fit this pattern. They occur in contexts where Paul explores how the gospel and the grace of God teach us to live. Nowhere does doing the commands of the Law of Moses constitute 'doing good'.

The one possible exception to this is 2 Timothy 3:16–17, which affirms that 'all Scripture is inspired by God and is useful for teaching . . . so that everyone who belongs to God may be proficient, equipped for *every good work*'. That 'Scripture' includes a reference to the law is clear from the only other reference to 'Scripture' in the Pastoral Epistles, 1 Timothy 5:18, which introduces a quotation from Deuteronomy 25:4. While it must be granted that 2 Timothy 3:16–17 does link 'doing good' with the law, the link is not direct. To recall a pattern of usage noted above, the text does not say 'obeying' or 'doing' the law will lead to 'good works'. Instead, Paul uses four terms to explain the usefulness of Scripture: 'teaching, rebuking, correcting and training in righteousness' (NIV). This posture is not one of seeing Scripture, including the law, as a binding norm to be obeyed, but as a valuable and necessary source for ethics to be read with profit. I will explore this distinction further in chapter 6. For now, suffice it to say that 2 Timothy 3:16–17 does not supply evidence of Christian 'good works' being a response to the law *as law*.

According to Paul, if for Jews doing good concerns keeping the law, for Christians doing good is the outworking of the fruit of the Spirit.

---

[41] A 'good work' is also found in Phil. 1:6, but there it refers to the activity of God in saving believers rather than a positive human activity.
[42] Betz 1979: 309.

Paul's selective use of texts from Deuteronomy

Along with noticing the many specific terms Paul does not use of Christians with respect to the law that are regularly used of and by Jews, it is also instructive to notice his selective use of some key Old Testament texts. It is striking that when Paul cites prominent texts from Scripture that endorse obeying the law, he does so without endorsing law observance. For an example of Paul's explicitly avoiding language about obeying the law for Christians, see the section 'Deuteronomy 9:4 and 30:11–14 in Romans 10:6–9' in chapter 5. The same goes for other texts from Deuteronomy.

Perhaps the most famous text in the Hebrew Bible, besides the Decalogue, is the Shema (Deut. 6:4–5). Bursting with theological and ethical implications, with its affirmation of monotheism and the command to 'love the LORD your God', the Shema is 'central to the whole book of Deuteronomy'.[43] And there is no doubt that the Shema impacted Paul's thought profoundly. To take just one example, evidence for the influence of the Shema on 1 Corinthians can be felt in Paul's call to undistracted devotion to the Lord in 7:32–35, his emphasis on love and edification in chapters 8–14 and in his teasing out of the implications of monotheism in the treatment of idolatry in 8:1–6.[44] Paul knew the Shema by heart and its imprint on his Christology and ethics is unmistakable.

The framework of the Shema in its various contexts in Deuteronomy concerns obedience to the law. Yet this aspect of the relevant texts is entirely absent from Paul's appropriation of the Shema. Consider the verses introducing the Shema in Deuteronomy 6 and the presentation of related material in Deuteronomy 11 and Numbers 15. In the following citations of these texts I have included in brackets the relevant words from the LXX that characterize Israel's relationship to the law (e.g. the verbs *phylassō*, *poieō* and *entellō*). While Paul quotes and alludes to various elements from such texts, such as the oneness of God and the double command to love God and neighbour, he never uses any of these terms for the way in which Christians relate to the law. It is hard to conceive such omissions as anything but deliberate.

In the opening words of Deuteronomy 6 and in Deuteronomy 11 Israel is not only told to keep the law, but the verses underscore the

---

[43] Craigie 1976: 169.
[44] See Rosner 2007a: 126–127.

uncompromising, undivided and comprehensive nature of this obedience with phrases such as 'the entire commandment' and 'his every commandment', and the heaping up of synonyms for the law ('statutes', 'ordinances', 'decrees', 'commandments'). The nation is to 'keep his charge, his decrees, his ordinances, and his commandments always'.

> Now this is the commandment – the statutes and the ordinances – that the LORD your God charged me to teach you to observe [*poiein*] in the land that you are about to cross into and occupy, so that you and your children and your children's children may fear the LORD your God all the days of your life, and keep [*phylasesthai*] all his decrees and his commandments that I am commanding [*entellomai*] you, so that your days may be long. Hear therefore, O Israel, and observe [*phylaxai poiein*] them diligently, so that it may go well with you, and so that you may multiply greatly in a land flowing with milk and honey, as the LORD, the God of your ancestors, has promised you.
>   Hear, O Israel: The LORD is our God, the LORD alone. (Deut. 6:1–4)

> You shall love the LORD your God, therefore, and keep [*phylaxē*] his charge, his decrees, his ordinances, and his commandments always. (Deut. 11:1)

> Keep [*phylaxesthe*], then, this entire commandment that I am commanding [*entellomai*] you today, so that you may have strength to go in and occupy the land that you are crossing over to occupy. (Deut. 11:8)

> If you will only heed his every commandment that I am commanding [*entellomai*] you today – loving the LORD your God, and serving him with all your heart and with all your soul. (Deut. 11:13)

Likewise, in Numbers 15 Israel is to remember and do all of God's commandments:

> The LORD said to Moses: Speak to the Israelites, and tell them to make fringes on the corners of their garments throughout their generations and to put a blue cord on the fringe at each corner.

> You have the fringe so that, when you see it, you will remember all
> the commandments of the LORD and do them [*poiēsate autas*], and
> not follow the lust of your own heart and your own eyes. So you
> shall remember and do all my commandments [*poiēsēte pasas tas
> entolas*], and you shall be holy to your God. I am the LORD your
> God, who brought you out of the land of Egypt, to be your God:
> I am the LORD your God. (Num. 15:37–41)

The notes that these key Old Testament texts strike in terms of
obedience to the law are completely absent from Paul's exhortations
to believers in Christ. Examples of key texts from across the Hebrew
Scriptures and also from Jewish intertestamental literature could easily
be multiplied. The way in which these Jewish texts conceive of the
people of God, namely as being under the law and its demands, is
deliberately avoided by Paul.

Paul's labels for the law as law-covenant

Paul has his own way of clarifying the sense in which Christians are
not under the law.[45] In my discussion of Romans 2 above, law as
'letter' (*gramma*; or 'legal code') emerged as a distinctively Jewish
perspective on the law. Aside from 'letter', three other terms in Paul's
letters describe the law as a possession of the Jews, but not of Christians: 'decrees', 'commandments' and 'book'.

In Ephesians 2:15 and Colossians 2:14 Paul writes of Christians as
being freed from the law as 'decrees', *dogma*, that is, 'rules or regulations to be observed' (BDAG 1a). And in Romans 7:7–12, in a
context of the law leading to death rather than life, as noted above,
Paul uses 'commandment', *entolē*, as a synonym for 'law'.

In Paul's quotation of Deuteronomy 27:26 in Galatians 3:10 he
changes 'the words of this law' in the citation of Deuteronomy to 'the
book [*biblion*] of the law': 'Cursed is everyone who does not observe
and obey all the things written in the book of the law.' In referring to
the curse of the law Paul shifts from the law as oral proclamation
to the law as written document, in a manner reminiscent of his use
of 'letter' as a reference to the law as an external and objective code.[46]

---

[45] In chapter 2 we observed that in 1 Tim. 1:8–10 Christians do not use the law as
law, *nomimōs* (lawfully).
[46] Cf. Childs 2008: 137: 'For Paul the letter of Scripture is the Mosaic Torah in its
written documentation.'

Tellingly, as Watson points out, in other texts in Deuteronomy, 'the book of the law' is associated with the curse of the law.[47] Paul conceives of the law as a letter that kills, as a book that brings a curse, as decrees that stand against us, and as commandments to be obeyed. In every case, according to Paul, this is not how the law relates to Christians. Intriguingly, such negative characterizations of law also appear in English idiom, with being prosecuted according to 'the letter of the law' and having 'the book thrown at one' being decidedly unpleasant experiences. The good news is that when it comes to the Law of Moses, God does not hold us to the letter of the law, nor does he throw the book at us!

Whereas at the end of other chapters I conclude with a summary paraphrase of what Paul says about the subject at hand, this chapter closes with what Paul says about Jews with respect to the law but does not say of believers in Christ.

Not in Paul's own words (a summary and paraphrase)

Paul never says, as he does of Jews, that believers in Christ rely on the law, boast about the law, know God's will through the law, are educated in the law, have light, knowledge and truth because of the law, do, observe and keep the law, on occasion transgress the law, or possess the law as letter or a written code, as a book, as decrees, or as commandments. Paul also never says, as he does of Jews, that Christians learn the law, walk according to the law, and expect good fruit and good works to flow from obedience to the law.

---

[47] Watson 2004: 432. Cf. Deut. 28:61; 29:19–20, 26; 30:10 (also Josh. 23:6).

Chapter Four

'Under the law of Christ'
Replacement of the law

Christ is given lordship over mankind in place of the Law.
(Adolf Schlatter)[1]

In a real sense conformity to Christ, His teaching and
His life has taken the place for Paul of conformity to
the Jewish Torah. . . . We should accept on a priori
grounds that attributes ascribed to the Torah revealed
on Sinai would by the Apostle be transferred to
Christ.

(W. D. Davies)[2]

This is what Paul finds wrong in Judaism: it is not
Christianity.

(E. P. Sanders)[3]

In the new era the prophetic-eschatological good news of
salvation/restoration in Christ has displaced halakhic law
as the foundational guide to community life.

(Roy E. Ciampa)[4]

Paul's negative stance towards the law goes beyond explicit critique
(see chapter 2) and critical silence (see chapter 3). Not only does the
apostle say that believers are not 'under the law', and not say that we
'keep', 'obey', 'transgress' or possess the law as 'letter' or legal code,
or 'walk according to the law', but something else is put in the privi-
leged place normally occupied by the law. This motif of substitution
is the focus of this chapter.

[1] Schlatter 1999: 242.
[2] Davies 1982a: 148–149.
[3] Sanders 1977: 552.
[4] Ciampa 1998: 296.

In New Testament theology the theme of replacement as a way of relating the Old and New Testament is regularly associated with the Fourth Gospel. In John, Jesus is the new Moses, enacts a new exodus, eclipses the great Jewish feasts and institutions that marked God's saving work in the past, replaces the Jerusalem temple, and, by dying during Passover week, is the ultimate Jewish Passover sacrifice. Hebrews stands out among the New Testament letters as developing similar ideas, especially in relation to Jesus vis-à-vis sacrifice and priesthood.

Paul's letters make similar moves, even if less explicitly than John and Hebrews. In Colossians, for example, Christ effectively replaces the Jerusalem temple as the new and greater locus of the presence of God (1:19). The reality found in Christ replaces the keeping of sacred days and laws of clean and unclean foods (2:16–17). And in his death Christ is 'cut off' from the old world, thereby replacing the rite of physical circumcision (2:11–13).[5]

How prevalent is the motif of replacement in Paul's thought with respect to the law? Commentators on Paul's letters familiar with his Jewish roots sometimes make passing remarks that point to its subtle presence:

- With reference to Romans 15:16 Dunn notes that whereas in *4 Maccabees* 7.8 'priestly service' is offered to the law, Paul offers 'priestly service' to his gospel.[6]
- In connection with Ephesians 6:4, where fathers are to instruct their children 'in the Lord', Hoehner notes that 'the father's training and admonition is not . . . centered around the law as in the rabbinics, but, rather, [is] Christocentric'.[7]
- N. T. Wright argues that the underlying view of Christ in Colossians (esp. in 1:15–20) is that 'he has taken the position which Judaism assigned to the Jewish Law'.[8]
- In Galatians 1:6–9, according to Ciampa, Paul describes the Galatian Christians' pending apostasy in terms that can be compared with scriptural material about turning from the law; Paul's treatment of apostasy from his gospel may be compared to the way Jews describe apostasy from God and his law.[9]

---

[5] See Beetham 2008.
[6] Dunn 1988b: 860. Gk. *hierourgeō*.
[7] Hoehner 2002: 798.
[8] N. T. Wright 1986: 25.
[9] Ciampa 1998: 238–239.

- In 1 Corinthians 7:32–35 Paul explains that he prefers singleness because marriage makes life more complicated and can be a distraction from devotion to Christ, whereas in several rabbinic texts, worldly preoccupations, such as a wife, are seen as a potential distraction from the study of Torah.[10]

A motif of replacement with respect to the law is in fact deeply embedded in Paul's thought. Paul not only does not say certain things about the law in Romans 2 and elsewhere with reference to Christians (see chapter 3), but he shifts the focus from the law to something else by using the same words and concepts: believers do not rely on the law, but on Christ; do not boast in the law, but in God through Christ; do not find God's will through the law, but in apostolic instruction, wisdom and the gospel; are not instructed by the law, but by the gospel; and are not obliged to obey the law, but rather apostolic instruction.[11]

Six further lines of evidence show how deep and wide is the replacement of the law in Paul's letters. These include (1) a Christ–Torah antithesis; (2) substitutes for the Law of Moses; (3) teaching on Christians fulfilling the law; (4) instructions on how to walk; (5) the language of newness; and (6) 'circumcision is nothing' complements.

The regular use of the rhetoric of 'not this, but that instead' in the material in question sharpens the polemical edge of Paul's engagement with the law. It is also striking that the things that sit in the place of the law in the Christian life are remarkably similar across all six strands. If the law held a central place in the life of Jews, one of the findings of this chapter is to notice that which is central for the Christian life according to Paul.

Concerns were raised in his own day and have been raised ever since that Paul's releasing believers from the Law of Moses will lead to lawless behaviour. Does Paul's abolition of the law leave a vacuum when it comes to morality? Or, in the words of Romans 6:1, 'What then are we to say? Should we continue in sin in order that grace may abound?' The material covered in this chapter is effectively Paul's answer to this question. The Law of Moses substitutes, and others, supply reassurance that Paul's law-free gospel will not lead to licence. On the contrary, the resources of the gospel are a far better place from which to keep the commandments of God.

[10] Ciampa and Rosner 2007: 715.
[11] In chapter 5 I consider Paul's selective quotation of Deut. 9:4 and 30:11–14 in Rom. 10:6–9, where he substitutes references to Christ and faith in the message of the gospel in place of obligations to obey the law.

The Christ–Torah antitheses

Terence Donaldson observes that there is at least one thing on which Paul did not change his mind after the Damascus road experience: 'Both before and after his conversion Paul saw Christ and Torah as being in some way mutually exclusive categories.'[12]

The two most commonly cited texts in connection with Paul's so-called Christ–Torah antithesis are in Galatians 2 and Philippians 3. In both texts, if once the law held a central place for Paul the Jew, for Paul the Christian that place is firmly and exclusively occupied by Christ. Galatians 2, as Hurtado puts it, 'describes Paul's own existential move to a faith stance in which he entrusted himself wholly to the redemptive efficacy of Jesus' crucifixion and surrendered his previous promotion of full Torah observance as requisite for being found righteous by God'[13]:

> For through the law I died to the law, so that I might live to God. I have been crucified with Christ; and it is no longer I who live, but it is Christ who lives in me. And the life I now live in the flesh I live by faith in the Son of God, who loved me and gave himself for me. (Gal. 2:19–20)

Unpacking these verses and the theology they espouse would take us too far from our immediate concerns.[14] Suffice it to say, two existences are contrasted. Paul's life 'to God', his faith-union with Christ, takes the place of his life under the law. As Bruce puts it, 'A change of lordship, from law to Christ, has taken place.'[15] The change is styled as moving from death to life. Believers share both Christ's death to the old order under the law (Gal. 4:4) and his resurrection to new life.

In a similar way in Philippians 3:4–14, to gain Christ Paul must give up something:

> Yet whatever gains I had, these I have come to regard as loss because of Christ. More than that, I regard everything as loss because of the surpassing value of knowing Christ Jesus my Lord. For his sake

---

[12] Donaldson 1989: 655–656.

[13] Hurtado 2004: 428.

[14] For example, concerning the interpretation of the opening clause, 'For through the law I died to the law', Bruce (1982: 142) somewhat pessimistically counsels that 'certainty is unattainable'.

[15] Ibid. 144.

> I have suffered the loss of all things, and I regard them as rubbish, in order that I may gain Christ. (Phil. 3:7–8)

The 'gains' Paul gainsays are identified in verse 6 as 'righteousness under the law'. In Hurtado's words, 'for Paul identifying himself with Jesus' crucifixion seems to have involved forsaking his Torah zealotry for devotion to Jesus as God's Son'.[16]

The question of the origin of Paul's Christ–Torah antitheses has a long and debated history. Suggestions range from Paul's pre-conversion despair over keeping the law and expectations about the Torah in the messianic age, to his convictions about Christology, soteriology and/or ecclesiology, to sociological explanations.[17] Whatever the answer, it is clear that for Paul if salvation is through Christ crucified, salvation cannot come through Torah: 'if justification comes through the law, then Christ died for nothing' (Gal. 2:21).

Paul's conversion and calling marked a sea change in his life and a paradigm shift in his thinking, 'a transfer of allegiance from one set of world-structuring convictions to another'.[18] The message of a crucified and resurrected Messiah meant that Christ took the place of the Torah.

Law of Moses substitutes

Paul uses three phrases in Galatians, 1 Corinthians and Romans that have some connection, one way or another, to the Law of Moses: 'law of Christ', 'law of faith' and 'law of the Spirit of life in Christ Jesus'.[19] Unfortunately, the interpretation of these intriguing expressions has reached no consensus. The big question of interpretation in each case concerns whether the 'law' in the 'law of Christ/faith/Spirit' is the Law of Moses or not. Are Paul's alternatives to the Law of Moses the law reconfigured somehow in connection with Christ, faith and the Spirit? Or are they something entirely different, such as Christ's moral teaching, Christ's example, love or something else? Various mediating positions, such as understanding Paul's referring to the Law of Moses read with the emphasis on love, are also possible.

---

16 Hurtado 2004: 430.
17 See Donaldson 1989 on these and more explanations.
18 Ibid. 682.
19 Other genitival phrases using *nomos* appear that are not juxtaposed with the Law of Moses, such as 'law of righteousness', 'law of sin', 'law of marriage', etc.

Galatians 6:2

Chronologically, of the three phrases Paul uses 'the law of Christ' first in Galatians: 'Bear one another's burdens, and in this way you will fulfil *the law of Christ* [*ton nomon tou Christou*]' (Gal. 6:2). There are good reasons to think that its use here is polemical, most likely coining it as a counter to his opponents.[20] As it turns out, this polemical streak can be detected for all three phrases throughout their usage, whatever their precise interpretation. In context, all four occurrences of the three phrases appear in contrast to and as a substitute for the Law of Moses.

The biggest question facing interpreters of 'the law of Christ' concerns whether 'the law' refers to the Mosaic law. Dunn exemplifies those who answer in the affirmative:

> Paul refers in this shorthand way to the Jesus-tradition as indicating how Jesus interpreted the law in his teaching and actions . . . this does not mean a law other than the Torah, the (Jewish) law. It means that law as interpreted by the love command in the light of the Jesus-tradition and the Christ-event.[21]

In support of this position, it is noteworthy that the referent for *nomos* in Galatians is consistently the Law of Moses; of the thirty-one occurrences of *nomos* prior to 6:2 only 5:18 and 5:23 do not unambiguously refer to Torah (being possible references to law in general). The genitive in 'the law of Christ', *tou Christou*, would then be understood quite plausibly as something like law 'determined by' or law 'belonging to' Christ. And connecting 'the law of Christ' to love is given credence in the light of Galatians 5:14, 'the whole law is summed up in a single commandment, "You shall love your neighbour as yourself,"' and Romans 13:8–10, both of which cite Leviticus 19:18. Jesus' own summary of the law as love of God and neighbour (Matt. 22:36–40; Mark 12:28–31) gives further support.

However, as David Horrell points out,[22] there are reasons to doubt identifying the Law of Moses as the referent for 'law' in the phrase 'the law of Christ'. While 'the law of Moses' (1 Cor. 9:9) and 'law of God' (Rom. 7:22, 25) refer to the Torah, for Paul Christ is consistently

[20] See Betz 1979: 300–301.

[21] Dunn 1993a: 322–323. Dunn's interpretation of 'the law of faith' and the 'law of the Spirit' goes along similar lines.

[22] Horrell 2005: 226–227.

set over against the law. In Galatians Christ is the one who redeems from the curse of the law (3:13) and it is in Christ that Paul has died to the law. Even if the previous references to 'law' in Galatians all use *nomos* to refer to the Law of Moses, the addition of *tou Christou* means it is better to take 'law of Christ' to mean something different. The polemical context of Galatians, where Paul is forcefully opposing the imposition of the law on believers in Christ (e.g. 4:21a), also renders a positive reference to the Law of Moses in Galatians 6:2 unlikely.

If 'the law of Christ' is not the Law of Moses in the light of Christ, what is it? A reference to the moral teaching of Jesus seems unlikely. With respect to Jesus tradition, there are only three explicit citations of sayings of Jesus (1 Cor. 7:10–11; 9:14; 11:23–25) and eight or nine allusions to or echoes of Jesus' teaching in Paul's letters.[23] Three prominent allusions that concern ethical matters are Luke 6:27–28 // Matthew 5:44 in Romans 12:14 concerning non-retaliation; Mark 7:15 in Romans 14:14 concerning (non-)defilement of unclean food; and Mark 9:50 in 1 Thessalonians 5:13, which has to do with living at peace.[24] But there are no quotations of Jesus or allusions to sayings of Jesus in Galatians. Specific teaching from Jesus is important to Paul and his communities, but it is not prominent enough in Paul's letters to be unambiguously labelled 'the law of Christ'.

The context of Galatians favours taking 'the law of Christ' to mean behaviour in keeping with the Christ's example. Richard Hays argues convincingly that Paul has in view 'Christ's example of burden-bearing'. 'Law' then has the meaning of 'normative pattern', which all who are in Christ are called to fulfil in their relationships with others. As Hays notes, the theme of Christ's redemptive self-giving appears throughout the letter: 1:3–4; 2:20; 3:13–14; 4:4–5.[25] In this following of Christ's example of self-sacrifice on behalf of others Paul leads the way, as 2:19–20 attests (cf. 1 Cor. 4:9–16). In this sense 'fulfilling the law of Christ' is the equivalent of Paul's hope for the Galatian believers that 'Christ is formed in you' (4:19).

[23] See Dunn 1997: 650–651.
[24] It is worth noting that the first two cases revolve around biblical interpretation (of Lev. 19:18 and the food laws in Leviticus respectively) and the third echoes a biblical theme. When it comes to ethics, both Jesus and Paul regularly stand in the biblical and Jewish tradition.
[25] See Hays 1989: 277–287. Cf. Barclay 1988: 133–134, who takes a compromise position: 'When Paul talks of "fulfilling the law of Christ" he means fulfilling the law in the way exemplified by Christ, i.e. fulfilling it through love.'

1 Corinthians 9:21

A variation on 'the law of Christ' occurs in 1 Corinthians:

> To the Jews I became as a Jew, in order to win Jews. To those
> under the law I became as one under the law (though I myself am
> not under the law) so that I might win those under the law. To
> those outside the law I became as one outside the law (though I
> am not free from God's law but am *under Christ's law* [*ennomos
> Christou*]) so that I might win those outside the law. (1 Cor.
> 9:20–21)[26]

Paul would not want the Corinthians to think he would ever act like
a person who is not committed to obeying God. Thus, to avoid any
misunderstanding he adds the words 'though I am not free from God's
law but am under Christ's law'. 'Free from God's law' contains the
third use of the same word for 'without law' in this verse, *anomos*, but
this time the near context suggests the meaning 'free fr[om] obedience
to God' (BDAG 85d). In one sense Paul is 'without law', but in
another he is not.

The translation suggested by BDAG (85d) helpfully clarifies the
significance of all the legal language in 1 Corinthians 9:21: 'I identified
as one outside Mosaic jurisdiction with those outside it; not, of
course, being outside God's jurisdiction, but inside Christ's.'

Paul is not bound by the Law of Moses but is bound to obey God
as one living under the authority of the Lord Jesus Christ. Fee
explains, 'This does not mean that in Christ a new set of laws has
taken the place of the old, although in terms of specifics it would
certainly refer to those kinds of ethical demands given, for example,
in Rom. 12 and Gal. 5–6.'[27] 1 Corinthians suggests 'lawlessness'
(especially in the forms of idolatry, sexual immorality and greed) was
prevalent in Corinth and that may also have led Paul to emphasize
that the fact that he is not under the law does not mean he participates
in such 'lawless' behaviour. Like Paul, the Corinthians must live under
Christ's lordship.

---

[26] The word translated 'outside the law' by the NRSV (*anomos*) that Paul uses in this
text usually means 'evil' or 'wicked' in the LXX, as in English 'lawless' or 'outlaw'.
However, Paul uses it in v. 21 to mean 'not under the law' of Moses.
[27] Fee 1987: 430. Cf. Thiselton 2000: 704, commenting on 1 Cor. 9:21: 'the law of
Christ should not be restricted to any body of traditional sayings of Jesus. Christians
stand under the direction of the gospel as that which witnesses to Christ in a broader
and more comprehensive sense.'

Thus in 1 Corinthians 'law of Christ', expressed differently from in Galatians, carries a different but related meaning. It is equivalent to living under Christ's lordship, a concept reinforced throughout the letter.[28] If Corinthian problems can be attributed to their cultural background, Paul's various responses may be ascribed to his understanding of the crucified Christ and his lordship over against all human and spiritual powers; in almost every case Paul pits Christ against the prevailing culture.[29] He appeals for unity in the name of Christ (1:10), who is the power and wisdom of God (2:23–24) and the foundation of the church (3:11). The church must be cleansed of the incestuous man because of Christ's sacrifice (5:7). To have relations with a prostitute is to violate Christ (6:15). Eating food sacrificed to idols must be avoided for the sake of one for whom Christ died (8:11) and in imitation of Christ (11:1). With respect to head coverings, he notes that Christ is the head of every man (11:3). The Lord's Supper must be celebrated by discerning 'the body' of Christ (11:29). Spiritual gifts are to be exercised in order to build up the body of Christ (12:27). The resurrection of believers is grounded in the resurrection of Christ (15:3–23). Finally, all of history is about the subjection of all things under Christ's feet and his presentation of the fully redeemed kingdom/ creation to God the Father (15:24–28). Throughout the letter 'Christ' appears 64 times, 'Lord' 66 times and 'Jesus' 26 times.

Romans 3:27 and 8:1

If in Galatians, the law of Christ concerns behaviour in keeping with Christ's example, and in 1 Corinthians it is equivalent to the related idea of living under the lordship of Christ, two different examples of Law of Moses substitutes occur in Romans. The first is 'the law of faith':

> Then what becomes of boasting? It is excluded. By what law? By that of works? No, but by *the law of faith* [*nomou pisteōs*]. For we hold that a person is justified by faith apart from works prescribed by the law. (Rom. 3:27–28)

Some interpreters understand 'the law of faith' and 'the law of works' as two different ways of using the Law of Moses. Understood

[28] Overlapping expressions that also focus on Christ crucified in 1 Corinthians include 'the mind of Christ', 'the word of the cross' and 'the wisdom of God'.

[29] In a similar vein K. Barth (1933: 103–104) argues that 'what is at stake in Christianity is the rule of God and nothing else. That is the Either-Or with which he confronts the Corinthian Church all along the line.'

in terms of works, the law leads to boasting; understood in terms of faith, it does not.[30]

However, as Moo argues, at this point in Romans Paul has made the law and faith mutually exclusive; 3:21–26 and 3:28 are what lead Paul to ask in 3:31, 'do we then nullify the law through faith?' (NET). 'This question does not make sense unless Paul has, in this context, fully separated "faith" from the law of Moses.'[31] Indeed, the distinction between doing and believing, with the former aligned with the law, is maintained throughout Romans (see 2:25–29; 3:2; 4:2–8; 9:31 – 10:8).

It is better to understand Paul as contrasting two different 'laws' in Romans 3:27. The referent to 'law of works', as Moo puts it, 'would naturally bring to mind *the* law, the torah'.[32] Paul has forged such a link between the law and works in Romans (see 2:6–16, 25–27; 3:20) that the connection may be assumed. Thus with the contrast between 'the law of faith' and 'the law of works' Paul asserts that 'the characteristic demand of the Mosaic covenant – works – is contrasted with the basic demand of the New Covenant – faith'.[33] The 'law of faith', as Thielman suggests, may even refer to the new covenant.[34]

Similar expressions to 'law of works' and 'law of faith' are found in Romans 8:1–2: 'There is therefore now no condemnation for those who are in Christ Jesus. For *the law of the Spirit of life in Christ Jesus* [*nomos tou pneumatos tēs zōēs en Christō Iēsou*] has set you free from the law of sin and of death.' As Schreiner puts it, 'it is hard to conceive of Paul that the law in conjunction with the Spirit frees people from sin, since elsewhere Paul emphasizes that those who are "under the law" are under sin'.[35] The law promised life (see chapter 2, 'The law as a failed path to life') but proved to be death (7:10). It is better to take 'the law of the Spirit of life' in contrast to 'the law of sin and of death'.

In each of the cases in Galatians, 1 Corinthians and Romans 'the law of Christ/faith/the Spirit' is a substitute for the Law of Moses. In three pithy expressions Paul sums up the solution to the plight of living under the Law of Moses. The 'law of faith' and the 'law of the Spirit' point to the crucial nature of faith in Christ and the work of

---

[30] See Moo 1996: 248 for a list of proponents, including Cranfield, N. T. Wright and Dunn.

[31] Ibid.

[32] Ibid. 249, italics original.

[33] Ibid. 250.

[34] Thielman 1994: 183.

[35] Schreiner 2010: 22.

the Spirit, and 'the law of Christ' points us to living our new lives after his example and under Christ's lordship.

Fulfilling the law

In chapter 3 we noted that Paul never says that Christians observe, keep, do or obey the law (or transgress it). He does, however, as Betz observed, say that believers in Christ 'fulfil' the law. Paul's notion of Christian fulfilment of the law appears in three texts, each using the verb *plēroō*:

> For God has done what the law, weakened by the flesh, could not do: by sending his own Son in the likeness of sinful flesh, and to deal with sin, he condemned sin in the flesh, so that the just requirement of the law might be fulfilled [*plērōthē*] in us, who walk not according to the flesh but according to the Spirit. (Rom. 8:3–4)

> Let no debt remain outstanding, except the continuing debt to love one another, for whoever loves others has fulfilled [*peplērōken*] the law. The commandments, 'You shall not commit adultery,' 'You shall not murder,' 'You shall not steal,' 'You shall not covet,' and whatever other command there may be, are summed up in this one command: 'Love your neighbour as yourself.' (Rom. 13:8–9 TNIV)

> You, my brothers and sisters, were called to be free. But do not use your freedom to indulge the sinful nature; rather, serve one another humbly in love. For the entire law is fulfilled [*peplērōtai*] in keeping this one command: 'Love your neighbour as yourself.' (Gal. 5:13–14 TNIV)

In part due to the nature of biblical commentaries the discussion of these three texts is usually undertaken with just one or at best two in view. However, in order to appreciate Paul's teaching on Christians fulfilling the law, all three need to be taken into account. The three texts together raise a number of questions: What distinguishes Christian fulfilment of the law from Jewish doing of the law? Do Christians fulfil the law by righteous living or does Christ fulfil the law for believers? What has love got to do with it?

The first thing to notice is that when Paul speaks of Christian fulfilment of the law, he is not referring to isolated laws, but the law as a whole that is fulfilled: 'the entire law is fulfilled' (Gal. 5:14); 'the just requirement[36] of the law might be fulfilled' (Rom. 8:3); 'whoever loves has fulfilled the law', including 'whatever other command there may be' (Rom. 13:8–9 NIV). All three references to fulfilling the law have in mind not isolated laws but the law as a whole.

The verb *plēroō*, when referring to the law in Romans and Galatians, goes beyond mere obedience to the law and also indicates that the law has in some sense been brought to completion. Barclay notes that the verb is never used in the LXX or in Second Temple Jewish texts in Greek in relation to the law.[37] While this is largely correct, there is one exception. In the *Testament of Naphtali* 8.7–9 *plēroō* is used in the sense of 'obeying' certain commands:

> For the commandments of the law [*hai entolai tou nomou*] are twofold, and through prudence they must be fulfilled [*plērountai*]. For there is a time for a man to embrace his wife, and a time to abstain from that for his prayer. So there are two commandments [*dyo entolai*]; and, unless they be done in their order, they cause sin.

While this text shows that *plēroō* may denote the 'doing' (*prassō*) of commands, it is an isolated instance. Pauline usage suggests another meaning.

The usage of *plēroō* in Romans is enlightening. Leaving aside Romans 8:4 and 13:8, *plēroō* is used four times in the letter. In three of these it has the sense of 'to make full' (BDAG 828a): (1) evildoers are '*[f]ull* of envy, murder, strife, deceit, craftiness' (Rom. 1:29); (2) 'May the God of hope *fill* you with all joy and peace in believing' (Rom. 15:13); and (3) 'I myself feel confident about you, my brothers and sisters, that you yourselves are *full* of goodness, filled with all knowledge, and able to instruct one another' (Rom. 15:14). The fourth example illustrates the sense of *plēroō* in connection with the law: 'by the power of signs and wonders, by the power of the Spirit of God, so that from Jerusalem and as far around as Illyricum I have *fully* proclaimed the good news of Christ' (Rom. 15:19). Here Paul uses *plēroō* in the sense of bringing his ministry in those areas to completion (cf. BDAG 829b: 'to bring to completion an activity'). The

---

[36] Paul uses the Gk. *dikaiōma* with its usual LXX meaning of 'right or just requirement'. Whereas the plural *dikaiōmata* designates specific commandments in the LXX and in the NT (e.g. Luke 1:6; Heb. 9:1, 10; and Rom. 2:26), the singular *dikaiōma* refers to the righteous behaviour required by the law in general or as a unity. Cf. Moo 1996: 482: *dikaiōma* in Rom. 8:4 'denotes the summary (note the singular, as opposed to the plural in 2:26) of what the law demands of God's people'.

[37] Barclay 1988: 138.

use of *plēroō* in Colossians 4:17 illustrates the same meaning: 'And say to Archippus, "See that you *complete* the task that you have received in the Lord."' This meaning of the verb fits well in the contexts of Christian fulfilment of the law, where it denotes bringing the obligation to obey the law to its completion.[38]

In Romans 8:3 Paul points to the law as a failed path to righteousness and life: what 'the law could not do, God has done' (my tr.). Jesus' substitutionary death satisfies the righteous requirement of the law, 'to deal with sin'. As Moo explains, in Romans 8:3–4 'the law's just demand is fulfilled in Christians not through their own acts of obedience but through their incorporation into Christ. He fulfils the law; and in him, believers also fulfil the law.'[39]

The second part of Romans 8:4, which identifies those for whom the law is fulfilled as those 'who walk not according to the flesh but according to the Spirit', is better taken in a descriptive rather than an instrumental sense. It is not that 'the just decree is fulfilled in us by our walking', but those in whom the just decree is fulfilled are 'those who walk' in a certain manner. The just demand of the law is fulfilled, or brought to completion, *in us*, not by us. The incorporation of believers into Christ means that his perfect obedience to the law renders them 'no condemnation' of the law that leads to sin and death (Rom. 8:1, my tr.). The passive voice of *plēroō* in Romans 8:4 ('so that the just requirement of the law *might be fulfilled* in us') 'points not to something we are to do but to something that is done in and for us',[40]

However, the fulfilment of the law is not accomplished only *for believers*, but also *through believers*. Even if we understand Romans 8:4 in forensic terms, and the actual obedience of believers is not in view there, the obedience of believers is not far away. The clause in Romans 8:4 about the conduct, or walk, of believers, draws attention to the fact that Paul does not think that Christ's substitutionary death and fulfilling of the law's just requirements leaves believers without moral direction. However, the believer's walk is not according to the

---

[38] A few English versions translate *plēroō* in Galatians 5:14 as 'to sum up': 'For the whole law is summed up in a single commandment, "You shall love your neighbor as yourself"' (NRSV; cf. NIV 1984).

[39] Moo 1996: 484. One of Moo's arguments for this view (483) is that 'the passive verb [in Rom. 8:4], "might be fulfilled" points not to something that we are to do but to something that is done in and for us'. However, cf. Schreiner 1998: 405, who cites 2 Cor. 10:6: Paul will act 'whenever your obedience is fulfilled', where the passive points to the obedience of believers themselves.

[40] Moo 1996: 483. This point holds even if on occasion the verb can be used in the passive to indicate human activity, as in 2 Cor. 10:6: 'whenever your obedience *is fulfilled*' (my tr.).

law (see chapter 3), which has been made powerless by the flesh. Instead, those for whom Christ has fulfilled the law 'walk . . . according to the Spirit', that is, 'according to the values of the "new age", created and dominated by God's Spirit as his eschatological gift'.[41]

Romans 13:8–9 and Galatians 5:13–14 stress the same thing, spelling out that this completion of the law by believers is in connection with love. The fulfilment of the law through love is effectively the law's replacement. As Moo states, commenting on Romans 13:8, 'Christians who love others have satisfied the demands of the law *in toto*.'[42] If in Romans 8 Christ fulfils the law *for us*, in Romans 13 and Galatians 5 Christ fulfils the law *through us*.

With Paul's teaching on the Christian fulfilment of the law we meet the basis of our justification, in Christ's perfect obedience on our behalf, our safe position of being in union with him, and the fact that our new status leads to a new way of living, in love as the fulfilment of the law.

Walking in newness of life

'How to walk and please God' (1 Thess. 4:1, my tr.) was a question asked and debated in every quarter of Judaism in the first century. The standard Jewish answer, based firmly on Scripture, was to walk 'according to the law'. I reviewed some of the evidence for this in chapter 3, 'The absence of "walk according to the law" in Paul's ethics'.

In this light it is indeed striking that Paul never says that believers in Christ are to walk according to the law. But it is of course not the case that Paul has abandoned an interest in conduct pleasing to God, or even in the standard Jewish metaphor for such conduct.

However, instead of walking according to the law, Paul recommends walking according to a different set of norms: not as the Gentiles do (1 Cor. 3:3; 2 Cor. 10:2; Eph. 4:17), nor in idleness (1 Thess. 4:12), or as enemies of the gospel (Phil. 3:18); but according to or by the Spirit (Rom. 8:4; Gal. 5:16), apostolic example (Phil. 3:17), apostolic teaching (2 Thess. 3:6) and the truth of the gospel (Gal. 2:14); in Christ (Col. 2:6), in love (Rom. 14:15; Eph. 5:2), in newness of resurrection life (Rom. 6:4) and in good works (Eph. 2:10); as in the day (Rom. 13:13), as children of light (Eph. 5:15); by faith (2 Cor. 5:7); wisely (Eph. 5:15; Col 4:5).[43]

[41] Ibid. 485.
[42] Ibid. 814.
[43] The walking motif is obscured in many English Bible translations, which prefer to speak of more literal 'conduct'.

How is the change from the Jewish stress on walking in obedience to the law to other standards of conduct to be explained? One explanation would be to note that biblical-Jewish tradition has a second strand of metaphorical walking, in addition to walking according to the law, namely walking wisely. Walking as a figure for conduct is also found in the wisdom books. In Proverbs, for example, a 'wise' (13:20; 28:26) and 'blameless' (2:7; 19:1; 28:6, 18) walk 'in the ways of the just' (2:20, my tr.), 'the way of righteousness' (8:20) and 'insight' (9:6) is recommended, as opposed to walking in 'ways of darkness' (2:13), 'the way of evildoers' (4:14). If Paul is tapping into this tradition, which Ephesians 5:15 and Colossians 4:5 might suggest, then inferring a replacement of the law would be unnecessary.

However, many of the positive norms Paul employs in the context of his use of the walking metaphor suggest that he does in fact present the Christian walk as a replacement for the Jewish walk of obedience to the law. In particular, the language of 'newness', 'light' and the 'Spirit' associate the Christian walk with the new age of the Spirit, a time when the Mosaic dispensation has come to an end.

Walking 'in *newness* [*kainotēs*] of life' in Romans 6:4 is Paul's description of life under grace, not under the law (see 6:15). The polemical edge to this new life is clear from the context in Romans. At the end of Romans 5 Paul states that 'the law was brought in so that the trespass might increase' (5:20 NIV) and then feels obliged to explain how life under grace does not do likewise. That the noun 'newness' points not only to resurrection life but can point also to life not under the law is evident from its other use in Romans 7:6: 'But now, by dying to what once bound us, we have been released from the law so that we serve in the *new way* of the Spirit, and not in the old way of the written code' (TNIV). Paul's use of the adjective *kainos* offers further confirmation that a walk in 'newness of life' is the attractive alternative to life under the law: Paul writes of a 'new covenant' (1 Cor. 11:25; 2 Cor. 3:6), the 'new creation' (2 Cor. 5:17; Gal. 6:15) and a 'new humanity' in Christ (Eph. 2:15; 4:24).

The other part of the phrase 'newness of *life*', namely 'life', also suggests that the Christian walk under grace is set in contrast to and substitutes for living under the law. 'Life' consistently connotes 'eternal life' in Romans. When Paul speaks of 'life' in Romans, especially in Romans 5 – 8, the implicit contrast with 'death' is never far from view. In Romans 5 Adam's trespass leads to death for all. And in Romans 7:5, 10 and 13 it is the law that leads to death. The fact that the new life in Christ is the solution to life under the law is made explicit in 8:2: 'the law of the Spirit of life in Christ Jesus has set you free from the law of sin and of death'. Paul's walk 'in newness of life' is the happy substitute for a walk 'in oldness of death' under the law.

Walking in the *light* or in the daytime in Ephesians 5:15 and Romans 13:13 respectively is not only an apt figure for appropriate conduct, but it too points to life in the age of eschatological fulfilment. Jewish apocalyptic theology regularly employed 'light' language. Specifically, the visions of Isaiah 59 – 60 may have influenced Paul's language of walking in the light.[44] In Isaiah 59:9–11 sinful Israel is depicted as blind men walking in darkness but hoping for light, and in Isaiah 60:19–20 the glory of God is an 'everlasting light'. Then in Isaiah 60:1–3 the bright light of salvation dawns when the Lord returns to his people and 'nations shall walk to your light' (my tr.).[45]

Walking in *the Spirit* in Galatians 5 and Romans 8 in the contexts of both letters is set in opposition and as an alternative to walking according to the law. Furthermore, Beale argues convincingly that the fruit of the Spirit in Galatians 5:22, which fleshes out what walking in the Spirit involves, is a general allusion to Isaiah's promise that the Spirit would bring about abundant fertility in the coming new age.[46] Isaiah 32 and 57 prophesy that in the new creation the Spirit would be the bearer of plentiful fruitfulness, which Isaiah often interprets to be godly attributes such as righteousness, patience, peace, joy, holiness, and trust in the Lord, traits either identical or quite similar to those in Galatians 5:22–23. To walk in the Spirit is thus to experience the ethical blessings of the new age of the Spirit, an age in which the dispensation of the law has passed away.

Dunn draws similar conclusions in his comments on the polemical thrust of Galatians 2:14 ('they did not walk according to the truth of the gospel', my tr.):

> The characteristic Jewish use [of walking for conduct] was in commendation of a walk in the law/statutes/ordinances/ways of God (hence 'halakah'). In no doubt deliberate contrast, Paul speaks of a walk toward the truth of the gospel. Evidently, he was implying

[44] A suggestion made to me by Gordon Conwell Theological Seminary student Jesse Peterson.
[45] The Hebrew has *hālak*, but in this context it is not usually translated literally. On the contrast of walking in newness of life as the superior eschatological alternative to the OT 'walk in the law', see Dunn 1988a: 315–316.
[46] See Beale 2005.

with polemical intent that 'the truth of the gospel' provided a different and superior beacon for conduct.[47]

good reasons for concluding that at least some of Paul's imagery is set in polemical contrast to and functions as a for Jewish walking in obedience to the law. The Christian wness of life' / 'in the light' / 'in the Spirit' / 'according to f the gospel' replaces life under the law.

guage of newness

ur words regularly translated 'new' or 'newness': *neos* (2×),), *kainos* (6×), *kainotēs* (2×). Apart from one 'new moons' , the rest of the occurrences in Paul's letters appear as ways rizing the new age and new covenant that have been inaug- he death and resurrection of Jesus Christ. It is striking that e eleven are set in contrast to the old covenant of the law. t obvious is the contrast with the old covenant in Paul's two o the new covenant in 1 Corinthians 11:25 and 2 Corinthians me notion of the new situation in Christ replacing the old under the Law of Moses can be found in the following when read in context: 'newness of life' (Rom. 6:4), 'the new life of the Spirit' (Rom. 7:6), 'one new humanity' (Eph. 2:15) and 'a new creation' (Gal. 6:15; 2 Cor. 5:17 [2×]). The other three occurrences appear in descriptions of the new life without drawing any contrast to the old covenant: believers as a 'new batch' of dough (1 Cor. 5:7) and part of the new humanity (Eph. 4:24; Col. 3:10).

That the new covenant replaced the old covenant is explicit in Jeremiah 31:32: 'it will not be like the old covenant that they broke' (my tr.). However, a possible objection to reading the language of newness in Paul's letters as underscoring a replacement of the old covenant is the appearance in new-covenant prophetic texts of intimations of the continued role of the law. Two texts in particular make this point:

I will put my spirit within you, and make you follow my statutes and be careful to observe my ordinances. (Ezek. 36:27)

But this is the covenant that I will make with the house of Israel after those days, says the LORD: I will put my law within them, and

---

[47] Dunn 1993a: 462. See too Ciampa 1998: 169.

I will write it on their hearts; and I will be their God, and they shall be my people. (Jer. 31:33)

In both passages the accent is on the fundamental change in the human beings that the new covenant brings, the transformation of people's hearts. Parallel to Jeremiah 31:33 is Jeremiah 32:39: 'I will give them singleness of heart and action' (TNIV).[48] And the same is implied in Ezekiel's promise of God's Spirit within God's people. While the new-covenant prophetic texts indicate both continuity and discontinuity with the past, Williamson is surely right that 'the newness of the new covenant must not be underestimated'.[49] As it turns out, Ezekiel's language of obedience to the law in the LXX (*phylassō* and *poieō*) is not used by Paul in his letters to characterize how believers in Christ relate to the law (see chapter 3). Keeping the law is evidently not a part of the prophecy Paul felt the need to emphasize.

'Circumcision is nothing' complements

After an extensive examination in chapter 1 I concluded that 1 Corinthians 7:19 was an example of Pauline polemic against the Law of Moses, in which the repudiation of the law of circumcision, a key command in the law, was followed by its replacement by something else. A key argument in favour of this interpretation is that the same rejection of circumcision occurs twice in Galatians, and what Paul prefers to circumcision in those texts is clearly not some other part of the Law of Moses but something else:

Circumcision is nothing and uncircumcision is nothing. *Keeping God's commands* is what counts. (1 Cor. 7:19 TNIV)

In Christ Jesus neither circumcision nor uncircumcision counts for anything; the only thing that counts is *faith working through love*. (Gal. 5:6)

Neither circumcision nor uncircumcision means anything; what counts is *the new creation*. (Gal. 6:15 NIV)

---

[48] See Williamson 2007: 165. In his discussion of the new covenant in Paul, Williamson comments, 'As children of the promise who have been born of the Spirit we are free from the letter of the Mosaic covenant, which was vastly inferior to the light of the transforming glory we now have in the face of Jesus Christ.'

[49] Ibid. 180.

A fourth text may be added to the three from 1 Corinthians and Galatians. In Romans 14, in the context of discussing the unimportance and non-binding nature of the Jewish food laws and sabbath for Christians, Paul explains what is important in the Kingdom of God: 'For the kingdom of God is not food and drink but *righteousness and peace and joy in the Holy Spirit.*'

In this section it is worth taking a closer look at what Paul regards as eclipsing the Law of Moses. If the law does not count for Paul, what does?

Obedience to apostolic instruction

In chapter 1 I concluded that 'keeping the commandments of God' (ESV) in 1 Corinthians 7:19 was a reference to Paul's own instructions, in context perhaps his call to flee sexual immorality and glorify God in one's body. At first blush it may seem odd that what trumps obedience to the law is obedience to an apostle. However, as Ciampa observes, 'the theme of obedience is not lacking in Paul's theology'. Ciampa cites some of the relevant data (with particular reference to Romans):

> Romans begins and ends with the theme of 'the obedience of faith' (1.5; 16.26). Within the letter Paul speaks of what God has accomplished through Christ 'to bring the Gentiles to obedience' (15.18). In 6.16 he speaks of 'obedience leading to righteousness' (or possibly to 'justification'). Paul's message has to do with obedience from the heart (6.17) to the truth (Rom. 2.8; Gal. 5.7), the gospel (Rom. 10.16; 2 Thess. 1.8), or Christ (2 Cor. 10.5–6). It is Christ's own obedience which provides the righteousness (and obedience) of his people (5.19; cf. Phil. 2.8).[50]

What distinguishes new-covenant obedience from simply obeying the law? Or in other words, what makes the former better than the latter? While not being easy to pin down, new-covenant obedience involves an internalizing of the demands of God, a key feature of new-covenant prophecies. The best clues as to its character are supplied by the other 'circumcision is nothing' complements. New-covenant obedience involves love produced by faith in Christ, the new creation, righteousness, peace and joy in the Holy Spirit. Recalling chapter 2 and Paul's use of Leviticus 18:5 as a summary

---

[50] Ciampa 2007: 109.

of the law as law, if obedience under the old covenant was meant to lead to life, obedience under the new is the fruit of new life in Christ.

Love produced by faith in Christ

In Galatians 5:1 Paul brings two of the major themes of the letter to a head, namely imprisonment under the law and the liberating redemption wrought by Christ: 'For freedom Christ has set us free.' This climactic indicative is followed by its corollary, namely the imperative to 'stand firm' and 'not submit again to a yoke of slavery'. Galatians 5:3 makes it clear that the crushing weight of this yoke is the obligation to obey the whole law, which is what, Paul insists, 'every man' signs up for 'who lets himself be circumcised'. In 4:4 the grave consequences of seeking to be 'justified by the law' (my tr.) are to be cut off from Christ and fall away from grace.

In Galatians 5:5–6 Paul presents a more positive description of maintaining freedom in Christ. It is only 'through the Spirit, by faith [in Christ]' (v. 5a) that this freedom can be maintained and people can stand firm. The life of faith lives in confident expectation of final vindication before God: 'we eagerly wait for the hope of righteousness' (v. 5b).

In Galatians 5:6 Paul continues to pit circumcision and the law against grace and faith: 'For in Christ Jesus neither circumcision nor uncircumcision counts for anything; the only thing that counts is faith working through love.' Freedom from the law does not lead to sin. On the contrary, as Paul makes clear in 5:13–14, the true intent of the law, serving one another in love, is fulfilled by those who have faith in Christ and are in union with him:

> For you were called to freedom, brothers and sisters; only do not use your freedom as an opportunity for self-indulgence, but through love become slaves to one another. For the whole law is summed up in a single commandment, 'You shall love your neighbor as yourself.'

And true faith in Christ, unlike keeping the law, produces love.[51]

In Galatians Paul fights on two fronts: against the view that being under the law is essential for justification, and the related position that being under the law is necessary for moral progress and restraining sin. Galatians 5:6 refutes the second. In the verses following, 5:13–6:10, Paul fills out the implications of his insistence that faith in Christ

---

[51] The verb in 5:6, translated by the NRSV as 'faith *working* through love', is *energeō*. BDAG (335c) defines it as 'bring someth[ing] about through use of capability', with suggested glosses being 'work, produce, effect'.

produces love, along with joy, peace, patience, and so on, by the work of the Spirit in the life of believers.

The new creation

Along with love produced by faith in Christ, Paul places something else in antithesis to circumcision in Galatians, namely 'new creation!' (Gal. 6:15). Paul uses the same phrase in 2 Corinthians 5:17: 'So if anyone is in Christ, there is *a new creation*: everything old has passed away; see, everything has become new!' The two passages are syntactically identical.[52] And they both set up a contrast in terms of an eschatological once–now motif: the former state of being under the law (in Galatians) and being outside Christ (in 2 Corinthians) is eclipsed by new creation.

In Galatians the contrast between the age of circumcision and the new creation is explained in terms of Paul's conviction concerning the cross's bringing 'the end of the world' in 6:14: 'May I never boast of anything except the cross of our Lord Jesus Christ, by which the world has been crucified to me, and I to the world.'

But new creation in both Galatians and 2 Corinthians is not simply about eschatology. Paul is not just saying that the age to come is more important than this age. As in Galatians 5:6, in Galatians 6:15 Paul contends that the status of being in Christ, being part of the future new creation, brings moral transformation in the present. It recalls Paul's own story in Galatians 1 – 2 of being severed from the law as a result of the revelation of Christ in him and the new life he now leads by faith in the Son of God (2:20). As Paul puts it in Galatians 1:4, Christ 'gave himself for our sins to set us free from the present evil age'. The details of this liberation, which is paradigmatic for all believers, are laid out in Galatians 5 – 6. Thus 'new creation' is a broad description of life in the new age, which begins now and is the equivalent of life in Christ by the Spirit (cf. 5:25).[53]

Righteousness, peace and joy in the Holy Spirit

The fourth instance of Paul's exalting something over observing the law is in Romans 14:17, where he asserts that 'the kingdom of God is not a matter of eating and drinking [in obedience to the law or otherwise], but of righteousness, peace and joy in the Holy Spirit' (TNIV).

[52] The wording is emphatic, formulated without subject, verb or article: *kainē ktisis*.
[53] Cf. Hubbard 2002: 232: 'Paul's new creation . . . functions as an alternative formulation of his central Spirit affirmation – the Spirit creates life (2 Cor. 3:6).'

In Romans 14:1 – 15:6 Paul is dealing with a dispute between the strong and the weak over the question of observance of certain laws (diet and days) from the Law of Moses. While the strong, championing Christian freedom, hold that believers in Christ may 'eat anything' (14:2 NIV), the weak observe kosher laws and observe the sabbath. As I concluded in my discussion of this passage in chapter 1 (see under 'Definition of terms: "Paul", "law" and "believer"'), Paul allows for the expression of Jewish cultural tradition, living under the law's direction, but not its dominion. In order to give both sides some perspective, in Romans 14:17 he plays down the significance of the food laws and tells them what is truly important in the kingdom of God.

Whereas Paul can speak of the kingdom of God as a future inheritance (as in 1 Cor. 6:9–10; 15:50; Gal. 5:21), here it is a present reality in the life of Christians (as in 1 Cor. 4:20). And the character of this life under God's rule is described in terms of 'righteousness and peace and joy' springing from the Spirit. It is no accident that two of these three qualities appear in the fruit of the Spirit in Galatians 5:22 ('joy' and 'peace').

Both 'righteousness' and 'peace' are used in Romans in connection with justification and reconciliation with God. However, in this context, as Moo argues, they probably have more to do with 'relations among believers'.[54] What counts in the kingdom is right relations in the community, 'righteousness', and harmony and mutual support among believers, 'peace'. When these two are in place, the result is 'joy'. 'Righteousness, peace and joy' are each manifestations of life in step with the Holy Spirit.[55]

What Paul underscores in Romans 14:17, in place of the law, is primarily ethical, but it is ethics arising from the gospel. The three blessings are in effect gifts of the Spirit for the eschatological age. And as Moo notes, this summary of the community's life under God's rule is an outworking of his exposition of the gospel in Romans. This can be seen in the use of three similar terms in Romans 5:1–2, 'Paul's transitional encapsulation of the argument in chaps. 1–4'[56]:

Therefore, since we have been declared *righteous* by faith, we have *peace* with God through our Lord Jesus Christ. Also through Him,

[54] Moo 1996: 857.
[55] The phrase *en pneumati hagiō* modifies all three qualities, each being associated in early Jewish and Christian teaching with the new age of the Spirit.
[56] Moo 1996: 857.

we have obtained access by faith into this grace in which we stand, and we *rejoice* in the hope of the glory of God. (HCSB)

What Paul stresses as vitally important in Romans 14:17 is simply the outworking of our justification and reconciliation to God for our corporate life in the kingdom of God: being declared righteous with God must lead to righteousness in human relationships, and finding peace with God must lead to living at peace with others. In other words, the joy of being right with God and Christian hope should spill over into the joy of Christian fellowship.[57]

The centre of Paul's theology

The late twentieth century witnessed a debate in New Testament studies concerning the centre of Paul's theology.[58] Proposals ranged from the very broad, such as Jesus Christ, life under the lordship of Christ, Christological soteriology, and reconciliation, to the more narrow and specific, including justification by faith, the Son of God, dying with Christ, and even the transformation of time.

The debate stalled partly because what was meant by 'centre' was often not made clear and the occasional and unsystematic nature of Paul's letters kept pushing back against the very search for a centre, however it was defined. The absence of controls and objective criteria for assessing proposals also made progress difficult. In some cases suggestions about the centre of Paul's theology revealed more about the interpreters and their tradition than they did about Paul.

While I have no intention of reopening the question of the centre of Paul's theology, the material reviewed in this chapter is defin- itely of interest to the general question of what mattered most to Paul. The material I have rehearsed in this chapter emerged from the stylistic question of what Paul puts in the place of the law, that which had previously taken centre stage in his life and thought as a devout Jew. In this sense the data have been gathered with some controls in place.

---

[57] Cf. 2 Tim. 2:22: 'pursue *righteousness*, faith, love, and *peace*, along with those who call on the Lord from a pure heart', where 'righteousness' and 'peace' are virtues of Christian fellowship.

[58] See R. P. Martin 1993: 92–95. Cf. Plevnik 1989: 477–478: 'Any centre of Pauline theology must include all those components of the apostle's gospel: his understanding of Christ and of God, his understanding of God's salvific action through Christ, involving the Easter event and its implications, the present lordship, the future coming of Christ, and the appropriation of salvation.'

In the summary below, the breadth of this collection of matters of great importance in Paul's letters covers not only salvation and Christ-ology, but also ethics and eschatology. Compared to many of the suggestions for the centre of Paul's theology, in Paul's replacement of the law there is an accent on faith in and union with Christ the Lord and on the new life of the Spirit.

In Paul's own words (a summary and paraphrase)

Believers in Christ do not rely on the law, but on Christ; do not boast in the law, but in God through Christ; do not find God's will through the law, but in apostolic instruction, wisdom and the gospel; are not instructed by the law, but by the gospel; and are not obliged to obey the law, but rather must obey apostolic instruction.

Christians are not under the Law of Moses, but under the law of Christ, the law of faith and the law of the Spirit. We have died to the law, Christ lives in us and we live by faith in the Son of God. Above all else, including righteousness under the law, we value knowing Christ Jesus our Lord. We do not keep the law, but fulfil the law in Christ and through love. We do not seek to walk according to the law, but according to the truth of the gospel, in Christ, in newness of resur-rection life, by faith, in the light and in step with the Spirit. Instead of the oldness of the letter, we participate in newness of life, the new life of the Spirit, and the one new humanity. What counts is not the law, but faith expressing itself through love, the new creation, keeping the commandments of God, and righteousness, peace and joy in the Holy Spirit.

Chapter Five

'Witness to the gospel'
Reappropriation of the law
as prophecy

The typological reading of the external elements of the older regime [the Mosaic law and covenant] is a basic feature of Pauline theology, and this tends not to receive enough attention.

(Henri Blocher)[1]

The death and resurrection of Jesus was an apocalyptic event that had brought the old world order to an end. . . . [Paul] moved to an entirely new hermeneutical perspective, within which the Law functioned primarily as *promise and narrative prefiguration of the gospel.*

(Richard B. Hays)[2]

The law functions on both sides of the great divide between letter and Spirit. When the veil covering the reading of Scripture is removed the law becomes *the goal reaching out through Christ toward the eschatological redemption of God's entire cosmos.*

(Brevard Childs)[3]

The coming of Christ means for Paul that the law has lost its defining covenantal function and instead exercises *a primarily prophetic role.*

(Markus Bockmuehl)[4]

---

[1] Blocher 2004: 499, italics added.
[2] Hays 1996b: 163, italics original.
[3] Childs 2008: 138, italics added.
[4] Bockmuehl 2000: 169, italics added.

> For Paul 'the law is upheld precisely because *the redemptive-historical purposes and anticipations of the law* are upheld'.
>
> (D. A. Carson)[5]

> For Paul, 'Scripture [including the law] is a *witness to the gospel.*'
>
> (Dietrich-Alex Koch)[6]

To this point in our investigation of Paul and the law I have emphasized Paul's negative stance towards the law, both his explicit and implicit rejection (chapters 2 and 3) and replacement of the law (chapter 4). But these two moves are not the whole story. A third more positive take on the law is also evident across the Pauline corpus: the law has ongoing value and validity. According to Paul, if the law as law-covenant and legal code is *for Jews*, what is the law *for us* as Christians? Paul in fact uses the very phrase 'for us' (*di hēmas*) with reference to the positive meaning of the law for Christians on three occasions.[7]

The phrase 'for us' occurs twice in 1 Corinthians 9:9–10a, where Paul reads the law in a sense intended for Christians. In context Paul wishes to bolster his argument for the support of ministers by the congregations to whom they minister.[8] Having used the argument from analogy with reference to military service and agriculture, he cites Deuteronomy 25:4, appealing to something more than 'human authority' (1 Cor. 9:8: *kata anthrōpon*):

> For it is written in the Law of Moses: 'Do not muzzle an ox while it is treading out the grain.' Is it about oxen that God is concerned? Surely he says this for us [*di hēmas*], doesn't he? Yes, this was written *for us* [*di hēmas*]. (1 Cor. 9:9–10a TNIV)

The apostle asserts that the law, in particular the injunction not to prevent a working ox from eating some of the grain, was written 'for our sake' (NRSV); it gives instruction pertinent to Christian conduct.

---

[5] Carson 2004a: 139, italics added.

[6] Koch 1986, italics added. Translation of the title *Die Schrift als Zeuge des Evangeliums*, an allusion to Rom. 3:21.

[7] The phrase occurs three times in Paul and nowhere else in the NT.

[8] See Ciampa and Rosner 2010: 404–407 for a full discussion.

The same kind of point is made in 1 Corinthians 10:11, following 10:1–10 where Paul draws lessons from Israel's wanderings in the wilderness narrated in Numbers, and claims that such narratives 'were written down for our [moral] instruction [*nouthesian hēmōn*]' (RSV).[9] If Christians do not read the law as legal code, it is still to be read as teaching us how to live. This construal of the law as wisdom for Christian living is the subject of chapter 6, the next chapter of this book.

The third occurrence of 'for us' in Paul's letters appears in Romans 4. In this chapter Paul expounds a text from the law, Genesis 15:6 ('Abraham believed God and it was reckoned to him as righteousness', my tr.), to demonstrate that the law witnesses to the righteousness of God in the gospel (see Rom. 3:21). Romans 4 ends with these words:

> The words 'it was credited to him' were written not for him alone, but also for us [*di hēmas*], to whom God will credit righteousness – for us who believe in him who raised Jesus our Lord from the dead. He was delivered over to death for our sins and was raised to life for our justification. (Rom. 4:23–25 NIV)

Here the law, in particular the example of Abraham being justified by faith, was written for our sake, that of believers in Christ, who exercise the same faith as Abraham. In this sense the law was written for Christians when it is read as testifying to the gospel. If Christians do not read the law as legal code or law-covenant, we do read it as witnessing to faith in Christ. This construal of the law as prophecy of the gospel is the focus of attention in this chapter.

The conviction that the law testifies to Christ is in fact a major presupposition of New Testament thought. In the Gospels Jesus affirms that 'all the prophets and the law *prophesied* until John [the Baptist] came' (Matt. 11:13) and 'the Scriptures *testify* about me' (John 5:39, my tr.).[10] Likewise, on the road to Emmaus Jesus spoke to the two disciples of the prophetic witness 'about himself' of both the law and the prophets:

---

[9] Cf. Rom. 15:4: 'For whatever was written in former days was *written for our instruction*, so that by steadfastness and by the encouragement of the scriptures we might have hope.'

[10] The verbs 'to prophesy' and 'to testify' are *prophēteuō* and *martyreō*. John 5:45, 'your accuser is Moses', indicates that the referent of 'the scriptures' in v. 39 includes the law.

Then he said to them, 'Oh, how foolish you are, and how slow of heart to believe all that the prophets have declared! Was it not necessary that the Messiah should suffer these things and then enter into his glory?' Then beginning with Moses and all the prophets, he interpreted to them the things about himself in all the scriptures. (Luke 24:25–27)

Paul is presented in the closing verses of the book of Acts as engaged in teaching about Christ from the law: 'From morning until evening he explained the matter to them, testifying[11] to the kingdom of God and trying to convince them about Jesus both from the law of Moses and from the prophets' (Acts 28:23). This text depicts Paul teaching and bearing witness to Christ, 'both from the law of Moses and from the prophets'. Reading the Law of Moses in tandem with the prophets as testifying to Christ will emerge as a key feature of Paul's reading of the law as prophecy.

Paul himself reading the law as prophecy can be seen in Galatians 3:6–8, in connection with Abraham's justification in Genesis 15:6 and 12:3:

So also Abraham 'believed God, and it was credited to him as righteousness'.

Understand, then, that those who have faith are children of Abraham. Scripture *foresaw* that God would justify the Gentiles by faith, and *announced the gospel in advance* to Abraham: 'All nations will be blessed through you.' (NIV)

In hermeneutical terms there is a big difference in the ways legal codes and prophecy are read; if a legal code commands and decrees, prophecy forecasts and proclaims in advance (along with exhorting and encouraging). In Galatians 3 Paul speaks of the law's 'fore-seeing'[12] and 'declaring the gospel beforehand',[13] terms indicative of the latter rather than the former.

Paul's reading of the law as a testimony to Christ is too big a subject to investigate comprehensively in a single chapter. Instead of

---

[11] Gk. *diamartyromai*. BDAG 232b: 'to make a solemn declaration about the truth of someth. *testify of, bear witness to*'.

[12] Gk. *prooraō*. BDAG 873a: 'to see in advance, *foresee* w. an eye to the future'. Cf. Acts 2:31 (quoting Ps. 16): '*Foreseeing* this, David spoke of the resurrection of the Messiah . . . '

[13] Gk. *proeuangelizomai*.

combing through all of his letters with this theme in mind, a task that deserves a whole book, in this chapter I propose to do three things to clarify and confirm the shape of Paul's reading of the law as prophecy:

1. Look at an intriguing example of Paul's reading a text from the law that demonstrates all three movements that characterize Paul's interactions with the law, namely repudiation, replacement and reappropriation as prophecy.
2. Consider the prophetic character of the Law of Moses.
3. Investigate Romans as a test case of Paul's following through on his conviction that the law is a witness to the gospel.

Deuteronomy 9:4 and 30:11–14 in Romans 10:6–9

In Romans 10:5–13 Paul explores the connection between the righteousness and faith introduced in verse 4, which announced a 'righteousness for everyone who believes'. His exposition includes several quotations of Scripture. The first quotation, of Leviticus 18:5 in Romans 10:5, points to the law as a failed path to life (see chapter 2). The second, a composite quotation of Deuteronomy 9:4 and 30:11–14 in Romans 10:6–9, is somewhat unusual, to say the least.

The subject of Deuteronomy 30:11–14 is the commandment God gave to Moses for Israel. Paul omits this and attributes the quotation instead to a personified 'righteousness that comes from faith'. As Hays explains, in 'an apparently capricious act of interpretation' Paul takes two admonitions from Deuteronomy to obey the law and 'turns them into a cryptic prophecy of the Christian gospel'.[14] Paul, it seems, deliberately leaves out the positive references to the law in the Deuteronomy 30 citation. The following quotations italicize these elements:

Deuteronomy 9:4 LXX
Do not say in your heart, when the Lord your God casts out these nations from before you, 'it is because of my righteousness [*dikaiosynas mou*] the Lord has brought me in to inherit this good land'.[15]

---

[14] Hays 1989: 73–74.
[15] All LXX translations are my own.

Deuteronomy 30:11–14 LXX

*For this commandment that I am commanding you today [hoti hē
entolē autē hēn egō entellomai soi sēmeron]* is not excessive nor is it
far from you. It is not in heaven above, that you might say, 'Who
will go up to heaven for us and take it for us that we might *hear
and do it [kai akousantes autēn poiēsomen]*?' Nor is it beyond the
sea, that you might say, 'Who will go over to the other side of
the sea for us *so that we might hear and do it [kai akoustēn hēmin
poiēsei autēn]*?' The word is very near to you. It is in your mouth
and in your heart and in your hands *to do it [auto poiein]*.

Romans 10:6–10a

But the righteousness that comes from faith says, 'Do not say in
your heart [cf. Deut. 9:4], "Who will ascend into heaven?"' (that
is, to bring Christ down) 'or "Who will descend into the abyss?"'
(that is, to bring Christ up from the dead). But what does it say?

'The word is near you,
  on your lips and in your heart'

(that is, the word of faith that we proclaim); because if you confess
with your lips that Jesus is Lord and believe in your heart that God
raised him from the dead, you will be saved. For one believes with
the heart and so is justified, and one confesses with the mouth and
so is saved.

Three times Moses reassures the Israelites that they are in a position
to 'do' (*poieō*) the law (at the end of vv. 12, 13 and 14). These are
conspicuous by their absence in Paul's citation of the text. As Ciampa
notes, 'while the text from which Paul is quoting gives great emphasis
to the need to obey the Law of Moses, Paul omits these elements,
introducing references to Christ and the gospel message in their
place'.[16] As Watson explains, Paul senses that the texts from Deuteronomy 'must be rewritten so that they testify to the righteousness of
faith, and against the righteousness of the Law as articulated in the
Leviticus [18:5] citation'.[17]

Paul does not affirm the passage's message that the Law of Moses
is a gift from God that they are able to obey. A key element of the law

16 Ciampa 2007: 108.
17 Watson 2004: 338.

as law-covenant is the human obligation to 'do' or 'obey' it. The omissions from the Deuteronomy 30:11–14 citation in Romans 10:6–9 demonstrate that Paul's avoidance of such verbs in connection with how believers in Christ relate to the law (see also chapter 3) is neither unwitting nor an oversight. The deliberate omissions from the citations of Deuteronomy in Romans 10:6–8 suggest that Paul does not think that Christians should 'observe' the Law of Moses.

If what Paul leaves out implies the repudiation of the law *as law*, what he replaces 'hearing and doing the commandments of the law' (my tr.) with is telling. He rewrites the text so that it testifies to the righteousness of faith and against the righteousness of the law articulated in the Leviticus 18:5 citation. The 'word' that is 'near' is the word of faith preached by Paul. Paul reads Deuteronomy as affirming that the presence of God's word in the community of God's people empowers the obedience of faith. If the main point of Deuteronomy 30:11–14 is that God's commandments were not difficult to find and obey, Paul wants to affirm that the same may also be said of the gospel message he preaches, perhaps with the implicit force of an a fortiori argument, how much more is the gospel Paul preaches 'near you, on your lips and in your hearts'?

Is this simply a mischievous and cavalier misreading of the texts from Deuteronomy? Is it a blatant misuse of them in the service of Paul's polemic? There are two considerations that suggest Paul is reading the Deuteronomy texts as a prophecy of the gospel, albeit a cryptic one, not entirely out of keeping with their original intent. The contexts in Deuteronomy 9 and 30 supply some clues.

Ellis points out that

> Deut. 30.6 speaks of the 'circumcision of the heart', which Jer. 31.31 identifies with the New Covenant. Deut. 30:11–14 does not merely concern the 'location' of the law but an attitude towards it, in which they love the Lord God 'with all their heart' (Deut. 30.6, 10, 16).[18]

In his view, implicit in this is 'an attitude of faith, which alone can fulfil the law (cf. Rom. 8.4), and so [Paul] applies the principle to his own day'.[19] With reference to Deuteronomy 9:4, the other text Paul quotes, Seifrid points out that 'the monetary language that Paul draws

---

[18] Ellis 1957: 123.
[19] Ibid.

from carries with it the reminder of Israel's rebellious heart and its need for a new, saving work of God'.[20] Both texts, it seems, look beyond themselves in ways conducive to Paul's reading of them.

Ciampa argues that Deuteronomy 30:1–14 'moves back and forth between the present, the near future and the distant future'.[21] In the present Israel is challenged to keep God's near and accessible commandments. The near future is a time of judgment for not keeping the commandments, brought on by a deafness and blindness that reflected uncircumcised hearts. And a distant future is envisioned when God's presence and word would be restored to his people and they would love and obey him again, when they return to God and see the end of their exile. According to Ciampa, 'Paul seems to understand that God himself has turned his chosen people's hearts back to him through the death and resurrection of Christ (that one, world-transforming, act of obedience) and the proclamation of the same.'[22] Is there evidence that the law as a whole is to be read in this prophetic manner?

The 'prophetic' character of the law

When Blocher et al. (see quotations at the beginning of this chapter) talk about the typology, promise and narrative prefiguration, goal, prophetic role and redemptive-historical purposes and anticipations of the Law of Moses, what are they referring to? Does the proposal of Paul's reading the law as prophecy have any basis in the character of the Law of Moses itself? Does the law have a prophetic character?

A comprehensive study of the Pentateuch is beyond the scope of this book and would certainly derail my intentions to write something on Paul and the law of readable length. Instead, I will review five recent studies of the Pentateuch that together present a compelling case for regarding the law as having a prophetic dimension. The five studies are markedly different in terms of focus and approach, which makes it more remarkable that they all point in the same direction. My intention is not to endorse every detail of these studies; I suggest some qualifications and offer some critique in some cases along the way. The impression left by them, nonetheless, is inescapable: the Law of Moses, viewed from many angles, has a prophetic character.

[20] Seifrid 2007: 657.
[21] Ciampa 2007: 109
[22] Ibid.

In other words, there is the potential for Paul's reading of the law as prophecy in the law itself, as we saw in his reading of Deuteronomy 9:4 and 30:11–14 in Romans 10:6–9 (see above). When Paul reads the law as prophecy, he is not reading against the grain.

It is not that the law's primary genre is prophecy. The most prominent genres of the law are law and narrative. While law is prominent in the second half of Exodus, Leviticus and Deuteronomy, narrative dominates Genesis, the first half of Exodus and most of Numbers. But law and narrative are certainly not the only genres; other subgenres are present, such as song, oracles and wisdom elements. When a composite text of varied genres (the law) is read as part of a larger composite text (the law and the prophets) in a new context (after the death and resurrection of Christ), it is not surprising that certain elements take on new significance. Five independent studies of the Pentateuch highlight these elements.

Walter Moberly and a canonical approach to the patriarchal narratives

R. W. L. Moberly, *The Theology of the Book of Genesis*, notes that there is a difficulty in calling the law 'the law' in the light of the fact that the patriarchs, who dominate the first book of the law, exist before the law is given through Moses.[23] Rabbinic literature also wrestles with this tension. Moberly contrasts the rabbinic difficulties with the patriarchal non-observance of the law (which they tended to resolve by arguing that Abraham actually kept the Mosaic law) with Paul's use of Abraham to 'relativize' the Torah. Commenting on Paul's discussion of Genesis 12:3 and 15:6 in Galatians 3 and Romans 4, Moberly writes:

> If Abraham can be righteous in a context that specifies faith but not torah observance, and if this same Abraham can be a channel for a promise of blessing to the nations of the earth, then this correlates with and *anticipates* what God has done in the death and resurrection of Jesus and fundamentally relativizes the signifi-cance of torah – which is not thereby deprived of all significance, but no longer has its classic Jewish significance.[24]

My point is simply to note that Moberly observes that Paul's reading of the law in Galatians 3 and Romans 4 picks up on a tension in

[23] Moberly 2009.
[24] Ibid. 125, italics added.

Genesis that was noticed by the rabbis, even if their explanation differs from Paul's. The prominence of faith, as prior to the giving of the law and law observance, is something the following study also picks up on.

John Sailhamer and the way of Abraham

J. Sailhamer's study *The Meaning of the Pentateuch* argues that the Pentateuch as a whole presents the way of Abraham, who lived by faith before the law, as better than that of Moses, who failed to keep the law once it was given.[25] With this in mind, the central message of the Pentateuch is that human beings are made righteous before God by faith and not by works of the law. According to Sailhamer, a close reading of the text reveals a complex literary strategy that was used to convey an eschatological hope in a future king from the line of David who would some day bless the world. In short, he understands the Pentateuch as underscoring the failure of the Sinai project of law and the importance of faith.

We do not have to buy into Sailhamer's theories about the composition of the Pentateuch and its updating by prophetic editors at the end of the Old Testament period to appreciate his insights about the final form of the text; at the end of the day he is reading the final form of the text. When enquiring about the meaning of the Pentateuch, Sailhamer asks the following pertinent questions:

- If the Pentateuch is supposed to be about the law, why is there no mention of it for sixty or so chapters?
- Why does Moses, whose name is virtually synonymous with the law, never enter the land of promise, while Abraham, whose name is synonymous with faith, walks freely throughout the same land?
- Why is a whole generation excluded from the land except two individuals who demonstrate faith in God's promise?
- Why do major sections of the law appear after major transgressions of the people?
- Why is there such a coincidence of law, sin, faith and righteousness?

If faith is the big idea, in what particular promise were the Israelites to place their faith? Key poems placed in strategic locations in the text indicate that the Israelites expected a king from the line of Judah who would defeat the powers of chaos and restore creation. According

[25] Sailhamer 2009.

to Sailhamer, later editors confirmed this understanding and inserted the eschatological term 'in the latter days' before these poems to indicate that this was the eschatological hope of the prophets (e.g. Gen. 49:1; Num. 24:14; Deut. 31:29; cf. Deut. 4:30). Thus this would happen when a new covenant would be made, a covenant that is expected in the book of Deuteronomy (chs. 29–30).

Francis Watson and the God of promise

Francis Watson's strategy in *Paul and the Hermeneutics of Faith* is to study the relationship between Torah, Paul as a Jewish reader of Torah, and contemporary non-Christian Jewish readings of Torah.[26] The purpose of Genesis, for example, according to Paul, is to identify the God of promise as the primary agent in the Abraham narrative, rather than Abraham himself, who simply believed God. This may be contrasted with the narrative of the heroic Abraham found in many Jewish readings (e.g. 1 Macc. 2.50–54; also *Jubilees*, Philo, Josephus and Eupolemus), where Abraham was found faithful when he was tested. In the latter, Abraham's faithfulness is detached from Genesis 12 and connected to his heroic obedience at the sacrifice of Isaac in Genesis 22. Paul emphasizes instead the promise of universal blessing in Genesis 12:3, and, in the light of Genesis 15:6, the primacy of faith. According to Watson, 'at stake here is not simply the question of the Gentile membership of the people of God [the emphasis of the New Perspective on Paul], but the priority and unconditionality of divine action in its universal scope'.[27]

According to Watson, Paul's reading contrasts with that of contemporary Jews:

> Apart from Paul, Jewish interpreters regard the promise motif as secondary to a story whose primary aim is to celebrate Abraham's outstanding piety and virtue. . . . In contrast, Paul consistently focuses on the promise motif whenever he speaks of Abraham.[28]

In connection specifically with the Mosaic laws, Watson observes that the post-Sinai history of Israel in the wilderness is a history of catastrophe. Israel's journey from Sinai to the Promised Land is framed by two censuses, one in the wilderness of Sinai, and the other on the plains of Moab by Jordan at Jericho. At the conclusion of the second

[26] Watson 2004.
[27] Ibid. 186.
[28] Ibid. 268–269.

census it is clear that the entire generation of those numbered at Sinai has perished: 'The first census turns out to be an enumeration not for military service but for slaughter.'[29] Watson's conclusion is that 'in moving from Leviticus to Numbers, then, we find that the law's conditional promise of life [cf. Lev. 18:5] is overtaken by the reality of death'.[30] Paul's treatment of Israel's experience in the wilderness in 1 Corinthians 10 tallies with this reading; for Paul, the wilderness generation died because they transgressed the law (specifically by committing idolatry, sexual immorality and grumbling).[31]

In Watson's view the Torah contains an internal conflict by providing two opposing accounts of God's plan of redemption. This leads him to adopt an antithetical hermeneutic that rejects the teaching of some texts, such as Leviticus 18:5, and affirms that of others, such as Genesis 15:6 (and Hab. 2:4). If Deuteronomy 30 anticipates a return to God as 'a matter of appropriate human action', the Song of Moses in Deuteronomy 32 sees it as 'a matter of definitive, unsurpassable divine saving action, which reorients human action towards itself and so represents a breach with the law'.[32]

While I think such tensions can be better explained in other ways,[33] Watson does mount a strong case for Paul's reading of the priority of grace and faith over works and law in the Torah itself: 'For Paul [the Torah] is most fundamentally the divine promise, in which God announces an unconditional saving action, universal in its scope, that lies beyond the horizon of the scriptural writers themselves.'[34]

Gary Millar and Deuteronomy

According to J. G. Millar, *Now Choose Life*, in the context of the Pentateuch the book of Deuteronomy is Moses' attempt to spell out for God's people the theological and ethical consequences of the

[29] Watson 2004: 355.

[30] Ibid.

[31] They did not die because they failed to keep the law perfectly (not even Joshua and Caleb did that), but because they were guilty of gross rebellion and fundamental faithlessness.

[32] Ibid. 464.

[33] Cf. Ciampa 2007: 116: 'It seems unlikely, however, that Paul finds two opposing abstract and static approaches to redemption in Scripture, two contradictory voices, one of which must be rejected and the other upheld. If we grant that Paul perceives that Christ's coming has brought about the transition from curse to blessing that was anticipated in Deuteronomy 30 in a surprising way, it opens up the possibility that Paul views some texts as reflecting divine guidance and instruction for the times before the coming of Christ and others provide clues for the situation in which Paul's readers find themselves as believers in Christ. That was then, this is now (Rom. 10:4).'

[34] Watson 2004: 357.

exodus deliverance.[35] Put another way, Deuteronomy explains the nature of an obedient response to God's grace. The collections of laws in chapters 5 and 12–26 stipulate that the Lord is to be worshipped at the place and in the way he chooses (cf. e.g. ch. 12) and insist that nothing is to be done to defile the land, which is the place where God is encountered (cf. 12:7).

Curiously, various elements strike a pessimistic note and point beyond the book to the need for the future decisive action of God. That little can be expected from God's people is signalled in chapter 2, where they are unfavourably compared to the Moabites and Ammonites. It is also expressed throughout chapters 5–11, where repeated calls to obey or remember (e.g. 5:1, 31–33; 6:1–14; 7:12–15) suggest a negative expectation. Israel's spiritual incapacity is repeatedly underscored (e.g. 29:4). Nothing less than a circumcision of the heart is required, which only God can perform (30:6; cf. 10:16). Moses predicts Israel's apostasy (31:16–18; 32:19–21, 26) and he himself dies outside the land (ch. 34), suggesting that there is little hope for the nation. Moses' song ends with the one reference to atonement in the entire book (32:43). The new-covenant teaching of Jeremiah and Ezekiel, in which the problem of the human heart is resolved, is thus anticipated in Deuteronomy.

In connection with Paul, the 'latter days', to which Deuteronomy 4:30 refers, when 'you will return to the LORD your God and heed him', of which the Hebrew prophets also speak (cf. Jer. 23:20; 30:24; 48:47; 49:39; Ezek. 38:16; Dan. 2:28; 10:14; Hos. 3:5), is the time in which Paul locates his ministry; believers are those 'on whom the fulfilment of the ages has come' (1 Cor. 10:11). Paul writes as a minister of the new covenant, a covenant that Deuteronomy does not name but ultimately points forward to.

William Horbury and messianism in the Greek Pentateuch

William Horbury's study of views of monarchy and messianism in the Greek Pentateuch focuses on future-oriented passages.[36] By messianism he means the expectation of a Davidic king in the last times. He notes, for example, the history of interpretation of Deuteronomy 17:15, which concerns the appointment of a king of the Lord's choosing when the nation takes possession of the Promised Land. While the text was understood as either permissive or imperatival, in

---

[35] Millar 1998.
[36] Horbury 2006.

the Greek Pentateuch 'it could be understood as a prophecy of rule, especially of the appointment of a king in the time of Samuel, and as a command to set up an indigenous ruler, who is associated with the Pentateuchal prophecies of a succession of Jewish rulers'.[37]

Horbury also notices that in spite of the prestige of the priesthood in the Greek age, non-priestly monarchy is to the fore in the LXX of the Pentateuch:

> In the Septuagintal treatment of this subject its future dimension is underlined, for example in Deut 17, 14–20, . . . in connection with Deut 28,36. The last days in particular have begun to form a topic (Gen 49,1; Deut 32,35 LXX), and a number of passages speak of the advent of a great individual Israelite ruler in the last days (Gen 49,10c, Num 24,7,17; Deut 33,5).[38]

The expected ruler is portrayed variously in the LXX Pentateuch, including as a prophetic ruler, in connection with Deuteronomy 18:15–22, and a conquering human sovereign-king in the line of Judah.

Such studies underscore the way in which prophetic elements of the Law of Moses were amplified in early Jewish interpretation. Evidently Paul was not the first Jew to read the law as bearing testimony to a future king or even to the Messiah of the end times.

The law as prophecy in Romans

To this point in our investigation we have seen Paul cite passages from Deuteronomy as proclaiming the gospel (in Rom. 10), noted Paul's assertions in Romans 4 and Galatians 3 that the law was written as a prophecy of key features of the gospel, and reported a number of studies that observe the prophetic character of the Law of Moses. In order to fill out the picture of Paul's own reading of the law as prophecy, in this section we will undertake a thorough examination of Paul's precept and practice in the letter to the Romans.

Among Paul's letters Romans presents itself as an obvious candidate for such an investigation. While the reasons for Romans are hotly debated, two purposes present themselves from the text: first, in Romans Paul explains and defends his gospel to the Christians

---

[37] Ibid. 96–97.
[38] Ibid. 126.

in Rome to introduce himself in the hope of later creating a base for financial support of his mission to Spain from the Roman church (see Rom. 15:24); and, secondly, having heard of a split between Jewish and Gentile believers in Rome he presents his gospel as a basis for his plea that the two groups 'accept each other' (14:1 – 15:13, my tr.). The first purpose means that the letter presents a remarkably comprehensive presentation of Paul's gospel. And the second ensures that the basis of that gospel in the Hebrew Scriptures is brought to the surface. In Romans, more than any other letter, we would expect Paul to explain the relationship between his gospel and the law and the prophets.

The precept of the law as prophecy in Romans

At first blush, in Romans Paul asserts in just two passages that he reads the law as a prophecy of the gospel: 3:21, which states that the law and the prophets attest the righteousness of God, and 4:23–24 (see above), where the example of Abraham's being justified by faith in Genesis 15:6 was written 'for us' who believe. However, in this case first impressions are misleading. A more careful reading of Romans finds Paul making the assertion no fewer than five times: 1:2; 3:21; 3:31; 4:23–24; and 16:25–26.[39] And as we will see in the next section, Paul's precept in this matter is backed up by his consistent practice in the letter with numerous examples of reading the law as prophecy. In fact, the law as prophecy of the gospel emerges as a major theme of Romans.

As part of his self-description as the sender of the letter, Paul writes the following in Romans 1:1–3a: 'Paul, a servant of Jesus Christ, called to be an apostle, set apart for the gospel of God, which he promised beforehand [*proepangellō*] through his prophets in the holy scriptures, the gospel concerning his Son'. Paul asserts that the gospel concerning Jesus Christ, for the proclamation of which he was set apart, was 'promised beforehand' (BDAG 868d) in certain writings. The question for our purposes is whether the reference to 'the holy scriptures' in Romans 1:2 includes the law. Two considerations confirm that it does.

First, the phrase 'through his prophets' cannot be taken as ruling out a reference to the law. Acts 3:21–22 is a case in point, where Peter's speech uses similar language to Romans 1:1–3a and cites Moses as an example of such a holy prophet:

---

[39] A possible sixth occurs in Rom. 9:6a: 'It is not as though the word of God had failed.'

[W]ho [i.e. Jesus] must remain in heaven until the time of universal restoration that God announced long ago through his holy prophets. Moses said, 'The Lord your God will raise up for you from your own people a prophet like me. You must listen to whatever he tells you.'

Secondly, Paul's use of *graphē* in Romans supports taking 'the holy Scriptures' (*graphais hagiais*) in Romans 1:2 as including the law. The word occurs four times in the singular and three times in the plural in the letter. The first two instances of the singular, 'scripture', introduce quotations from the law, while the last two quote the prophets:

1. 'For what does the scripture say? "Abraham believed God, and it was reckoned to him as righteousness"' (Rom. 4:3, quoting Genesis).
2. 'For the scripture says to Pharaoh, "I have raised you up for the very purpose of showing my power in you, so that my name may be proclaimed in all the earth"' (Rom. 9:17, quoting Exodus).
3. 'The scripture says, "No one who believes in him will be put to shame"' (Rom. 10:11, quoting Isaiah).
4. 'God has not rejected his people whom he foreknew. Do you not know what the scripture says of Elijah, how he pleads with God against Israel?' (Rom. 11:2, quoting 1 Kings).

These references in Romans to 'scripture' point back to the opening of the letter, serving to fill out the way in which the gospel was promised beforehand in the holy scriptures (Rom. 1:2). It is the same prophetic scriptures to which Paul refers on those four occasions. The scriptures Paul quotes illustrate his reading of both the law and prophets as prophecies of the gospel. We could read into all four an ellipsis to make clear the programmatic nature of Romans 1:2. 'The scripture' to which Paul refers in Romans 4:3, 9:17, 10:11 and 11:2 is the scripture 'through which the gospel was promised beforehand' (Rom. 1:2, my tr.).

The three instances of 'scriptures', in the plural, in Romans include one at the beginning of the book and one at the end. Romans 16:25–26 forms an inclusio with Romans 1:1–3, underscoring again the role of the prophetic scriptures in 'declared the gospel beforehand' (to recall the language of Gal. 3:8):

Now to God who is able to strengthen you according to my gospel and the proclamation of Jesus Christ, according to the revelation of the mystery that was kept secret for long ages but is now disclosed, and through *the prophetic writings* [*graphōn prophētikōn*] is made known to all the Gentiles, according to the command of the eternal God, to bring about the obedience of faith.

Given the way in which Paul refers to passages from both the law and the prophets as 'scripture', *graphē*, in Romans (see the four instances above, which include two from each), there is every reason to take the reference to 'prophetic Scriptures' (HCSB) in Romans 16:25–26 as a general reference to both the law and the prophets.

The third occurrence of 'scriptures' in the plural in the letter is in Romans 15:4: 'For whatever was written in former days was written for our instruction [*didaskalia*], so that by steadfastness and by the encouragement of *the scriptures* we might have hope.' The specific scripture Paul has in mind here is Psalm 69:9, from the example of which he draws a point about Scripture in general. However, unlike the other six occurrences of *graphē* in the letter discussed above, the context in Romans 15 does not concern reading the law and the prophets as prophecy, but reading the Scriptures for moral instruction, Christian conduct. In this case, the citation of the psalm supports Paul's presentation of the Messiah, who did not please himself (Rom. 15:1), as the pattern to which believers are to be conformed. The use of the law as wisdom for living is addressed in the following chapter, chapter 6.

Having dealt with Romans 1:2 and 16:25–26, and touched on 4:23–24 in the introduction to this chapter, the remaining two instances of Paul teaching about the law as prophecy of the gospel appear in Romans 3. Read in their respective contexts they are in full accord with the other three passages. The first is in Romans 3:21–22a:

But now, irrespective of law, the righteousness of God has been disclosed, and is attested by the law and the prophets [*martyroumenē hypo tou nomou kai tōn prophētōn*], the righteousness of God through faith in Jesus Christ for all who believe.

As Cranfield notes, this 'attestation of the gospel by the OT is of fundamental importance for Paul [which] is indicated by the solemn way in which he insists on it here in what is one of the great hinge sentences on which the argument of the epistle turns'.[40] Indeed,

---

[40] Cranfield 1975: 203.

along with its tone and placement, we may note the uncommon language it uses as underlining its significance: Paul nowhere else in his letters uses the phrase 'the law and the prophets', and this is the only time Paul uses the verb *martyreō* in reference to the witness of Scripture.[41]

Romans 3:21 sets up a contrast between the failure of law to save and the testimony of the law (along with the prophets) to God's saving action in Christ. Many commentators take 'apart from law' to mean 'apart from doing the law'.[42] But, while it is true theologically that we are saved not by works, and Paul affirms this elsewhere, the point here seems to be something more than just this. Here it is not that righteousness is 'received apart from law', but righteousness is 'disclosed apart from law'. Paul's 'but now' signals a new stage of salvation history. As Moo puts it:

> In the new era inaugurated by Christ's death God has acted to deliver and vindicate his people 'apart from' the law. It is not primarily the law as something for humans to do, but the law as a system, as a stage in God's unfolding plan, that is in view here. 'Law' (*nomos*), then refers to 'the Mosaic covenant,' that (temporary) administration set up between God and his people to regulate their lives and reveal their sin until the establishment of the promise in Christ.[43]

In Romans 3:21 *nomos* has the same referent in both sides of the contrast. The righteousness of God has been disclosed apart from the law *as law-covenant*, but it is testified to by the law (and the prophets) *as prophecy*.

The contrast is between Romans 1:18 – 3:20 and 3:21–26 and a shift from the old era to the new era. But it is important to understand the nature of the temporal shift. It is not that we move from the wrath of God to the righteousness of God; Paul affirms that the old era displayed God's forbearance (3:26). Rather, as Carson puts it, 'the law-covenant could not effect righteousness or ensure that anyone be

---

[41] The imagery of the law court, in the background of 1:18 – 3:18 and to the fore in 3:19–20, explains the use of 'testimony' language, *martyreō*: the law and the prophets are summoned as witnesses to 'the righteousness of God through faith in Jesus Christ for all who believe' (Rom. 3:22). Cf. Dunn 1988a: 165.

[42] E.g. Calvin, Cranfield and Murray.

[43] Moo 1996: 223.

declared righteous . . . [U]nder the new era what is needed is righteous-ness that is manifested apart from the law'.[44]

But with this shift in salvation history, going from BC to AD if you like, the law does not cease to be relevant. Rather, its function changes; even if the law-covenant did not disclose the saving righteousness of God, it does (along with the prophets) bear witness to it. Carson makes the same point:

> According to Paul God gave the law not only to regulate the conduct of his people and to reveal their sin until the fulfilment of the promises in Christ. He also gave it because the law has *a prophetic function*, a witness function: it pointed in the right direction; it bore witness to the righteousness that is now being revealed.[45]

The question of most interest for our present purposes is this: To what in particular do the law and the prophets testify? Precisely what does the law prophesy? Most commentators, if they answer this question, do so in general ways with little attempt at validating their opinion from the rest of Romans. Fitzmyer and Dunn are exceptions. Fitzmyer suggests that Romans 4:23–24 'illustrate' the Old Testament's bearing witness to the gospel.[46] And Dunn points in the same direction, namely to the rest of the epistle: 'The testimony he will subsequently elaborate, particularly in chaps. 4 and 9–11, is of a community in the character of God's saving purpose through Israel, which is not to be confused with a national or ethnic continuity as such.'[47]

The possibility that Paul's exposition of the gospel in the chapters following Romans 3:21 serves to illustrate the witness of the law and the prophets will be explored in the following section, 'The law as prophecy in practice in Romans'. In my view Paul follows through on his conviction and confirms the prophetic role of the law and prophets at numerous points in the letter. Before proceeding to that task, there is one final verse in Romans that completes the picture of Paul's teaching on the law as prophecy, namely 3:31.

---

[44] Carson 2004a: 122. Cf. Campbell 1992: 180–181: 'Paul's statements [in Rom. 3:21–22a] amount to a deliberate contrast between different functions of the same body of writings – a contrast made possible by wordplay on the signifier *nomos*. As part of a soteriological condition or response, the Torah now seems defunct for Paul, but as an inspired and authoritative testimony to the acts of God, the writings still serve their appointed function.'

[45] Carson 2004a: 123, italics added.

[46] Fitzmyer 1993: 344.

[47] Dunn 1988a: 166.

The relationship between 3:27–31 and the passages preceding and following it, 3:21–26 and 4:1–25, is critical to its interpretation. In short, Romans 3:27–31 picks up on the critical nature of faith in the justification of both Jews and Gentiles, a theme introduced in 3:22, 26. As to what follows,[48] Paul makes three points in 3:27–30 that he then goes on to develop in 4:1–25:

1. Faith excludes boasting (3:27) – seen in the life of Abraham (4:1–2).
2. Faith, apart from works of the law, is necessary to preserve grace (3:28) – seen in the lives of Abraham and David (4:3–8).
3. Faith is necessary for both Jews and Gentiles to be justified (3:29–30) – seen in Abraham's being justified before he received the sign of circumcision (4:9–25).

Paul then climaxes Romans 3:21–30 by answering the objection that this emphasis on faith in the new era of universal salvation, when righteousness is manifested apart from the law-covenant for both Jews and Gentiles, abolishes the law altogether: 'Do we then overthrow [*katargeō*] the law by this faith? By no means! On the contrary, we uphold the law [*alla nomon histanomen*]' (Rom. 3:31).

Paul denies that the new thing God has done in the sacrificial death of Christ (3:25) does away with the law. It is not that Christians end up 'under the law' after all; Paul 'does not uphold *nomos* ("law") as *lex*, as ongoing legal demand'.[49] Rather, the law is upheld, that is 'validated', and its 'validity reinforced' (*histēmi*; BDAG 482b), though not *as commandments in the new age*, but *as prophecy of the new age* in which both Jews and Gentiles will be justified by grace through faith. Paul abolishes the law as law-covenant, but upholds it as prophecy.[50]

The upholding of the law (3:31b) is in effect

the unpacking of the last clause of Romans 3:21: the law and the prophets testify to this new 'righteousness from God' that has come in Christ Jesus, and thus their valid continuity is sustained in that to which they point. . . . The law is upheld precisely because the

---

[48] See Carson 2004a: 139.
[49] Ibid.
[50] Cf. Fitzmyer 1993: 367: 'In insisting on faith as the one principle of salvation, and in linking it to the one God, Paul affirms the basic message of the OT, and in particular that of the Mosaic law itself, rightly understood.'

redemptive-historical purposes and anticipations of the law are upheld.[51]

The connection of 3:31 with 3:21 is given more credence when it is recognized that 4:1–25 is effectively an exposition of Genesis 15:6 from the law, and Psalm 32:1–2 from the prophets.[52]

To sum up, in investigating Paul's teaching about the law as prophecy in Romans we have found five statements affirming the belief that the law points to salvation in Christ:

1. The gospel of God was promised beforehand through his prophets in the holy Scriptures, which includes the law (1:2).
2. The disclosure of the righteousness of God is attested by the law and the prophets (3:21).
3. We uphold the law as prophecy, in stressing the critical role of faith in justifying both Jews and Gentiles (3:31).
4. The account of Abraham's faith being credited to him as right-eousness was written for believers in Christ (4:23–24).
5. The revelation of the mystery, which is the gospel about Jesus Christ, is disclosed through the prophetic Scriptures, which includes the law (16:25–26).

It is noteworthy that two of the texts, the first and fifth, which envelop the letter, in their use of the noun 'prophets' and the adjective 'prophetic' respectively, supply precedent for labelling this teaching 'the law as prophecy'. In Romans 1:2 Paul affirms that the gospel was promised in advance in the holy Scriptures 'through his prophets' (*dia tōn prophētōn*); and in 16:26 this gospel is disclosed 'through the prophetic writings' (*graphōn prophētikōn*).

The law as prophecy in practice in Romans

Having considered Paul's precept with regard to the law as prophecy in Romans, what of his practice? Does Paul follow through and make use of the law as prophecy in his exposition and defence of the gospel? How prevalent in Romans is the testimony of the law to 'the righteous-ness of God through faith in Jesus Christ for all who believe'?

[51] Carson 2004a: 139.
[52] Cf. Murray 1959: 124: 'By appeal to Abraham and David (4:1–8) the apostle shows that the doctrine of justification by faith was imbedded in the Old Testament itself, and that it was at the centre of the revelation which had been entrusted to the Jews and in possession of which they boasted.'

Significantly, three of the five passages in Romans in which Paul affirms the prophetic function of the law refer to the law as part of a larger body of writings: in 1:2 and 16:26 the law is included in 'the holy scriptures' and 'the prophetic writings' respectively; and in 3:21 Paul refers to 'the law and the prophets'. Furthermore, as we noted above, when Paul cites 'scripture' on four occasions in Romans, two of the texts are from the law and two from the prophets. It is worth considering whether this pattern in Paul's precept is repeated in his practice. Does Paul appeal to *the law along with the prophets* when showing that he upholds the law as prophecy?[53]

As it turns out, in Romans Paul regularly cites the law as a prophecy of the gospel in tandem with the prophets, something not unexpected in the light of Romans 1:2, 3:21 and 16:25–26. Six times Paul quotes the law in its prophetic capacity and in every case there is in the same context a quotation or quotations from the prophets. In spite of the thicket of exegetical issues that typically slow progress in the interpretation of Romans, the following brief summary affirms little that is controversial. There is solid evidence that Paul cites the law and the prophets together in Romans as a witness to his gospel:

- In Romans 4 the law and the prophets testify to righteousness by faith apart from the law: in connection with Abraham's faith in Genesis 15:6, 22 (Rom. 4:1 – 4:9–25); and David's forgiveness in Psalm 32:1–2 (Rom. 4:6–8).
- In Romans 9 the law and the prophets testify to the partial hardening of Israel that has accompanied the gospel: in Genesis 21:12; 18:10, 14; 25:23; Exodus 33:19; 9:16 (Rom. 9:6–18); and in Malachi 1:2–3; Isaiah 29:16; 45:9; 10:22–23; 1:9; Hosea 2:23; 1:10 (Rom. 9:25–29).[54]
- In Romans 10 the law and the prophets testify to righteousness by faith: in Deuteronomy 9:4; 30:11–14 (Rom. 10:6–9);[55] and in Isaiah 28:16; 53:1; Joel 2:32 (Rom. 10:11–15).
- In Romans 10 the law and the prophets testify to not all Israelites accepting the gospel: in Deuteronomy 32:21 (Rom. 10:19); and in Psalm 19:4; Isaiah 65:1–2 (Rom. 10:18, 20–21).

[53] We will restrict ourselves to quotations from the law. This is not to deny the importance of other levels of influence, such as allusions, echoes, use of language, etc. Focusing on more explicit and direct appeal to the law makes its own compelling case.

[54] Cf. Seifrid 2007: 639: 'The law itself defines the children of Abraham and of Israel as those created by the word of promise.'

[55] See the discussion of this text above in the section 'Deuteronomy 9:4 and 30:11–14 in Romans 10:6–9'.

- In Romans 11 the law and prophets testify to the hardening of Israel; 'As it is written' in Deuteronomy 29:4 // Isaiah 29:10; 'And David says' in Psalm 69:22–23 (Rom. 11:8–10).
- In Romans 15 the law and the prophets testify to Gentiles glorifying God; in Deuteronomy 32:43; 2 Samuel 22:50 // Psalms 18:49; 117:1; Isaiah 11:10.

The six examples illustrate Paul's conviction that the gospel of salvation through faith in Christ for all who believe does not overthrow the law, but rather upholds the law as prophecy (3:31).

The issue of Jews and Gentiles in the people of God is a recurring theme in Paul's reading of the law as prophecy in Romans; it occurs in five of the examples, with only the first from Romans 10 as an exception. However, it would be unwise to conclude that according to Paul the witness of the prophetic Scriptures is limited to or even focused on this question. Paul tends to cite Scripture explicitly more often when dealing with questions with which his Jewish readers and opponents took issue. The concentration of quotations in Romans 9 – 11, which deals with the election of Israel and the inclusion of the Gentiles, bears this out.[56]

It is also noteworthy that, in citing the law and the prophets as testimony to the gospel in the above six examples, Paul has chosen to cite texts drawn first from the law and then from the prophets; this sequence is clearly discernable. The only partial exception is the quotation of Psalm 19:4 in Romans 10:18, which is followed by a quotation from Deuteronomy and then Isaiah in that order. I am not suggesting that this pattern of citing the law and then the prophets is contrived or even conscious on Paul's part. However, it is striking that the only place in his letters where he refers to Scripture as 'the law and the prophets' is in Romans 3:21, which (along with 1:2 and 3:31) sets up his appeal to the law and the prophets as a witness to the gospel in the rest of the letter.

In Paul's own words (a summary and paraphrase)

The law was written for us Christians and is part of the prophetic writings which disclose my gospel and proclamation of Jesus Christ,

---

[56] According to UBS4, there are sixty-two OT quotations in Romans, with thirty-two in Rom. 9 – 11. In fact, up to a third of all of the quotations of Scripture in all of Paul's letters, depending on how one counts them, occur in Rom. 9 – 11. Cf. Seifrid 2007: 638: 'The long drought of direct citation of the Scriptures in chapters 5–8, which Paul breaks in 8:36, is followed by a flood of citations in chapters 9–11.'

which was a mystery kept secret for long ages, and is now made known to the Gentiles to bring about the obedience of faith. This gospel was promised beforehand through the prophets in the holy Scriptures, that is, through the law and the prophets. The law and the prophets testify to the message of the righteousness of God through faith in Jesus Christ for all who believe. When it comes to this gospel, the law is upheld and the word of God has not failed.

In particular, in Romans the law bears witness to Abraham's faith as a model for all believers, to the partial hardening of Israel that has accompanied the gospel, to righteousness by faith, to not all of Israel accepting the gospel, to the hardening of Israel, and to the Gentiles glorifying God as a result.

Chapter Six

'*Written for our instruction*'
Reappropriation of the law as wisdom

Any continuing role for the Torah (Jewish law) in Paul's
ethics is a matter of continuing controversy.

(James D. G. Dunn)[1]

The OT plays a rather subsidiary role in Paul's ethic
(though there has been a strong upsurge of support
in recent years for the opposite view).

(Christopher M. Tuckett)[2]

It is likely that these [the laws of Deuteronomy] and other
scriptural laws have exercised a far more pervasive
influence over Pauline parenesis than the small number
of explicit citations and direct allusions would suggest
(as argued by Brian Rosner).

(Francis Watson)[3]

While Rosner probably tries to argue for too much and
some of his links are more convincing than others, his
work has been widely received as an important corrective
to the approach of von Harnack and others opposed to
Paul's use of the Old Testament [for ethics].

(Richard Burridge)[4]

The question of continuity and discontinuity between the Old and
New Testaments is at the heart of many studies of biblical theology.

[1] Dunn 2003: 11.
[2] Tuckett 2000: 424.
[3] Watson 2004: 425.
[4] Burridge 2007: 95.

In the case of Paul and the law, discontinuity is underlined by Paul's firm insistence that Christians are not under the law (see chapter 2), his avoidance of the language of keeping, doing and obeying the law and walking according to the law for Christian conduct (see chapter 3), and his replacement of the law by other things (see chapter 4). Continuity, on the other hand, can be seen in Paul's use of the law as a witness to the gospel (see chapter 5). Can it also be seen in Paul's using the law for ethics? Answering this question is the task of this chapter.

In my view Paul's positive appropriation of the law for moral teaching is evidence neither of inconsistency (contradicting his insistence that believers are not under the law), nor an indication that his abrogation of the law is only partial (civil and ceremonial, but not the moral law). The key to understanding Paul's use of the law for ethics is hermeneutical. If the law *as law-covenant* has been abolished, the law is still of value for Christian conduct as Scripture and *as wisdom*.

The following six steps will be taken in order to defend and expound the thesis that when it comes to regulating conduct in the churches, Paul reads the law as wisdom for living:

1. Review the debate over the extent to which Paul is indebted to the law for his moral teaching.
2. Consider the use of the law in the Psalms as a forerunner to Paul's use of the law as wisdom.
3. Observe the 'wisdom' character of the law.
4. Examine the character of Paul as a wisdom teacher.
5. Investigate the ways in which Paul refers to the law and its functions that suggest that he reads it as wisdom.
6. Investigate some examples of the use of the law as wisdom in Paul's letters.

Paul, Scripture and ethics

The view that the law did not play an important role in Paul's moral teaching is widely held in Pauline studies. It is represented not only by Protestant but also by Roman Catholic and Jewish scholars. In my book *Paul, Scripture and Ethics*, first published in 1994, I listed more than thirty such scholars,[5] and similar views on the subject continue

---

[5] Rosner 1999: 3–4.

to be expressed to this day. Indeed, this chapter on Paul's use of the law for ethics would be very brief if it were to be written by such scholars.

Although it is a broad and diverse tradition of Pauline interpretation, Adolf von Harnack probably exercised the greatest single influence upon it through his forcibly written 1928 essay 'The Old Testament in the Pauline Letters and in the Pauline Churches'.[6] Harnack surveyed Paul's letters (ten in total), looking for indications that Paul based his practical teaching on the Hebrew Scriptures in general and on the Torah in particular. According to Harnack, six of the letters do not quote the Old Testament, and special circumstances explain the appearance of the Old Testament in the other four:

> From the beginning Paul did not give the Old Testament to the young churches as the book of Christian sources for edification. Rather, he based his mission and teaching wholly and completely on the gospel and expects edification to come exclusively from it and from the Spirit accompanying the gospel.[7]

Three factors help explain Harnack's position: (1) the influence of Marcion – Harnack wrote the definitive work on Marcion in his day and refers to him sympathetically in the essay several times; (2) the Lutheran theological construction, law versus gospel, which Harnack adopts in its most absolute form; and (3) the ignoring of the Pastoral Epistles, which Harnack regards as post-Pauline (though 2 Tim. 3:16–17 contradicts his position).[8]

Andreas Lindemann and R. G. Hamerton-Kelly are examples of those in more recent times who echo Harnack's conclusions:

> Paul understands the Old Testament, his Bible, no longer as Torah in the proper sense; it is no longer the source of the instruction of God for the conduct of people in so far as they are Christians.[9]

> The Mosaic Law played no constructive role in Paul's ethics.[10]

---

[6] Harnack 1995.

[7] Ibid. 44.

[8] See Rosner 1995: 6–8.

[9] Lindemann 1986: 263, my tr.

[10] Hamerton-Kelly 1990: 74. See Rosner 1994: 4 for a list of a further thirty-one scholars who express similar views.

My first book was effectively in response to Harnack et al., taking 1 Corinthians 5 – 7 as a test case, a passage Harnack describes as having hardly any links with the Law of Moses or the Old Testament.[11] I argued that Paul's teaching in this sample of his ethics can be reliably traced back into the Scriptures, in many cases by way of Jewish sources. In 1 Corinthians 5 a case of incest is condemned and discipline employed because of the teaching of covenant and temple exclusion in Leviticus and Deuteronomy.[12] In 6:1–11 going to court before unbelievers is prohibited with the Scriptures' teaching on judges in mind, especially the example of Moses' appointing judges in Exodus and Deuteronomy.[13] In 6:12–20 going to prostitutes is opposed by using the scriptural doctrine of the Lord as the believer's husband and master, and with advice that recalls early Jewish interpretation of Joseph's fleeing Potiphar's wife.[14] And in 7:1–40 several key texts from the law (as understood by much early Jewish interpretation) inform what is said about marriage, singleness and divorce.

While the question remains open for some, many are coming to see Scripture and especially the law as a critical and formative source for Paul's moral teaching. In his study of Paul's reading of the Pentateuch Francis Watson writes, 'It is likely that . . . these [the laws of Deuteronomy] and other scriptural laws have exercised a far more pervasive influence over Pauline parenesis than the small number of explicit citations and direct allusions would suggest (as argued by Brian Rosner).'[15] Recall the quotations from Watson and Burridge at the start of this chapter.

Christopher M. Tuckett, whose article in 2000 on the role of the Old Testament in Paul's ethics, 'Paul, Scripture and Ethics', concludes in opposition to my work that 'the OT plays a rather subsidiary role in Paul's ethic'. But it is significant that he admits that in saying this he is swimming against the rising tide of scholarship: 'there has been a strong upsurge of support in recent years for the opposite view'.[16]

Indeed, my views are hardly novel. Whereas scholars such as Adolf Schlatter and W. D. Davies saw Paul and his teaching as essentially Jewish, E. P. Sanders's influential work portrayed him as something fundamentally different. Since the publication of Sanders's *Paul and*

---

[11] Rosner 1999.
[12] Cf. Rosner 1991b, 1992a.
[13] Rosner 1991a.
[14] Rosner 1992b.
[15] Watson 2004: 425.
[16] Tuckett 2000: 424.

Palestinian Judaism in 1977, comparisons of aspects of Paul and his thought with early Jewish thought have abounded. Much work in Pauline studies since, by scholars who endorse or critique the New Perspective, has stressed the Jewish matrix of Paul's thought and his scriptural inheritance.

Along with a number of studies that stress the continuity between Paul's moral teaching and biblical/Jewish antecedents,[17] the growing interest in the New Testament use of the Old Testament[18] has also contributed to an awareness of the continuing influence of the law on Paul's moral teaching. The case against recognizing Paul's indebtedness to the law in matters moral comes down to a failure to take seriously the intertextual nature of Paul's letters.[19] Counting citations of the law is too blunt an instrument to gauge Paul's dependence. A more attentive reading is needed, noticing not just quotations, but also allusions, echoes, language and ideas. The genre of Paul's letters, with his authority residing squarely in his own apostleship, means that he has no need to make his indebtedness to the law explicit. And quotations of the law are just the tip of the iceberg of Paul's dependence.

Richard Hays offers a helpful summary of four ways that Paul uses the Hebrew Scriptures when he regulates conduct in the churches.[20] These uses underscore the subtle and varied ways in which the Law and the Prophets are a crucial and formative source for Paul's ethics. Only the first of his four categories represents an explicit and direct usage. The other three are more subtle and indirect.

First, according to Hays, Paul sometimes reads Scripture as a word of God spoken directly to the church. He was not averse to asking, 'what does the scripture say?' (Gal. 4:30). Concerning the temptation of personally taking revenge when wronged, he quotes Proverbs 25:21–22: 'If your enemies are hungry, feed them' (Rom. 12:20–21). With respect to the question of the financial support of ministers of the gospel he cites Deuteronomy 25:4, a text where God, he believes, 'speak entirely for our sake' (1 Cor. 9:10): 'You shall not muzzle an ox while it is treading out the grain' (1 Cor. 9:9).

Secondly, Scripture was often for Paul the implicit source for particular norms. He takes for granted in Romans 13:8–10, for example, that adultery, murder, theft and covetousness are wrong because of

---

[17] See e.g. Tomson 1990; Reinmuth 1985.

[18] For some of the fruits of this work see Beale and Carson 2007.

[19] See Hays 1989. Cf. Ciampa 2008 for a contribution taking into account the influence of the language and ideas of Scripture on the NT.

[20] Hays 1996a.

the Decalogue. Even when not made explicit, the ultimate basis for his moral judgments on a host of matters is instinctively Scripture. The language and arguments used in his condemnation of idolatry in Romans 1, 'the works of the flesh' in Galatians 5:19–21 and incest in 1 Corinthians 5 indicate that his moral vision is informed by Scripture.

Thirdly, Paul regularly drew attention to scriptural narratives as moral exemplars. He viewed the experience of Israel as paradigmatic for the church. In 1 Corinthians 10, for example, Paul refers to Israel's wilderness wanderings and sin with the golden calf in order to warn the church against idolatry, sexual immorality, putting Christ to the test and murmuring against God. What is striking is that in exhorting a predominantly Gentile church on this basis he describes the events as those of '*our* ancestors' (10:1). The church is to perceive itself as part of Israel's story, to hear the resonances between it and their own situation and to shape their lives accordingly. Similarly in 2 Corinthians 8:7–15 Paul encourages the church to take part in the collection for the poor in Jerusalem by referring to Israel's experience of God's provision of manna in the desert (Exod. 16:18 is quoted in v. 15).

Fourthly, in dealing with moral problems Scripture is consistently for Paul the narrative framework for the identity of the community. Paul's ethical judgments, as we will see below, are inseparable from his sense of the vocation of God's people. When Paul writes to the churches in need of moral discernment, he reminds them on the basis of Scripture of who they are and where they stand in relation to God's purposes. As Hays contends, Paul, with frequent reference to the promises to Abraham and the prophecies of Isaiah, uses Scripture to

> provide an overarching proleptic vision of God's design to redeem the world and situates the community of believers within the unfolding story of this dramatic redemption. Every ethical guidance that Paul gives to his churches finds its ultimate warrant in this narrative framework.[21]

There is another factor that makes counting quotations a misleading measure for gauging Paul's use of the law for ethics: Paul stands in a Jewish tradition as a moral teacher, notwithstanding his disagreements with other Jews concerning many matters relating to

---

[21] Ibid. 37.

the law.[22] And the 'pattern of teaching' to which Paul committed believers in Christ (Rom. 6:17) had much in common with early Jewish catechesis, which itself attempted to live in accordance with the law. Early Jewish moral teaching was often the lens through which Paul perceived the relevance of the law for ethics, refracting the dynamic witness of Torah in a variety of ways. In Jewish moral teaching certain passages from the law become prominent, certain moral scruples from the law are emphasized, certain ethical concerns from the law are connected, certain forms of parenesis found in the law are popularized, certain moral themes from the law undergo development, and certain interpretations of the law are promulgated.[23] It is only when such developments are kept in mind that the influence of the law on Paul's moral teaching can be fully appreciated.

The use of the law in the Psalms

Gordon Wenham regards the psalms to be especially pertinent to New Testament ethics in terms of sharing a similar moral vision: 'The ethics of the psalms ought to be of great interest to readers of the New Testament. Not only do we find echoes of their vocabulary throughout the New Testament but also many of the emphases of the psalms are reinforced there.'[24] In this section I wish to add that along with a shared interest in a range of topics concerning conduct, the hermeneutics of the use of the law in the Psalms is also instructive for subjects like Paul and the law.

While there are patent differences between the use of the law in Paul and in the Psalms,[25] the Psalms exemplify an appreciation for the law that goes beyond mere law observance, and in certain key respects show what it means to read the law as wisdom for living. Significantly, Psalm 119, the high point of teaching concerning the law in the Psalms, is often classified as a wisdom psalm celebrating the value of the law.

A broad study of the use of the law in the Psalms is needed to appreciate its full significance. While it is true that the majority of the psalms are prayers of praise or petition, many contain considerable ethical content. And as it turns out, the law itself is a major theme of

[22] See Rosner 1994: 26–58.
[23] See ibid. 54–55 for a list of twelve examples.
[24] Wenham 2012: 182.
[25] The most obvious difference is the psalmist's devotion to the law, which Paul does not echo.

the psalter. Gordon Wenham comments that '[t]he structure of the Psalter, which commends the law in the opening psalm and makes it the theme of the longest psalm [Ps. 119], immediately draws attention to the law's importance.'[26] In noting other ways in which the book of Psalms draws attention to the law, Wenham points out that Psalm 19:7–9 bears comparison with Psalm 119, sharing with it six terms for the law. With reference to the placement of Psalms 19 and 119 it is indeed striking that 'the first and last book of the Psalter have at their center a psalm praising the law'.[27] The psalter is 'itself divided into five books like the Pentateuch'.[28]

What do the rest of the psalms do with the law? Several psalms give clear evidence that the psalmists knew the Mosaic law and covenant: Psalm 78:5–8 condemns Israel for persistent disobedience to the law; Psalm 105:44–45 says that the Lord gave Israel 'the lands of the nations . . . / that they might keep his statutes / and observe his laws'; Psalm 81:9–10 quotes the prologue to the Ten Commandments and paraphrases the first two commandments; and Psalm 50:16–19 lists a string of offences, including theft, adultery and false witness, as a rejection of 'God's statutes, covenant and words' (my tr.).[29]

Wenham offers a helpful comparison of the ethics of the psalter and the laws of the Pentateuch.[30] Concerning the Decalogue he concludes:

> There is plenty of evidence that the psalmists know the Ten Commandments and place them at the heart of their ethical thinking. The demand to worship God alone is fundamental to the psalms, and the manward commandments are also thoroughly endorsed, whether it be respecting parents, marriage, life or property.[31]

However, it is not that the Psalms quote the commandments as rules to be obeyed and leave it at that. As Wenham notes, the laws of the Pentateuch 'indicate the floor of behavior, not the ideal of loving God with all your heart and loving your neighbor as yourself. To love one's neighbor means much more than not murdering him or not stealing

[26] Wenham 2012: 78. Wenham's book, especially chs. 5–8, is an insightful exploration of the subject of the ethics of the psalter, a neglected topic in scholarship on the Psalms.
[27] Ibid. 79.
[28] Ibid.
[29] Ibid. 106, commenting on Ps. 50, Wenham concludes that 'the psalmist is consciously recalling the Ten Commandments here'.
[30] Ibid. ch. 6, 'Laws in the Psalter'.
[31] Ibid. 109–110.

from him.'[32] This is a critical point in the study of biblical ethics that is often overlooked. Part of the answer to the objection that not being under law will lead to licence and moral decline is that being under law is overrated in terms of its moral value. The Psalms offer an enlightening case study in what it means to internalize and delight in the law. At many points the Psalms demonstrate a reflective and expansive application of the Ten Commandments that goes beyond mere legal compliance.

As noted above, *the first commandment*, 'You shall have no other gods before me' (Exod. 20:3), is paraphrased in Psalm 81:9. However, the influence of the first commandment goes much deeper, with the psalter's frequent stress on the uniqueness of God and his supremacy over other gods. The incomparability of God is the chorus of many psalms:

> There is none like you among the gods, O Lord,
> nor are there any works like yours.
>
> (Ps. 86:8)[33]

The psalmist's declaration of complete dependence on the one God is also revealing, as in Psalm 62:5–6:

> For God alone my soul waits in silence,
> for my hope is from him.
> He alone is my rock and my salvation,
> my fortress; I shall not be shaken.

Likewise, the denunciation of those who take no regard for this God arises from attention to the first commandment: 'Fools say in their hearts, "There is no God"' (Ps. 14:1).

In Psalm 24:3–4 obeying *the second commandment*,[34] against the worship of idols and images, is extended beyond mere cultic conformity to include actions of the hands and heart:

> Who shall ascend the hill of the Lord?
> And who shall stand in his holy place?

[32] Ibid. 182. See further Wenham 1997.

[33] For other examples see Pss 86:10; 95:3; 96:4; 97:9.

[34] 'You shall not make for yourself an idol, whether in the form of anything that is in heaven above, or that is on the earth beneath, or that is in the water under the earth. You shall not bow down to them or worship them.'

> Those who have clean hands and pure hearts,
>> who do not lift up their souls to what is false,
>> and do not swear deceitfully.

In Psalms 31:6 and 119:37 resisting idolatry is phrased in terms, respectively, of not 'paying regard to worthless idols' and not 'looking at worthless things' (ESV), indicating reflection on the rationale of idolatry, namely its futility. Similar 'meditation' on the first and second commandment can be seen in Psalm 115:3–8:

> Our God is in the heavens;
>> he does whatever he pleases.
> Their idols are silver and gold,
>> the work of human hands.
> They have mouths, but do not speak;
>> eyes, but do not see.
> They have ears, but do not hear;
>> noses, but do not smell.
> They have hands, but do not feel;
>> feet, but do not walk;
>> they make no sound in their throats.
> Those who make them are like them;
>> so are all who trust in them.

Evidence of expansion and reflective application of the laws of the Pentateuch can also be seen with the use of *the third commandment*, 'You shall not make wrongful use of the name of the LORD your God' (Exod. 20:7). It is not quoted directly in the psalter, but 'the proper use of God's name is frequently celebrated'.[35] Psalm 8, for example, begins and ends by praising God's name:

> O LORD, our Sovereign,
>> how majestic is your name in all the earth!

A positive take on the prohibition of misusing God's name is also seen in Psalms 96:8 and 99:3: 'Ascribe to the LORD the glory due his name'; 'Let them praise your great and awesome name. / Holy is he!' As Wenham puts it, 'The psalms underline the importance of the

---

[35] Wenham 2012: 103.

proper use of God's name by illustrating how it ought to be used, not by banning its misuse.'[36]

The fourth commandment, 'Remember the sabbath day, and keep it holy' (Exod. 20:8), is conspicuous by its absence from the Psalms.[37] Why this is the case is open to discussion. It may simply be that the regular use of the psalms on the sabbath removes any need to refer to it.

The impact of *the fifth commandment*, 'Honour your father and your mother' (Exod. 20:12), is felt in the psalter, even if it is not mentioned explicitly. Specifically, the Psalms celebrate the gift of children and the privilege of parenthood. In Psalms 89:26 and 103:13 the honouring of earthly fathers is implied in reverence for God our father: 'You are my Father, / my God, and the Rock of my salvation!'; 'As a father has compassion for his children, / so the LORD has compassion for those who fear him.' And in Psalm 127:3–5 children are seen as gifts from God:

> Children are indeed a heritage from the Lord,
> the fruit of the womb a reward.
> Like arrows in the hand of a warrior are the sons of
> one's youth.
> Happy is the man who has his quiver full of them.
>
> (My tr.)

Likewise Psalm 128:3–4:

> Your wife will be like a fruitful vine
> within your house;
> your children will be like olive shoots
> around your table.
> Thus shall the man be blessed
> who fears the LORD.

The sixth commandment, 'You shall not murder' (Exod. 20:13), follows a similar pattern. Rather than being cited simply as a law against literal killing, the emphasis shifts to something more generally applicable, namely depriving someone of their livelihood. Psalm 94:6 links murder to the broader theme of social justice:

---

[36] Ibid.

[37] A partial exception is the heading of Ps. 92: 'A Song for the Sabbath Day'.

> They kill the widow and the stranger,
> they murder the orphan.

In possibly more figurative uses of the imagery of murder, enemies in the Psalms are compared to savage lions or dogs who devour their prey (Pss 7:2; 17:12; 22:13, 16; 35:17) and to attacking bulls (Ps. 22:12).

The seventh commandment, 'You shall not commit adultery' (Exod. 20:14), is alluded to in Psalm 50:18, 'you keep company with adulterers', and according to its title is the focus of David's confession in Psalm 51 ('To the leader. A Psalm of David, when the prophet Nathan came to him, after he had gone in to Bathsheba'). The prohibition of adultery may also be behind the psalter's commendation of marriage and families (see on the fifth commandment above). Psalm 45, often classified as a royal wedding psalm, presents a glorious view of marriage, a kind of dignified obverse of the indignity of adultery.

The eighth commandment, 'You shall not steal' (Exod. 20:15), receives a sustained treatment in the psalter.[38] Stealing, especially from the poor, is often condemned. But such activity goes beyond what a criminal court would class as stealing. Several psalms seem to class economic exploitation as a kind of theft, extending the literal and narrow sense of the commandment not to steal. In particular, certain psalms speak of the poor being plundered (12:5), despoiled (35:10), ambushed and seized (10:9), and of evildoers eating up God's people 'as they eat bread' (14:4).

The ninth commandment, 'You shall not bear false witness against your neighbour' (Exod. 20:16), receives the fullest treatment of all the Decalogue laws in the psalter. A quite literal appropriation is evident at some points, as in Psalms 27:12 and 35:11: 'false witnesses have risen against me, / and they are breathing out violence'; and 'Malicious witnesses rise up; / they ask me about things I do not know.' But once again it is not just the narrow sense of the law that impresses the psalmists, in this case that of honest legal testimony, but rather the broader concern of the misuse of the tongue and also its proper use that is so widespread. Consider the following sample:

> How long, you people, shall my honour suffer shame?
> How long will you love vain words, and seek after lies?
>
> (Ps. 4:2)

---

[38] Cf. Ps. 69:4, where the psalmist complains, 'What I did not steal must I now restore?'

> You destroy those who speak lies;
>> the LORD abhors the bloodthirsty
>>> and deceitful . . .
> For there is no truth in their mouths;
>> their hearts are destruction;
> their throats are open graves;
>> they flatter with their tongues.
>>>> (Ps. 5:6, 9)

> Their mouths are filled with cursing and deceit
>> and oppression;
> under their tongues are mischief and iniquity.
>>>> (Ps. 10:7)

> Those who walk blamelessly, and do what is right,
>> and speak the truth from their heart;
> who do not slander with their tongue,
>> and do no evil to their friends,
>> nor take up a reproach against their neighbours;
> in whose eyes the wicked are despised,
>> but who honour those who fear the LORD;
> who stand by their oath even to their hurt.
>>>> (Ps. 15:2–4)

> Keep your tongue from evil,
>> and your lips from speaking deceit.
>>> (Ps. 34:13)

The theme of illicit desire, introduced by *the tenth commandment*, 'You shall not covet' (Exod. 20:17), is present in the psalter, along with its obverse, licit or good desire. In the Psalms the desires of the wicked are selfish:

> For the wicked boast of the desires of their heart,
>> those greedy for gain curse and renounce the LORD.
>>> (Ps. 10:3)

The psalmist prays that 'the desire of the wicked [will] come to nothing' (Ps. 112:10, my tr.). On the other hand, the psalmist prays in confidence that God will grant the desire of the righteous for God's salvation:

> O LORD, you will hear the desire of the meek;
>> you will strengthen their heart, you will incline your ear.
>>> (Ps. 10:17)

> You have given him his heart's desire,
>> and have not withheld the request of his lips.
>>> (Ps. 21:2)

In almost every case it is not the commandments as such, but the commandments reflectively extended and applied to varied contexts, that reveal the interest of the Decalogue in the Psalms.

The influence of the Law of Moses on the ethics of the Psalms extends well beyond the Ten Commandments and even the other laws in Exodus to Deuteronomy. The narratives of the law (the Pentateuch) are also put to good and extensive use in many psalms to draw moral lessons.[39] To cite just two examples, when Psalms 14 and 53 reflect on the flood, the tower of Babel and Sodom and Gomorrah, three stories of universal judgment in the book of Genesis, they draw conclusions for their own day and setting:

> They have all gone astray, they are all alike perverse;
>> there is no one who does good,
>> no, not one.
>>> (Ps. 14:3; cf. Ps. 53:3)

As Wenham concludes, 'Psalm 14 is a good example of a psalm that draws on biblical narrative to make an exceedingly significant evaluation of the human condition, the universal tendency to sin.'[40]

How are we to characterize the use of the Law of Moses in the Psalms? Psalm 119, a psalm in which nearly every verse contains a word for the law, sheds some light. The longest acrostic in the Bible, Psalm 119, falls into twenty-two sections, with every verse of each section beginning with a letter of the Hebrew alphabet. According to Wenham, 'the acrostic pattern underlines the comprehensiveness and perfection of the law as well as the psalmist's yearning to live by it'.[41] The psalmist considers the law from aleph to taw, or, if you like, from A to Z.

---

[39] See Wenham 2012: ch. 7, 'Narrative Law in the Psalter', upon which this brief summary builds.

[40] Ibid. 122.

[41] Ibid. 83.

In Psalm 119 the psalmist protests his love for God's law no fewer than a dozen times:

> Oh, how I love your law!
>   It is my meditation all day long.
>   (Ps. 119:97)[42]

Five times he uses the term 'delight' to describe his attitude towards the law:

> Your decrees are my delight,
>   they are my counsellors.
>   (Ps. 119: 24)[43]

His concern is not just to 'keep' the law (21×), but also to 'learn' it (13×), 'understand' it (10×), not 'forget' it (9×) and 'know' it (4×). Along with 'righteousness' (12×), he is concerned with 'steadfast love' (7×), 'faithfulness' (5×) and 'truth' (4×).[44]

The psalm's eight apparently synonymous terms for the law, each of which he uses between 19 and 25 times,[45] also point beyond reading the law as commandments to be obeyed and not transgressed. In particular, 'word', *dābār*, the second most common, occurring some 24 times, often refers to God's promises, as in the refrain 'I hope in your word' (Ps. 119:81, 114, 147; cf. 49, 74) or in the prayer 'Give me life according to your word!' (Ps. 119:25, 107 ESV); Psalm 119:89 is perhaps the most intriguing:

> The LORD exists for ever;
>   your word is firmly fixed in heaven.

Such material points to the fact that Psalm 119 is no 'paean to casuistry',[46] nor is its relationship to the law that of a heartless legalism. Instead, Psalm 119 witnesses to a deeply interior spirituality based on a love for God and his law. The psalms in general show an approach to the law that does not primarily view the law as commandments, but

---

[42] Cf. Ps. 119:47, 48, 113, 119, 127, 132, 140, 159, 163, 165, 167.

[43] Cf. Ps. 119:77, 92, 143, 174.

[44] These statistics are taken from Wenham 2012: 85.

[45] In the NRSV they are translated as 'law', 'word', 'ordinances', 'testimonies', 'statutes', 'commandments', 'precepts' and 'commands'.

[46] Wenham's turn of phrase (2012: 83).

rather as promise and teaching to be explored, internalized and applied to all of life's ups and downs.

Two other features of the ethics and use of the law in the Psalms fit well with this notion of a wisdom reading of the law. The first is a clear focus on the creation and its inherent moral order. As Wenham states, in the Psalms 'all of creation is a demonstration of God's wisdom, power, and benevolence'.[47] The second is the influence of the character of God on moral living: 'the righteous are meant to imitate God and represent him on earth'.[48] Both of these motifs are well known in the psalter and need not detain us further here.[49]

In all, four elements of the use of the law in the Psalms have affinities with what might be called 'reading the law as wisdom': (1) internalizing of the law; (2) reflective and expansive application of the law; (3) the created order as a basis for morality; and (4) the character of God as a basis for morality. All four prove to be of value when it comes to understanding Paul's own positive use of the law for matters of conduct.

Before moving to Paul's own use of the law as wisdom in both precept and practice we first need to notice the wisdom character of both the Law of Moses itself and of Paul's moral teaching in general. Both of these set the scene for understanding Paul's use of the law for ethics.

The 'wisdom' character of the law

In defending the idea that Paul reads the law as wisdom I am not arguing that the genre of the Law of Moses is wisdom. As noted in chapter 1, the Torah is a five-volume, multi-genre entity. Given that Jews like Paul read the law as a unity, it is not surprising that perspectives on the law's usefulness and purpose developed into strategies for reading it. In this section I simply wish to observe that there are several features of the law and its early interpretation that suggest that reading the law as wisdom is not to misread the law.

---

[47] Ibid. 131. On creation in the ethics of the Psalms see pp. 128–137, 'Narrative Law in the Psalter'.

[48] Ibid. 165. On the imitation of God in the Psalms see pp. 158–165.

[49] In this section on the use of the law in the Psalms I have devoted more space to the reflective and expansive applications of the laws, which are less well known, than to the place of creation theology and the imitation of God. All three will prove to be critical when we come to consider Paul's use of the law for ethics.

Connections between the law and wisdom

The seed of the notion of the law as wisdom is planted in Moses' description of the purpose of the law in Deuteronomy 4:6: 'You must observe them diligently, for this will show *your wisdom and discernment* to the peoples, who, when they hear all these statutes, will say, "Surely this great nation is *a wise and discerning people!*"' The greatness of the nation Israel, when they had taken possession of the land, would not consist in wealth or military power, but rather in the wisdom and discernment that result from being taught God's statutes and ordinances (Deut. 4:5) and their closeness to God (Deut. 4:4, 7).

The narrative introduction to the law in Exodus 18 and Deuteronomy 1 also points to the wisdom-teaching function of the law. There, Jethro, Moses' father-in-law, observes that Moses is overburdened with his responsibilities for God's people and recommends that Moses appoint judges to decide the minor cases. Moses takes his advice and installs as leaders *'wise* [LXX: *sophous*] and reputable individuals' (Deut. 1:15).[50]

Ezra, Psalms and Proverbs contain texts that similarly take the law to be a font of wisdom:

> For you are sent by the king and his seven counsellors to make inquiries about Judah and Jerusalem according to *the law of your God, which is in your hand.* . . . And you, Ezra, according to *the God-given wisdom that is in your hand*, appoint magistrates and judges who may judge all the people in the province Beyond the River who know the laws of your God; and you shall teach those who do not know them. (Ezra 7:14, 25, my tr.)[51]

> The law of the LORD is perfect,
>   reviving the soul;
> the decrees of the LORD are sure,
>   *making wise the simple.*
>   (Ps. 19:7)

> Your commandment *makes me wiser* than my enemies,
>   for it is always with me.
>   (Ps. 119:98)

---

[50] For the influence of these texts on Paul's instructions in 1 Cor. 6:1–8 see Rosner 1994: 94–107.

[51] The context is the commissioning letter of Artaxerxes.

Those who keep the law are *wise children*.
(Prov. 28:7a)

A convergence of law and wisdom can also be seen in a number of Jewish intertestamental texts. Most famously, Sirach 24 equates law with wisdom. In a speech of personified wisdom Sirach 24.19–27 moves from calling for attention to wisdom to calling for attention to the law, which itself 'overflows with wisdom':

> 'Come to me, you who desire me,
>   and eat your fill of my fruits.
> For the memory of me is sweeter than honey,
>   and the possession of me sweeter than the honeycomb.
> Those who eat of me will hunger for more,
>   and those who drink of me will thirst for more.
> Whoever obeys me will not be put to shame,
>   and those who work with me will not sin.'
> All this is the book of the covenant of the Most High God,
>   the law that Moses commanded us
>   as an inheritance for the congregations of Jacob.
> It overflows, like the Pishon, with wisdom [*sophian*],
>   and like the Tigris at the time of the first fruits.
> It runs over, like the Euphrates, with understanding [*synesin*],
>   and like the Jordan at harvest time.
> It pours forth instruction [*paideian*] like the Nile,
>   like the Gihon at the time of vintage.

In Sirach 24 wisdom is the Torah of Israel, a source of wisdom, understanding and instruction (terms used frequently in wisdom contexts). The law has the same status as wisdom in terms of its heavenly origins and in the way of living it enshrines. Eckhard Schnabel's study of law and wisdom from Sirach to Paul finds several connections between law and wisdom in the postbiblical Jewish literature; both law and wisdom link the concept of life to 'walking', both are compared to 'light' and both lead to righteousness, holiness and purity.[52]

Schnabel's research shows that the identification of law and wisdom is not definitively established until Ben Sira, although it appears that some psalms and postexilic biblical literature presume it.[53] As it turns

[52] Schnabel 1985: 344–345.
[53] Ibid. 1–7.

out, a wide range of Second Temple Jewish texts also reinforce the connection between the law and wisdom:

- Baruch 4.1 identifies the wisdom that originated at the time of the creation of the world with 'the book of the commandments of God, / the law that endures for ever'.
- Baruch 3.9 issues the summary instruction to the nation 'Hear the commandments of life, O Israel; / give ear, and *learn wisdom*!'
- *2 Baruch* 48.24 describes 'that Law that is among us' as '*that excellent wisdom* that is within us'.
- *Testament of Naphtali* 8.10 exhorts its readers, 'Therefore, be wise and sensible in God [*sophoi en theō kai phronimoi*], understanding the order of his commandments, and the rules of every deed.'
- In the *Letter of Aristeas* 31 the king of Egypt is urged to have the Law of Moses translated into Greek in the following terms: 'It is necessary that these books should be made accurate for your library since the law that they contain, in as much as it is of divine origin, is *full of wisdom* and free from all blemish.'
- Among the Dead Sea Scrolls *Beatitudes* offers a 'solid identification of wisdom with Torah'[54] in its first preserved lines: 'Blessed is the man who has obtained *wisdom*. He has walked in the law of the Most High and prepared his heart for her ways' (4Q525 2ii + 3.3–4).
- Philo refers to Moses as the 'wise Moses' (e.g. *Dec.* 1; *Migr.* 201), as 'perfectly wise' (*Alleg. Interp.* 3.140; cf. 147), as an 'all-wise and godly man' (*Dreams* 1.214) and as 'that man who is wise in all things' (*Sacrifices* 173). He refers to 'the wise decrees of Moses' (*Names* 168), holds that the Mosaic laws 'are enacted with great wisdom and excellence' (*Dec.* 162), believes that laws based on 'the ten laws' are 'wise laws' (*Spec. Laws* 4.61) and equates 'the laws of the kingdom' with 'wisdom' (*Migr.* 197).

Jews contemporary with Paul believe that the law was enacted with wisdom, teaches wisdom and is full of wisdom, requires wisdom for its proper interpretation, and may even be identified as wisdom.

The moral order of creation, law and wisdom

According to Philo, Moses' presentation of laws is unique because it begins with an account of creation: '[T]he same being was the father

---

[54] Kampen 2011: 309.

and creator of the world, and likewise the lawgiver of truth'.[55] Therefore, 'his laws [are] the most fruitful image and likeness of the constitution of the whole world'.[56] *Pesiqta Rabbati* 21.19 observes that '[t]he Ten Commandments were said in correspondance to the ten words with which the world was created.' Paul acknowledged this idea when he referred to the Mosaic law as 'the embodiment of knowledge and truth' (Rom. 2:20).

According to Philo, 'it is the task of wisdom to investigate accurately everything that exists in nature' (*Prov.* 1.1). As it turns out the law itself supplies a solid basis for being read as supplying wisdom by anchoring its laws in the order of creation. George Athas explains this point with specific reference to reading the laws of Exodus:

> The ancient concept of justice (*mishpat*) was not thought of in purely legal terms, as we largely do today. Rather, justice was setting everything in its proper assigned place so that it may fulfill its assigned function in relational harmony with the rest of creation. In this way, creation and justice go hand in hand.[57]

Exodus 23:8 is a clear example of such wisdom-based law: 'You shall take no bribe, for a bribe blinds the officials, and subverts the cause of those who are in the right.' Andrew Cameron spells out the wisdom dimension of this law:

> This divine command actually takes its warrant from a wrong but persistent pattern of human behaviour, and even though the language is different, its logic bears striking resemblance to some wisdom aphorisms (e.g. Prov. 17:23; Eccl. 7:7). This regularly recurrent pattern of human behaviour is a corruption of the predictability of human desire, which is itself an aspect of the divinely ordered cosmos.[58]

Cameron lists six other laws from Exodus that might be described as 'wisdom moments', namely Exodus 20:26; 22:21, 27; 23:2, 9, 12.

In Bruce Waltke's view, 'the Pentateuch unites creation and ethics; the order of creation supports the order of redemption'.[59] The wisdom

[55] *Moses* 2.48.
[56] Ibid. 2.52.
[57] Athas 2008: 53.
[58] Cameron 2008: 143–144.
[59] Waltke and Yu 2007: 205. Cf. Goldingay 2003: 42: 'When one rebels against the rules and regulations revealed by God in the Torah . . . he or she rebels against the order of creation.'

basis of many of the Mosaic laws may even be seen with reference to the Decalogue:

> The creation narratives undergird the Ten Commandments, which epitomize the ethics of Israel's faith. . . . The narrative affirms the priority of the one true God demanded by the first commandment. It also affirms that he exists apart from and sovereign over all creation; thus, to reimage him in the form of an idol or as the goddess Sophia, as prohibited by the second commandment, is a detestable distortion of his glorious person. This sublime God will not tolerate the attaching of his glorious name to anything false; this truth supports the third commandment. The stipulation of Sabbath in the fourth commandment is predicated on the day of rest in the climax of creation. Murder is prohibited because humans are made in the image of God, which gives them dignity. The ban on adultery is based on the moral order established by God, who gave Adam only one wife. The Creator gave the arable soil to all humanity to provide them with food and wealth (Gen. 1:29). To steal from the community what rightfully belongs to all or to steal from an individual what that person has lawfully earned as his or her wage from working the creation must not be tolerated. One must also protect the reputation of every human being, for all are made in God's image.[60]

Such connections show that there is a moral aspect to the Mosaic law that is based on the creation's moral order, such that, as Chris Wright puts it, in the Law of Moses obedience is not only to the God of covenant purpose and redemptive action, but also to the God of created order.[61] As Wright points out, Genesis 1 presents creation as a place of order, system and structure,

> which provides an objective basis for the exercise of moral freedom and sets limits to moral relativism. . . . There is a basic shape to the world which we did not invent, and therefore a corresponding shape to the moral response required of us. . . . Morality, in biblical terms, is preconditioned by the given shape of creation.[62]

Wright also claims that the established order of creation generates confidence in the reliability and predictability of life in this world.

[60] Waltke and Yu 2007: 206.
[61] See C. J. H. Wright 1995: 48–56.
[62] Ibid. 49.

This leads to the conclusion that there are causes and effects in the moral realm, just as there are in the physical, and 'it is part of wise living in this world to take note of them and behave accordingly'.[63] Such ethical consequentialism undergirds the moral vision of both wisdom and law in the Bible, both of which are based on God's sovereign providence and justice. Wright also points out that in the Law of Moses 'perhaps the most familiar of all the implications of the creation material is the affirmation that God made humans in his own image',[64] which underscores the sanctity of human life (cf. Gen. 9:8–17) and the equality of all human beings (cf. Lev. 24:22).

Oliver O'Donovan likewise sees a close relationship between the Mosaic law, wisdom and the created order. In fact, it is a critical role of the law to make the moral implications of the order of creation more widely known:

> The re-presentation of wisdom as law declares, in fact, the central point of Israel's faith, which is the meeting of the life-in-the-world with life-before-God. . . . Wisdom, with its cool observational detachment and its inherent restriction to the educated, was made available in the form of law. . . . In torah therefore the moral authority of the created order and the transcendent authority of the electing God were made one.[65]

According to O'Donovan, the law is a wise articulation of the created order.

The better interpreters of the law, both Jewish and Christian, have never regarded its regulations as mere arbitrary impositions forced upon us by the power of God's will without any connection to the structures of God's world or the impact of his salvation. According to Calvin, at the heart of the law's demands is the call to live in accordance with the image of God: 'if any man carries out in deeds whatever is enjoined there [in the law], he will express the image of God, as it were, in his own life'.[66] For Calvin, 'the law of Moses sets forth the pattern of the image of God as it would have been originally created'.[67]

Traugott Holtz draws similar conclusions in his discussion of the Jewish roots of Paul's ethics:

[63] Ibid.
[64] Ibid.
[65] O'Donovan 1986: 189–190.
[66] Calvin 1975: 415.
[67] Zachman 2009: 470.

The world is not without order. It is not up to the will of humans to make it. There are firm limits to the world and therefore to humans, which can only be transgressed as the price of the world itself, at the price of one's own life. Order has been firmly imprinted on the world, in which alone it functions, if it wishes to remain itself. According to Jewish belief, a belief shared by Paul, this order has been revealed to humanity in the *nomos* [the law].[68]

There is no doubt that the law itself encouraged a reflective and expansive application, taking into account the whole of life. The people were to hear the law read regularly in public assemblies. Parents were to teach it daily to their children. The king was to write out a copy of it. Joshua was to read the law daily. The Psalms celebrate meditation on it. And the prophets pointed back to it. All of these point to a teaching function or wise appropriation of the law that was to form both leaders and people in their thinking, that is, in their hearts and way of life. The repeated call of the law to love God, trust him, fear him, obey him, imitate him, and guard this law in their hearts reinforces the spiritual nature of the law that fits with a wise reading.

It is not that the wisdom-order-of-creation basis for each of the laws is equally clear; by their very definition laws can at times appear to be the arbitrary imposition of the divine will. But digging a bit deeper reveals that the law in general is based on the fact that the law-giving God is both our Redeemer and our Creator. This is a critical point for the study of Paul's use of the law for ethics. Even when the law does not meet Christians with the force of law, as law-covenant, its basis in the moral order of creation means that it still functions as instruction and wisdom for living.

Paul the wisdom teacher

The likelihood that Paul read the law as wisdom for living is increased when two facts about his ethics are recognized: first, its wisdom character; and secondly, Paul's emphasis on renewal from within.

The wisdom character of Paul's moral teaching

There is abundant evidence of a wisdom character to Paul's moral teaching. According to 2 Peter 3:15, 'our beloved brother Paul wrote to you according to the wisdom given to him'.

---

[68] Holtz 1995: 70.

Paul calls the Corinthians to 'become wise' (1 Cor. 3:18); deplores the fact that none of the Corinthians is wise enough to settle the dispute between brothers (1 Cor. 6:5); calls the Roman Christians to 'be wise about what is good' (Rom. 16:19 NIV); prays that believers will be filled with the perception of God's will in all wisdom (Col. 1:9–10); admonishes and teaches 'in all wisdom' (Col. 1:28) and expects believers to do the same (Col. 3:16); and tells the Colossian Christians to be 'wise in the way you walk' (Col. 4:5, my tr.) and the Ephesian Christians to 'be careful how you walk, not as unwise, but as wise' (Eph. 5:15, my tr.). Note not only how widespread is this material, but also how Paul uses language expected of Jewish Torah observance, transferring it to Christian wisdom.

The pervasive wisdom basis to Paul's ethics is also seen in his appeal to reason and discernment, and to the orders of creation, such as nature (Rom. 1:26), marriage (1 Cor. 7), state (Rom. 13:1–7)[69] and work (1 Thess. 5:14; 2 Thess. 3:6–7, 11), as well as convention (Rom. 13:13; 1 Cor. 7:35; 13:5; 14:40; 1 Thess. 4:12) and custom (1 Cor. 11:14). Furthermore, in Paul's ethics various motives are similar to, if not identical with, motivations in the wisdom literature. Examples include the appeal to 'common sense' (1 Cor. 5:6; 6:12; 9:7; 11:15–16; 2 Cor. 9:6; Col. 3:21; 2 Thess. 3:10); the appeal to a sense of shame (1 Thess. 4:4; 1 Cor. 11:6; 2 Cor. 9:4; Rom. 2:17–24; 16:17–18); and social reasons (1 Thess. 4:12; 1 Cor. 7:4; Rom. 13:1–6; Gal. 5:15; Col. 3:20–25).

Wisdom and internalizing the law

In discussing the use of the law in the Psalms (see above), I noted the habit of the psalmists, most clearly in Psalm 119, to internalize the law, a move borne out in the widespread reflective and expansive application of the law in the Psalms. The psalmist, as Wenham puts it, effectively 'yearns for the prophecy of Jeremiah 31:33, that God would write his law in the heart, to be fulfilled in him'.[70] 'The psalmist has internalized the law in a way that anticipates a Christian understanding of the place of the law in ethics.'[71]

One of the key features of Paul's teaching on the Christian life is the notion of renewal from within. Paul is a theologian of the heart.[72]

---

[69] See Rosner 1994: 113–115 for the roots of the teaching of Rom. 13 in the sapiential traditions of Scripture.

[70] Wenham 2012: 84.

[71] Ibid. 86.

[72] The word *kardia* occurs fifty-two times in Paul's letters (with forty-two times in Luke-Acts coming in a close second among NT authors).

In Romans God 'searches the heart' (8:27), the law and circumcision must affect the heart (2:15, 29), and obedience and faith must be 'from the heart' (6:17; 10:9–10). As Peterson concludes, 'with such concerns Paul reflects New Covenant expectations'.[73] Along with allusions to Jeremiah 31:33 with expressions like 'the work of the law is written on their hearts' (Rom. 2:15 HCSB), the background to the new-covenant texts in Jeremiah include promises that the nation will return to the Lord 'with their whole heart' (Jer. 24:7), when God will give them 'singleness of heart and action' (Jer. 32:39 NIV).

However, internalizing the law is not just connected to the prophecies of the new covenant in the Old Testament. Psalm 37 connects wisdom with the one who internalizes the law:

> The mouths of the righteous utter wisdom,
>   and their tongues speak justice.
> The law of their God is in their hearts;
>   their steps do not slip.
>
> (Ps. 37:30–31 NRSV)

In Proverbs 7:1–4 writing the laws 'on the tablet of your heart' is juxtaposed with calling wisdom 'your intimate friend'.[74] And 2 Baruch 48.24 describes 'that Law that is among us' as 'that excellent wisdom that is within us'. This observation is vital when it comes to understanding Paul's appropriation of the law for Christian conduct, forging another link between Paul's positive appropriation of the law and wisdom.

The law as wisdom in precept

Having observed the wisdom character of both the law and Paul's ethics, it remains to test the hypothesis that Paul reads the law as wisdom when regulating conduct in the churches. Before moving to an investigation of Paul's practice in the next section, it is worth considering whether Paul gives some indication as to how he regards the

[73] Peterson 2012: 136–137.
[74] Cf. Prov. 7:1–4: 'My child, keep my words / and store up my commandments with you; / keep my commandments and live, / keep my teachings as the apple of your eye; / bind them on your fingers, / write them on the tablet of your heart. / Say to wisdom, "You are my sister," / and call insight your intimate friend.' 2 Baruch 48.24 also describes the internalizing of the law in terms of wisdom: 'For we are all one celebrated people, / Who have received one law from One: / And the law which is amongst us will aid us, / And the surpassing wisdom which is in us will help us.'

law in relation to Christian conduct. In other words, what is Paul's precept with respect to his use of the law for questions of conduct? Three texts go some way towards answering this question: 1 Corinthians 10:11, Romans 15:4 and 2 Timothy 3:16–17.

On two occasions, in the midst of using the law for ethics, Paul attaches enlightening epithets to the law. When Paul uses the law for practical purposes as a pastor, it is not the law as 'commandments', 'book', 'decrees' and 'letter' or 'legal code' (see chapter 4) to which he appeals, but rather the law as 'instruction', as in 1 Corinthians 10:11, and 'teaching', as in Romans 15:4. These two texts reveal something of the apostle's hermeneutic when he reads the law for ethics. As it turns out, both are closely associated with wisdom.

In 1 Corinthians 10:1–10 Paul describes the exodus and desert experience of Israel as a pattern in which idolatry followed on the heels of redemption. He believes that some Corinthians are in danger of falling into the same pattern due to their attitudes and practices with regard to food sacrificed to idols (especially the practice of eating in pagan temples or participating in certain pagan meals). In verse 7 Paul quotes the LXX of Exodus 32:6 as proof that the Israelites committed idolatry. The references to eating and drinking in association with idolatry make Exodus 32:6 an obvious reference point for issues related to food sacrificed to idols. Paul marks Exodus 32:6 as his main text by its explicit citation (and important use of the key words for 'eating', 'drinking' and 'rising up'). Allusions to Numbers 11, 14 and other Old Testament texts in 1 Corinthians 10:5–10 fill out the picture by pointing to subsequent situations where the same association between eating, drinking and idolatry can be seen (along with other temptations the Corinthians are facing). Paul uses Exodus 32:6 to inform the Corinthians' understanding of the ethical and spiritual danger they are facing. As Hays suggests,

> by coaxing the reader to recall the golden calf story, he links the present Corinthian dilemma . . . to the larger and older story of Israel in the wilderness. This metaphorical act creates the imaginative framework within which Paul judges – and invites his readers to judge – the proper ethical response to the problem at hand.[75]

Exodus 32:6 serves as a warning to avoid following in the footsteps of our Israelite fathers.

[75] Hays 1989: 92.

In 1 Corinthians 10:11 Paul explains that Israel's experiences occurred as examples to the Corinthian believers and were recorded for their moral education: 'Now these things happened to them as a warning, but they were written down for our instruction [*pros nouthesian hēmōn*], upon whom the ends of the ages has come' (RSV). The word Paul uses for 'instruction' or 'admonition' (AV) or 'warning' (HCSB), *nouthesia*, occurs only once in the LXX, in Wisdom 16.6, which, speaking of Numbers 11, says 'they were provoked as a warning [*nouthesia*] for a short time'. Philo also uses *nouthesia*, and the cognate verb *noutheteō*, in *On the Migration of Abraham* 14 as descriptions of things that should be done with the law; the law offers 'instruction' and 'admonishes' those in need of correction. For Philo, the author of Wisdom, and the apostle Paul the Law of Moses was a valuable source of moral education, or, as BDAG (679c) defines *nouthesia*, of 'counsel about avoidance or cessation of an improper course of conduct'.

A similar story emerges from Romans 15. As part of Paul's extensive response to divisions in the Roman church over issues of diet and calendar in 14:1 – 15:13, in 15:1–2 he exhorts the strong, those who regard themselves as free from food and sabbath laws, not to behave without regard to the weak: 'We who are strong ought to put up with the failings of the weak, and not to please ourselves. Each of us must please our neighbour for the good purpose of building up the neighbor.' Paul cites Psalm 69:9 in Romans 15:3 as support for the exhortations in verses 1–2: 'For Christ did not please himself; but, as it is written, "The insults of those who insult you have fallen on me."' In verse 4 the apostle makes a general point about his use of the psalm: 'For whatever was written in former days was written for our instruction [*didaskalia*], so that by steadfastness and by the encouragement of the scriptures we might have hope' (Rom. 15:4). The practical nature of the entire paragraph is made clear with the references to 'steadfastness' and 'encouragement' in verse 4b, terms suggestive of moral exhortation, and in Romans 15:5–6 where Paul prays that God would so work that the believers in Rome would live in harmony and that God would be glorified by their unity.

Paul's assertion in Romans 15:4 is not merely that Psalm 69:9 was 'written for our [practical] instruction'. Rather, his point is more general: '*whatever was written in former days* was written for our instruction'. And Romans 15:4b makes it clear that the writings to which he refers are 'the scriptures', which in Romans are conspicuously both the law and the prophets (see in chapter 4 on Rom. 1:2; 3:21; 16:25–26). If in 1 Corinthians 10:11 Paul describes the law as 'instruction', *nouthesia*, in Romans 15:4, by extension, he says that the law is a source of moral 'teaching', *didaskalia*.[76]

What is noteworthy for our purposes is that both *nouthesia* and *didaskalia* are terms that have clear wisdom associations. Paul uses the cognate verbs *noutheteō* and *didaskō* in contexts that indicate that the functions of instructing, admonishing and teaching are undertaken in conjunction with wisdom: 'We proclaim him by *instructing* and *teaching* all people *with all wisdom* so that we may present every person mature in Christ' (Col. 1:28, my tr.); '*teach* and *admonish* one another *in all wisdom*' (Col. 3:16).

In the LXX, wisdom or the way of wisdom is 'taught' (*didaskō*) in Proverbs 4:11, 30:3 and Wisdom 7.21. Philo writes that 'the one who is being instructed [*ho paideuomenos*], having received the doctrines of wisdom [*ta sophia dogmata*] at his ears from his instructor [*para tou didaskontos*], derives a considerable amount of learning from him' (*Spec. Laws* 4.107). The law, wisdom and teaching are all associated in *Names* 125.

Parental instruction, a common wisdom motif, is often described in terms of *nouthesia* and cognates. In Ephesians 6:4 fathers are told to bring up their children 'in the discipline [*paideia*] and instruction [*nouthesia*] of the Lord'. As it turns out, as BDAG notes, citing texts from Philo in support, *nouthesia* is often paired with *paideia*.[77] In 1 Corinthians 4:14 Paul 'admonishes' (*noutheteō*) the Corinthians as his 'beloved children'. With respect to the wisdom associations of 'teaching', *didaskalia*, in Philo's *Sacrifices* 138, the man who is 'fond of wisdom' receives 'the best possible education [*paideumatōn didachtheisa*]'.

2 Timothy 3:16–17, where the practical usefulness of Scripture is explained, is particularly enlightening:

> All scripture is inspired by God and is useful for teaching, for reproof, for correction, and for training in righteousness, so that everyone who belongs to God may be proficient, equipped for every good work. (2 Tim. 3:16–17)

---

[76] The referent of *didaskalia* in Paul's letters, that which is taught, usually focuses on matters of conduct; cf. '*teaching* that is in accordance with godliness' (1 Tim. 6:3).

[77] Cf. BDAG (748d), '*paideia*' 1: 'the act of providing guidance for responsible living'; 2 'the state of being brought up properly'.

That the referent of 'all scripture' includes the law is evident from the fact that the only other point in the Pastoral Epistles where *graphē* appears besides 2 Timothy 3:16 is in 1 Timothy 5:18, where it is used in an introduction to a quotation of Deuteronomy 25:4: 'For the Scripture says, "You shall not muzzle an ox while it is treading out the grain."' Paul cites this law to bolster his case for the financial support of 'elders who direct the affairs of the church well . . . especially those whose work is preaching and teaching' (1 Tim. 5:17).

Four terms in 2 Timothy 3:16–17 explicate the usefulness of Scripture, including the law, in its capacity for 'teaching' (*didaskalia*), namely 'reproof' (*elegmos*), 'correction' (*epanorthōsis*) and 'training' (*paideia*) in 'righteousness' (*dikaiosynē*).[78] Three of the four are regularly associated with wisdom in various contexts.

1. Sirach uses *elegmos* for the rebukes of both wisdom and the law: 'Favours and gifts blind the eyes of the wise; / like a muzzle on the mouth they stop *reproofs*' (Sir. 20.29); 'Those who hate *reproof* walk in the sinner's steps, / but those who fear the Lord [the mark of wisdom] repent in their heart' (Sir. 21.6); 'You heard *rebuke* at Sinai / and judgments of vengeance at Horeb' (Sir. 48.7).

2. With respect of *paideia*, in Sirach 39 the person who 'seeks out the wisdom of all the ancients' (v. 1) 'will be filled with the spirit of understanding; / he will pour forth words of wisdom [*rhēmata sophias*; v. 6] . . . He will show the wisdom of what he has learned [*paideian didaskalias*], / and will glory in the law [*en nomō diathēkēs kyriou*] of the Lord's covenant' (v. 8) and 'nations will speak of his wisdom' [*tēn sophian autou*]'.

3. Philo uses 'wisdom' and 'righteousness' in lists of virtues in *Names* 79 and *Dreams* 1.80. Josephus wants to 'learn God's wisdom and righteousness' (*Ant.* 11.268). In *4 Maccabees* 1.18 'wisdom is manifested under the forms of judgement and righteousness'. And in *Psalms of Solomon* 17.29 the king will judge peoples and nations in the wisdom of his righteousness (*sophia dikaiosynēs*).[79]

According to 2 Timothy 3:15–16, the practical usefulness of the law and the rest of Scripture are the equivalent of the typical and

---

[78] *Epanorthōsis* is a rare term in biblical Greek; it is a NT hapax legomenon and occurs only twice in the LXX (1 Esd. 8.52; 1 Macc. 14.34), in the sense of 'restoration' or 'correction'.

[79] Cf. 1 Cor. 1:30, where Christ as wisdom from God is defined as '*righteousness*, sanctification and redemption'.

regular functions of wisdom. In 'providing guidance for responsible living',[80] the law functions for Christians in much the same manner as wisdom. This is in stark contrast with 1 Timothy 1:8–9 (see chapter 2), where the law used lawfully (*nomimōs*), that is, to condemn sinners, is for the lawless and not for the righteous.

When it comes to regulating Christian conduct, Paul reads the law as 'instruction' and 'teaching', *nouthesia* and *didaskalia*, terms redolent of wisdom, and he claims that the law is useful for teaching, reproof, correction, and training in righteousness, which are also the functions of wisdom. However, I am not claiming anything more than an implicit equation of law and wisdom in Paul's letters. His reading of the law as prophecy, which we observed in chapter 5, is a far more explicit element in his letters and teaching (see on Rom. 1:2; 3:21, 31; 16:25–26); Paul does not call the law 'wisdom' as overtly as he calls the law 'prophecy'. For Paul the law as wisdom is more presupposition than principle.

Nonetheless, the hermeneutical asides in 1 Corinthians 10:11 and Romans 15:4, explaining the practical value of the law and the explanation of the practical usefulness of the law in 2 Timothy 3:16–17, are enlightening. In associating the practical use of the law with wisdom they fit well into the larger picture of Paul's use of the law in practical contexts, to which we now turn.

The law as wisdom in practice

If Paul's precept points towards reading the law as wisdom when he regulates conduct in the churches, what of his practice? While a full investigation of Paul's use of the law for ethics is beyond the scope of part of one chapter,[81] the following survey across a range of subjects indicates that when it comes to moral teaching, Paul does indeed read the law as what may be described as wisdom for living. Not unlike the use of the law in the Psalms, Paul internalizes the law, undertaking reflective and expansive applications, based in part on the moral order of creation and the character of God that stand behind the law.

---

[80] BDAG (748d), '*paideia*' 1.

[81] Given that Paul writes with his own authority (cf. 1 Cor. 14:37) it is fallacious to think that determining his dependence on the law for ethics is simply a matter of noting quotations of the law. The genre of his letters means that the sources of his teaching are not always apparent. More subtle and indirect dependence must be considered to determine the influence of the law in Paul's moral teaching.

Tithing

The practice of giving 10 per cent of one's income is legislated in the Law of Moses (e.g. Lev. 27:30–33)[82] and is taken by many Christians to be part of God's law that must be obeyed. Does Paul enforce or even recommend tithing? Despite having numerous opportunities to do so in his many discussions of giving, Paul nowhere endorses tithing; Paul is consistent with his often-repeated insistence that Christians are not under the law. But does that mean that the laws of tithing are irrelevant to believers in Christ? Paul's discussions of giving range widely, covering contentment, greed, the futility of riches, being rich towards God, and so on. What advice does Paul give when it comes to how much believers should give? Three passages in particular address this subject.

First, in 2 Corinthians 9:7 Paul talks against any form of compulsion when it comes to giving: 'Each of you should give what you have decided in your heart to give, not reluctantly or under compulsion, for God loves a cheerful giver' (my tr.). His instructions on giving do not come with the force of law. There is no appeal to the moral law of the Law of Moses or any other law for that matter.

Secondly, in 1 Corinthians 16:2 Paul recommends giving that is deliberate and proportional to one's income: 'On the first day of every week, each one of you should set aside a sum of money in keeping with your income' (NIV). Paul's emphasis falls on the value of advanced planning and preparation rather than last-minute scrambling and pressure. The key word in the phrase 'in keeping with your income', *euodoō*, has the sense 'have things turn out well, *prosper,*

---

[82] Tithing in the OT was not entirely uniform. Goldingay (2010: 168–169) offers a helpful summary: '(1) Tithing emerges in Gen. 14, when Abraham offered a tithe to Melchizedek. God didn't tell Abraham to do this, Abraham volunteered it and Melchizedek accepted it; (2) In Gen. 28:8–10 [should be 28:20–22] Jacob tells God he will give God a tithe since God promises to bless him. Goldingay sees here another instinctual, but perhaps even selfish, manipulative act on Jacob's part; (3) At the end of Lev. 27, vv. 30–33 tithing is both assumed and an occasion for God to remind Israel that it should not be evaded – they are to tithe on everything, even the best of their flock and produce; (4) The most common perception of tithing is that it is for 'clergy' and this is anchored in Num. 18:21–32 where tithing goes to the Levites. Here we find a pervasive practice in ancient Israel – tithes take care of the people in the Temple; (5) But Deut. 12 and 22:22–29; 26:12–13 clarifies this situation. The calendar is cut into seven years at a time. In year one and two, four and five, a normal tithe; in year three and six, a special tithe; and in year seven a sabbath. The special tithe went to the aliens, orphans and widows. (At least 3/7 years concern the poor: year 3, 6 and 7.); (6) The other reference to tithing, other than warning Israel to resume tithes after not tithing, pertains to the warning that kings will tax through a tithe (1 Sam. 8:15–17).'

succeed' (BDAG 410a).[83] Paul recommends giving that is proportionate, a principle shared with the laws of tithing in the Torah. It would seem that Paul has been instructed by the notion of a tithe, even if he does not enforce it as a law. Or as Keener points out,[84] Paul's instruction that each one should give as he or she has prospered may be an application of Deuteronomy 15:14, the advice of which also seems to be indebted to the notion of tithing combined with the principle that those with more are expected to give generously: 'Provide liberally out of your flock, your threshing-floor, and your wine press, thus giving to him some of the bounty with which the LORD your God has blessed you' (Deut. 15:14).

Thirdly, in 1 Timothy 6:17 Paul appeals to the generous character of God in creation as a motivation to give liberally: 'Command those who are rich in this world to be generous and willing to share, not to put their hope in wealth, but in God, who richly provides us with everything for our enjoyment' (my tr.). Those who 'put their hope in wealth' experience the world as a problem of scarcity. Money's function is to identify numerically what goods we most want, according to how scarce they are. Therefore 'hope in wealth' is an agreement with that system of evaluation: whatever is scarce is valuable, and whatever valueless must be worthless. But the person who 'hopes in God' experiences the world as an expression of his abundance. On this view, we are so awash with good things that we generally have no reason to worry. For such a person, it follows that monetary wealth is simply a tool for orderly sharing of this great, God-given abundance that surrounds us. Of course, such sharing is transacted among others who experience their world as a problem of scarcity, a system that sustains the monetary value of things. But the Christian is not hoodwinked by that system, and simply uses that system to bless others with God's abundance. Such a person has 'seen into the matrix' and knows that abundance, and the possibility of sharing it, remains with or without any monetary system.[85]

---

[83] The translation 'in keeping with your income' may be read in a very modern way, as though each person's income would be consistent each week, while in Paul's world most people would be more likely to have good and bad weeks, weeks in which things turned out well financially and weeks in which they did not (weeks in which they were regularly employed and weeks in which they were not, or weeks in which they experienced greater or lesser benevolence on the part of others). The point is that those who made a lot of money in a given week would be expected to give more than those who did not.

[84] Keener 1993: 489.

[85] Thanks to Dr Andrew Cameron for comments on this text.

When it comes to giving and sharing possessions, it is indeed striking that Paul does not enforce the law of tithing. He does give commands (see 1 Tim. 6:17a), but not without exposing their foundations in the order of creation and character of God. And he has evidently been instructed by the law, as his appeal for proportionate giving suggests, a principle enshrined in the tithes and offerings, and as the echo of Deuteronomy 15:14 in 1 Corinthians 16:2 demonstrates.

The objection is sometimes heard that when tithing is not expected of Christians as some sort of obligation, giving declines. What can be said in response? On one level, the answer is, so be it. As Paul said in 2 Corinthians 9:7, giving is to be 'not reluctantly or under compulsion'. If we want Christians to give more liberally, the solution is not a return to living under the law. There are numerous gospel motives, along with appeals to the generosity of God and the goodness of his creation that encourage the generous sharing of possessions. Passages like 2 Corinthians 8 – 9 and 1 Timothy 6 show the way with such appeals.

Greed as idolatry

In Colossians 3:5 ('greed . . . is idolatry') and Ephesians 5:5 ('the greedy [person]' is an 'idolater') Paul condemns greed as idolatry.[86] In drawing this unflattering comparison Paul is not quoting the Law of Moses. Nonetheless, his opposition to greed in terms of idolatry bears the marks of the internalization and reflective application of various texts from the law.

Two prominent ideas in the law, especially when read in the light of early Jewish interpretation, prepare the way for the startling judgment in question. First, the solemn words of the first commandment, 'you shall have no other gods before me' (Exod. 20:3; Deut. 5:7), were seen early to have a comprehensive scope. The first commandment is not a warning against greed. However, as Martin Luther taught in his catechisms, it casts its bright light over all the others and is the source and fountain from which all the others spring. The Ten Commandments are interdependent. To break one of the later commandments is also to break the first. Indeed, ancient Jews took 'you shall have no other gods before me' to be foundational to the rest of the Decalogue and in some sense all-embracing: 'Whoever professes idolatry denies the Ten Words . . . whoever denies idolatry, professes all of the Torah.'[87] Thus the prohibition of idolatry was understood as having a broad reach.

[86] See Rosner 2007b.
[87] *Sifre Deut.* 54.

A second idea found in Deuteronomy that anticipates the comparison of greed with idolatry is the association of wealth with apostasy. The famous confession of Deuteronomy 6:5 ('You shall love the LORD your God . . . ') offers a positive restatement of the first commandment. Interestingly, the Targumim of the Shema extend its relevance beyond the cultic and literal to a specific ethical application. Instead of enjoining the love of God with all one's heart, soul and strength, it calls for full allegiance in terms of one's heart, soul and possessions or money. The identification of material things as a threat to fidelity to God is also underscored in Deuteronomy 8, which warns those entering the Promised Land not to allow their prosperity to lead them to forget the Lord (Deut. 8:12–14). The lesson is reinforced in the Song of Moses in Deuteronomy 32: newly acquired wealth will lead the people into apostasy (see vv. 10–15): 'Jeshurun ['the upright one', Israel] grew fat . . . / and abandoned God who made him' (v. 15).

Paul's indebtedness to the law is suggested further by comparable teaching in other parts of the Old Testament and in the New Testament outside Paul's letters that also build on these two ideas from the Law of Moses. For example, the sage prays that God will not give him riches, lest he 'may have too much . . . disown [God] and say, "Who is the Lord?"' (Prov. 30:7–9). Job explains that 'if I have put my trust in gold or said to pure gold, "You are my security" . . . I would have been unfaithful to God on high' (Job 31:24–28 NIV). In Luke's Gospel, with reference to the teaching of Jesus, the dangers riches pose to entering the kingdom of God are evident in the parable of the rich fool (12:13–21), the encounter with the rich ruler (18:18–30) and in the calls to renounce possessions and give to the poor (14:33; 18:22). Jesus' charge that people serve either God or Mammon (i.e. possessions; Matt. 6:24 // Luke 16:13) is conceptually comparable to Paul's greed as idolatry.

Stealing

Three times, Paul mentions the subject of stealing. On one occasion he alludes to the Decalogue commandment not to steal and uses the language of legal obligation. What is significant is that the context is his challenge to his Jewish opponents as to whether they transgress the commandments:

> But if you call yourself a Jew and rely on the law and boast of your relation to God and know his will and determine what is best because you are instructed in the law, and if you are sure that you

are a guide to the blind, a light to those who are in darkness, a corrector of the foolish, a teacher of children, having in the law the embodiment of knowledge and truth, you, then, that teach others, will you not teach yourself? *While you preach against stealing [ho kēryssōn mē kleptein], do you steal [klepteis]?*[88] You that forbid adultery, do you commit adultery? You that abhor idols, do you rob temples? You that boast in the law, do you dishonour God by breaking the law? For, as it is written, 'The name of God is blasphemed among the Gentiles because of you.' (Rom. 2:17–24)

For Jews, as we noted in chapters 3 and 4, the law remains a legal code that must be obeyed and not transgressed.

Secondly, in Romans 13:8–10 Paul cites the commandment not to steal in a discussion for Christians of how love fulfils the law:

Owe no one anything, except to love one another; for the one who loves another has fulfilled the law. The commandments, 'You shall not commit adultery; You shall not murder; You shall not steal [*ou klepseis*]; You shall not covet'; and any other commandment, are summed up in this word, 'Love your neighbour as yourself.' Love does no wrong to a neighbour; therefore, love is the fulfilling of the law. (Rom. 13:8–10)

In this passage it is not that Christians must 'keep' the laws listed, including 'you shall not steal'. Rather, in the argument of Romans, Paul makes the point that not being under the law does not lead to licence; the obligation to love brings the law to completion (see the section in chapter 4, 'Fulfilling the law'). Paul's point is that loving one's neighbour is the goal of keeping the law. But keeping the laws (even those of the Decalogue, such as laws against adultery, murder, stealing and coveting) does not mean that one will love one's neighbour. But if one loves one's neighbour, one will do more than just keep the law, fulfilling what Paul takes to be its real intent.

The third text is Ephesians 4:28, where Paul addresses Christians and instructs them not to steal: 'Thieves must give up stealing [*ho kleptōn mēketi kleptetō*]; rather let them labour and work honestly with their own hands, so as to have something to share with the needy.'

In regulating Christian conduct Paul does not treat the law as a commandment to be obeyed and not transgressed. But it is not that

---

[88] Cf. LXX Exod. 20:15 and Deut. 5:19: *ou klepseis*.

the commandment is irrelevant to Christians; going deeper than just the law itself, Paul reflects on the responsibility to work in order to be able to share with the needy.

As it turns out, the three Pauline texts about stealing illustrate the three moves of Paul vis-à-vis the law. His treatment of the law for Jews as a commandment not to be transgressed in Romans 2 is not repudiation, but his failure to speak of the law in this way in connection with Christians is an example of implicit repudiation of the law as law-covenant. The assertion in Romans 13:9 against stealing, that love fulfils the law, is an example of the replacement of the law. And his reflective application of the law against stealing in Ephesians 4:28 is instruction for living that exemplifies the reappropriation of the law as wisdom.

Murder

What relevance does the commandment against murder in the Decalogue (Exod. 20:13; Deut. 5:17) have for Paul's moral teaching? An investigation of its influence in Romans as a test case is revealing.[89]

The letter to the Romans refers on two occasions to the commandment not to murder, employing the lexeme *phon-* 'murder', which is used in the LXX murder commandment. The first is in Romans 1 in a vice list:

> They were filled with every kind of wickedness, evil, covetousness, malice. Full of envy, murder [*phonou*], strife, deceit, craftiness, they are gossips, slanderers, God-haters, insolent, haughty, boastful, inventors of evil, rebellious towards parents, foolish, faithless, heartless, ruthless. (Rom. 1:29–31)

In Romans 1:28–29 there are at least three vices that are probable allusions to the second-table Decalogue violations. Along with murder, there is probably a link between 'covetousness' and the commandment against coveting, and between 'rebellious against parents' and the commandment to honour one's parents. However, the full story of the background and rhetorical function of the vice list is not exhausted by noting Decalogue allusions. Paul's enumeration of wickedness may echo the accounts of primeval violence in the Old Testament and Jewish literature and also accounts of the decline of Roman civilization, as many commentaries point out. However, the movement in

---

[89] See Williamson 2007, which this section summarizes and builds upon.

Romans 1:18–32 from idolatry to sexual immorality and antisocial vices does mirror the order of the (MT) Decalogue and renders the allusion to the murder commandment in Romans 1:29 more likely.

Romans 1:18–32 does not directly address the subject of Christian conduct; Paul's purpose is to begin his indictment of all humanity, culminating in the verdict that 'the whole world may be held accountable to God' (3:19). The allusions to the Decalogue in general and the murder commandment in particular offer a bridging point for introducing pagans to the perspective of the Hebrew Scriptures on the plight and guilt of humanity.

Still, a secondary function of the text is to instruct believers in Christ implicitly; the negative portrayal of human behaviour in Romans 1:18–32 is complemented by the positive exhortations in Romans 12 – 15 to love, and the renewed mind of Romans 12 is the reverse of the depraved mind of Romans 1. In this sense, even if Paul does not cite the murder commandment as a command to be obeyed, his allusion to it in Romans 1:29 is part of his moral exhortation to believers.

In Romans 13:9 Paul quotes four of the commandments from the second table of the Decalogue:

> The commandments, 'You shall not commit adultery; You shall not murder [*ou phoneuseis*]; You shall not steal; You shall not covet'; and any other commandment, are summed up in this word, 'Love your neighbour as yourself.' (Rom. 13:9)

As we have noticed already in this book in connection with this text (see chapter 4), Paul does not cite these commandments to bind Christians as those who are under the moral law. In context, in Romans 13:8 the single obligation is to love, 'for the one who loves . . . has fulfilled the law'. The commandments, including 'You shall not murder,' are cited as commandments that no longer bind us, in that love brings the law to completion and effectively replaces it as law with something better. The four commandments are cited as examples of what love looks like as a minimum. Of course, the quotation of Leviticus 19:18, 'Love your neighbour as yourself' (v. 9), is itself from the law and shows that not being under the law does not render the law irrelevant to holy living; the law itself anticipates its own demise (see the section in chapter 5, 'The "prophetic" character of the law'). Indeed, as the rest of Romans shows, commandments like the one not to murder continue to influence Paul's ethics.

A full appreciation of the influence of the murder commandment in Paul's moral teaching requires some attention to contemporary Jewish use of the commandment, along with the use of the commandment in the Hebrew Scriptures. Williamson argues that this background provides a heuristic lens for recognizing the influence of the murder commandment.[90] In brief, murder was widely regarded as the quintessential antisocial sin, the opposite of love, other laws overlapped with murder, and the notion of murder was exploited in its capacity as a metaphor for social injustice, including anger and malicious speech. (For a similar expansive application of the sixth commandment see the discussion above in the section 'The use of the law in the Psalms'.)

With this in mind, Paul's extensive use of other expressions for murder-related activity in Romans is significant. In Romans 3:13–15 he quotes Scripture on murderous speech ('the venom of vipers is under their lips') and murderous deeds ('feet . . . swift to shed blood'). In Romans 7:11 Paul personifies sin and depicts it as a killer in his discussion of sin and the law. Romans 8:35–36 refers to being killed and persecuted for God's sake. In Romans 11:3 Elijah is quoted as pleading to God against Israel: 'Lord, they have killed your prophets . . . and they are seeking my life.' In Romans 12:14, 17–21 Paul refers to those who persecute God's people. And in Romans 14:13, 15, 20, 21 Paul warns the strong about destroying those who are weak in faith. The influence of the murder commandment is profound, in spite of Paul's nowhere saying or implying that believers are under the law.

Sexual ethics

A similar story can be told with respect to Paul's frequent teaching about sexual morality. Although there are numerous laws in the Law of Moses that deal with sexual matters, when it comes to regulating Christian conduct Paul does not tell believers to obey the laws against adultery, incest, prostitution, sexual immorality, homosexual relations, and so on. Nonetheless, his instructions bear the imprint of the law. It is clear that he holds to the same norms for sexual behaviour that are found in the laws of the Torah. This can be seen in his opposition to incest in 1 Corinthians 5 and homosexual conduct in 1 Corinthians 6:9 and 1 Timothy 1:10, where not only is his position identical with the law, but the language he uses to make his point echoes the law. Also, as two further examples, the critical influence of key texts from

[90] Ibid. 112–203.

the law can be detected in his exhortation against going to prostitutes in 1 Corinthians 6:18 and in his major discussion of marriage and divorce in 1 Corinthians 7. Even if Paul does not use the law as law, there is good evidence that he reads the law as pertinent moral instruction when he discusses sexual morality.

Incest

In 1 Corinthians 5 Paul responds to a report currently circulating publicly. It is so scandalous that he deals with it as soon as he is finished with the problem of disunity in Corinth in chapters 1–4. If the Corinthians' presenting problem is divisions, their most serious and pressing fault is the way they are tolerating in their midst (lit. 'among you') the presence of a man committing incest. Paul is incredulous and could not be more vehement in his opposition. His dismay reveals firm opposition to incest and a belief that incest is grounds for urgent church discipline. On both counts he is indebted to the law.

According to 1 Corinthians 5:1 the offence concerned *sexual immorality*, *porneia*, a flexible term meaning 'prohibited sexual relations', which is in this context specifically incest. 'A man has his father's wife' tells us something of the case, the details of which were only too well known to the Corinthians. The phrase 'father's wife', *gynaika tou patros*, echoes the language of Leviticus 18:8[91] and indicates that the relationship was with his step-mother, since Leviticus 18:7 uses a different term to forbid sexual relations with one's 'mother'. Given his apostolic authority, Paul has no need to reveal the source of his opposition to incest, but the link with Levitical legislation suggests his indebtedness to the law.

Incest of any sort, whether with one's mother or with the wife of one's father, is prohibited in the law and early Judaism and was sufficient cause for discipline. Many commentators on 1 Corinthians 5 mention Leviticus 18:8 and 20:11 as the critical background to Paul's decision to expel the sinner, noting the shared terminology 'woman' and 'father' (v. 1). Sexual intercourse with the 'wife' of one's father is also condemned in Genesis 49:4 (see 35:22) and Ezekiel 22:10–11. However, two verses in Deuteronomy are just as likely to have influenced Paul. First, Deuteronomy 27:20, 'cursed is the man who sleeps with his father's wife' (my tr.), is perhaps the reason Paul 'curses' the sinner in 1 Corinthians 5. Secondly, Deuteronomy 22:30, 'A man shall not marry his father's wife', may have been the impetus for

---

[91] 'You shall not uncover the nakedness of your father's wife [LXX: *gynaikos patros*].'

Paul to quote the Deuteronomic expulsion formula in 1 Corinthians 5:13. A variation of that formula appears in Deuteronomy 22:22 ('If a man is found sleeping with another man's wife . . . you must purge the evil from Israel', my tr.; cf. 22:24) and is presumably the penalty for the incest prohibited in Deuteronomy 23:1 (22:30). In quoting the Deuteronomic formula in 5:13 Paul, it appears, is simply following the Torah.

Judaism maintained this Deuteronomic resolve that incest be punished: *Mishnah Sanhedrin* 7.4 (incest is punishable by stoning); 9.1 and *Kerithot* 1.1 (incest is one of the first offences listed for 'cutting off'); *Jubilees* 33.10–13; *Tosefta Sanhedrin* 10.1; *Damascus Document* 5; and *Temple Scroll* 66. Josephus describes incest as 'the grossest of sins' and 'an outrageous crime' (*Ant.* 3.274); and of incest Philo asks, 'What form of unholiness could be more impious than this?' (*Spec. Laws* 3.13–14; cf. 3.20–21).

Homosexual conduct

Paul uses two terms in vice lists that refer to homosexual behaviour: *malakos* (1 Cor. 6:9) and *arsenokoitēs* (1 Cor. 6:9; 1 Tim. 1:10).[92] My purpose in this section is not to enter into a full discussion of the meaning of these terms. Rather, I wish to draw attention to evidence that Paul's opposition to homosexual conduct signalled by them may be traced in part back to the law.

There is a strong case for concluding that with the second word, *arsenokoitēs*, Paul employed a new term that was fashioned on the basis of prohibitions in Leviticus 18:22; 20:13.[93] The only other occurrence of the word that is possibly contemporary with Paul (it may be a Christian interpolation) is *Sibylline Oracles* 2.73. The relevant section of the Sibyllines is closely related to *Pseudo-Phocylides* (suggesting its Jewish origin), which is itself heavily indebted to Leviticus.

[92] The two terms are variously translated; cf. the following translations of them in 1 Cor. 6:9: RSV, 'homosexuals'; TEV, 'homosexual perverts'; NEB, 'homosexual perversion'; NIV 1984, 'male prostitutes nor homosexual offenders'; AV 'effeminate, nor abusers of themselves with mankind'. Ciampa and Rosner (2010: 241–242) understand them as a pair, referring to those taking the passive and active roles in same-sex relations. However, Ciampa (2011: 111–112) refines this position, taking them 'as two separate vices, with the first including those who willingly take the passive/dominated role in male homosexual acts but including a variety of other behaviors associated with effeminacy in the Roman world as well, including some inappropriate male sexual relations with women (and not being identified with just one behavior), and the latter as a term for males who willingly play the dominant role in same-sex acts'. See Ciampa 2011: 111–119 for details.

[93] See Ciampa and Rosner 2010: 241–242.

A link between Paul's use of *arsenokoitēs* and LXX Leviticus 20:13 is suggested by the successive occurrence of *arsēn* (male) and *koitē* ('sexual relationship'; cf. 'coitus' in English): 'If a man lies with a male [*arsenos koitēn*] as with a woman, both of them have committed an abomination.' As David Wright concludes, it seems likely that 'the *arsenekoit-* group of words is a coinage of Hellenistic Judaism or Hellenistic Jewish Christianity'.[94]

Further support for seeing the roots of Paul's view in the law may be gleaned from the appearance of *arsenokoitēs* in 1 Timothy 1:10. Gagnon points out that the vice there appears in a list said to derive from the Law of Moses (cf. 1:8–9), suggesting a link with the Levitical prohibitions, and at least half the vices in the list derive from the Decalogue: 'there is good evidence that *pornoi* and *arsenokoitai* belong together under the seventh commandment, in which case the obvious offense of the *arsenokoitai* is a violation of the male–female pre-requisite for marriage'.[95]

That parts of Leviticus played a role in forming Paul's opposition to homosexual behaviour does not lend support to the idea that he saw Christians as under the law. Rather, his unselfconscious appropriation of the language of the prohibition in Leviticus is evidence that he has been instructed and taught by the law. The law is a crucial and formative source for Paul's stance, even though he does not cite it as law.

But there is another part of the law that appears to have informed Paul's opposition. In Romans 1:26 Paul comments that homosexual acts are contrary to 'nature' (*physis*). Cranfield argues that the phrase means 'contrary to the intention of the Creator'.[96] Paul seems to base his opposition to homosexual acts here on the order of creation. Wenham explains with reference to Genesis 1 – 2:

> God created humanity in two sexes, so that they could be fruitful and multiply and fill the earth. Woman was man's perfect companion, like man created in the divine image. To allow the legitimacy of homosexual acts would frustrate the divine purpose and deny the perfection of God's provision of two sexes to support and com-plement one another.[97]

Despite never quoting the law on the subject, Paul's indebtedness to

[94] D. F. Wright 1984: 129.
[95] Gagnon 2000: 233–234.
[96] Cranfield 1975: 125.
[97] Wenham 1991: 363.

the law for his stance on homosexual behaviour can be seen clearly at a number of levels.

Fleeing sexual immorality

In 1 Corinthians 6:18–20 Paul caps off his argument in 6:12–20 against believers in Corinth going to prostitutes. The heart of Paul's exhortation is an appeal to Christian identity. According to Paul, the Corinthians' sanctified status (1:2) demands their sexual purity. They are obliged to maintain the holiness of God's temple (3:16–17). Thus the case of incest (ch. 5) and the use of prostitutes (6:12–17) represent a threat to their core identity as people belonging to God. In this light it is hardly surprising that Paul issues the strongest possible command with the words *flee sexual immorality*. The lack of grammatical connection to what precedes heightens their emotive force. Equally, the verb to 'flee' carries a sense of urgency; in the LXX people 'flee' from enemies, snakes, the kinsman avenger and other potent dangers. The sin to be fled here is sexual immorality, *porneia*, a target broader than just prostitution. An apt concluding appeal to chapters 5–6, the injunction is a blanket condemnation of all illicit sexual relations. Words cognate to *porneia* occur in 5:1, 9–11; 6:13, 15–16, 18 (2×).[98] As Barrett puts it, 'Temptations to fornication were so common in Corinth that mere disapproval was likely to be inadequate; strong evasive action would be necessary. The same was true of idolatry (x. 14).'[99]

Some have questioned the relevance of the Old Testament to Paul's ethical teaching on the basis that Paul overlooks the opportunity to quote Scripture in such a context. He could have cited any number of texts forbidding prostitution, pre- or extra-marital sex.[100] The fallacy with such reasoning is that the most fundamental reason someone is opposed to something will not necessarily be made explicit in his or her arguments against it. Paul's arguments in 1 Corinthians 6 against the use of prostitutes in effect presuppose that prostitution is wrong. Paul is like a passenger trying to convince a speeding driver, with appeals to road safety, expensive fines, no need to hurry, and so on, to slow down. The use of such proofs does not betray a lack of

[98] Outside chs. 5–6 *porn-* words occur only in 7:2 (reprising the warnings of the previous two chapters) and 10:8.

[99] Barrett 1968: 150.

[100] See Rosner 1994: 121–126. Cf. on prostitution (some mercenary, some religious): Gen. 34:31; Lev. 21:7, 9; Deut. 22:21; 23:17 (esp. LXX); Amos 7:17; 2 Kgs 23:7; Jer. 2:20; Ezek. 23:37, 40–41; Hos. 6:9–10; 7:4; 8:9–10.

interest in the law; even if left unmentioned, the relevant law might rest at the heart of their opposition. As it turns out, a possible quotation of a piece of early Jewish moral teaching, *Testament of Reuben*, in verse 18 reveals Paul's indebtedness to the Genesis account of Joseph's fleeing Potiphar's wife in Genesis 39.

The central command of 5:1 – 6:20 in verse 18, *flee sexual immorality*, finds an exact parallel in *Testament of Reuben* 5.5.[101] Even though the individual words are not uncommon, the specific injunction occurs in only these two places in ancient Greek literature (along with quotations of 1 Cor. 6:18 in the church fathers). On the other hand, Gregory of Nyssa suggested a link between Paul's advice in 1 Corinthians 6 and the example of Joseph in Genesis 39. LXX Genesis 39:12 uses the same verb, 'to flee',[102] to describe Joseph's successful escape from Potiphar's wife: 'he *fled* out of her house' (cf. Gen. 39:13, 15, 18). Another suggestive link with 1 Corinthians 6 is the fact that Genesis 39 forms a contrast to Tamar's prostitution in Genesis 38.[103]

It is possible that both sources influenced Paul. As it turns out, *Testament of Reuben* 5 was itself written with Joseph in mind (see 4.8). The author warns his readers not only to 'flee immorality', but also noted the relevance of God's indwelling to the state of chastity (cf. 1 Cor. 6:19) and concluded that Joseph had 'glorified' God (cf. 6:20). The Genesis Joseph account likewise describes Joseph as 'one in whom is the Spirit of God' (41:38) and that his chief motivation in the action was not to sin against God (39:9), akin to glorifying him. Thus *Testament of Reuben* witnesses to a traditional interpretation of Genesis 39 that may also have influenced Paul. Alternatively, Paul quotes *Testament of Reuben* 5.5 directly, not as sacred Scripture but as an appropriate ethical maxim, a text to which he was driven, because of its effective use of Joseph in its warnings against *porneia*.

Marriage and divorce

Paul's most extensive discussion of marriage, singleness and divorce is in 1 Corinthians 7. Paul answers a number of questions put to him by the Corinthians in a letter ('Now for the matters you wrote about'; 7:1 NIV). Although not indicated explicitly, much of what

---

[101] Paul adds the conjunction *oun*, 'therefore', not translated in TNIV. On the connection between the texts see Rosner 1999: 123–146; 1992: 123–127.

[102] Gk. *pheugō*.

[103] Gk. *pornē* occurs in LXX Gen. 38:15, 21–22; *porneia* in 38:24.

Paul says in the chapter finds its roots in Scripture and especially the law.[104]

Paul makes several points regarding marriage in 1 Corinthians 7:1–7, many of which derive from the law. The idea in 7:2–5 that the husband and wife are obliged to give themselves sexually to each other betrays the influence of Exodus 21:10, where the husband 'shall not diminish her [his wife's] food, clothing *or her marital rights* [a euphemism for sexual relations]' (my tr.).

In 1 Corinthians 7:3, to support his comments about the prophylactic effects of a healthy marriage against the dangers of sexual immorality, Paul expounds the intimacy and mutuality of marriage. Paul's views were starkly different from his contemporaries who were not Jews or Christians. The positive bodily union advocated in verses 3–5 complements Paul's insistence on sexual abstinence in 5:1–13 and 6:12–20. The quotation of Genesis 2:24 in 6:16, 'The two shall be one flesh', prepares the way for the discussion in 1 Corinthians 7:3–5: for Paul, marriage is grounded in the goodness of creation. 'One flesh', while denoting more than sexual union, does not signify less.

In 1 Corinthians 7:4 Paul explains why sexual relations are due in marriage: the spouse's body belongs to his or her partner. While a property ethic applied to sexuality was common in the ancient world, including the OT (e.g. Deut. 20:5–7; 28:30), the distinctive reciprocity of Paul's comments (the husband's body belongs to the wife and vice versa) recall the notes of mutual belonging in the Song of Solomon (2:16a; 6:3; cf. 7:10). Paul's affirmation that the two belong to one another in total mutuality may derive from Genesis 2:24, quoted in the previous chapter (1 Cor. 6:16), 'The two shall be one flesh.' A full quotation of this text is the basis of the statement in Ephesians 5:28 'In the same way, husbands should love their wives as they do their own bodies. He who loves his wife loves himself.'

Periodic abstinence from sexual relations for the purpose of prayer in 1 Corinthians 7:5 brings to mind similar voluntary deprivation before cultic activities (e.g. Exod. 19:15; Lev. 15:18; cf. 1 Sam. 21:4–6) and finds a specific parallel in *Testament of Naphtali* 8.8: 'there is a time for having intercourse with one's wife, and a time to abstain for the purpose of prayer'.

---

[104] See Rosner 1999: 147–176. Recall my point under 'Paul, scripture and ethics' earlier in this chapter concerning the way in which postbiblical Jewish texts often themselves build on teaching from the law. I cite them in this and other sections not as a rival influence on Paul, but as testimony to the influence of Scripture and as sometimes mediating Scripture to Paul.

Paul's prohibition of divorce in 1 Corinthians 7:10–11 is based on the teaching of Jesus, which was later preserved in Mark 10:2–12 // Luke 16:18. However, to label it a departure from the teaching of Scripture is somewhat misleading; for while Deuteronomy 24:1–4 presupposes the legitimacy of divorce, other texts allow it under certain circumstances (Deut. 22:19, 28–29; cf. Mal. 2:15–16).

In 1 Corinthians 7:12–16 Paul deals with problems in marriage caused by the intrusion of the gospel. His response, in brief, is that 'mixed marriages are essentially Christian marriages'.[105] The idea of a 'holy family' takes up Jewish ritual language and rests on the presupposition of family solidarity. The notion that God's loving concern extends to the whole family is illustrated in various Old Testament texts from the law (e.g. Gen. 6:18; 17:7–27; 18:19; Deut. 30:19; cf. Ps. 78:1–7). Rabbinic Judaism's view that proselyte children constituted full members of Israel is roughly parallel.

Paul explains in 1 Corinthians 7:32–35 that he prefers singleness because marriage makes life more complicated and can be a distraction from devotion to Christ. The priority in these verses of pleasing God may have been derived from Deuteronomy 6, which Paul alludes to in the next chapter (1 Cor. 8:6). Martin McNamara has noted the treatment of the Palestinian Targum to the Pentateuch of Deuteronomy 6 and its relevance to New Testament teaching on the undivided heart: 'Israel was commanded to love God "with all her heart" [Deut. 6:5]. In the targum full devotion to God is described as "a perfect heart", i.e. one completely set on God, not divided between him and created things'.[106] Furthermore, in several rabbinic texts worldly preoccupations, such as a wife, are seen as a potential distraction from the study of Torah (e.g. 'Abot R. Nat. a. 20).

In 1 Corinthians 7:39–40 Paul makes three points regarding the termination of marriage and remarriage for the benefit of Christian widows in Corinth. Peter Tomson argues that all three use 'formulations directly related to Rabbinic halakha'.[107] Roots in the law are also evident. In 7:39a Paul indicates that the death of a husband terminates the marriage bond, so that the widow has the right to remarry. Deuteronomy 24:3 stipulates the same provision with the words 'if the latter husband dies' (NASB). In 7:39b Paul states that the widow may marry whomever she wishes. This is similar to *Mishnah Giṭṭin* 9.3, a tractate expounding the halachic implications of

---

[105] Fee 1987: 298.
[106] McNamara 1972: 122–123.
[107] Tomson 1990: 120–122.

Deuteronomy 24:1–4, 'you are permitted to marry any man' (v. 39, my tr.). Finally, in 7:39c Paul adds the restriction 'only in the Lord'. Similar clauses were in Jewish circulation in Paul's day. For example, a Bar Kokhba divorce deed has the analogous specification 'you may go and be married to any Jewish man you want' (*DJD* 2, no. 19). The exclusion of marriage to a non-Jew has its basis in Scripture (Deut. 7:3; Josh. 23:12; cf. Ezra 9:1–4; Neh. 13:23–27).

Conclusion

When exhorting believers in Christ to live lives pleasing to God, Paul does not address them as those who are under the law. The above survey of the laws of tithing, stealing, idolatry, murder, incest, homosexual conduct, sexual immorality, marriage and divorce confirms this conclusion. Paul cites none of the relevant laws as commandments to be obeyed and not transgressed.

However, it is not the case that the law is irrelevant to Paul's teaching concerning subjects such as giving, theft, idol worship, antisocial vices and sexual ethics. There is ample evidence that Paul knows the relevant laws, along with other material in the law, such as the accounts of creation, the Joseph narratives and the Song of Moses. The law is a critical and formative source for his moral teaching on these topics. Rather than reading the law *as law*, Paul reads it *as wisdom* for living, in the sense that he has internalized the law, makes reflective and expansive applications, and takes careful notice of its basis in the order of creation and the character of God.[108]

Paving the way for Paul's wisdom hermeneutic with respect to the law is a comparable use of the law in the Psalms,[109] the wisdom character of the law itself,[110] the wisdom character of Paul's moral teaching in general,[111] and Paul's own claim that he reads the law in the capacity of wisdom.[112]

---

[108] Cf. Cameron 2008: 145: 'What might it look like to use OT law in the NT as data there for Christian wisdom? At least a few "tests" can be imagined: (1) We may see law peppered unsystematically throughout moral discussion, or allusions to it threaded throughout moral discussion, since it would function only as one of a number of sources for Christian wisdom; (2) We may see the purpose or ground of any given law functioning as the primary moral datum, rather than its deontic force *per se*; and (3) When law does appear, we may expect to see its inner logic expanded, and/or amplified, and/or reapplied.'

[109] See the section 'The use of the law in the Psalms' above.

[110] See the section 'The "wisdom" character of the law' above.

[111] See the section 'Paul the wisdom teacher' above.

[112] See the section 'The law as wisdom in precept' above.

In Paul's own words (a summary and paraphrase)

The law was written for us Christians to teach us how to live. It was written for our instruction and the events it records were also written down to instruct us. In fact, all of the law is useful for moral teaching, for reproof, for correction and for training in righteousness.

Chapter Seven

'Keeping the commandments of God'
A hermeneutical solution

Paul's controversial view of the Law was inextricably
bound up with the significance which he ascribed to Jesus
as Messiah and with the challenge this issued to all the
fundamental symbols of Jewish life.

(W. D. Davies)[1]

One of the most difficult areas in the study of Paul lies in
trying to understand the ways in which, and the extent to
which, Paul's perspectives on his ancestral faith were
reconfigured in the light of his vision of Christ.

(David Horrell)[2]

The subject of Paul and the law is rightly regarded as one of the
knottiest puzzles in the study of the New Testament. Paul affirms that
'the law is holy, just and good', insists that 'we uphold the law' and
asks rhetorically, 'Does the law not speak entirely for our sake?' Yet
the same Paul also holds that believers in Christ 'are not under the
law', believes that 'the law brings death and works wrath' and
maintains that 'Christ is the end of the law'.

Exegesis alone is not the key to solving the puzzle. Scholars continue
to debate the interpretation of 'works of' / 'righteous requirements
of' / 'end of' / 'fulfilment of' the law, and so on, along with 'law of
Christ / faith / the Spirit', and so on. However, the precise meaning
of particular terms and phrases in Paul's letters can actually become
a distraction from the main task of understanding Paul and the law,
which to my mind is to track the big moves he makes over against and

[1] Davies 1982b: 7.
[2] Horrell 2006: 89.

with the law. Whether 'law of Christ' is an example of replacement of the law or its reappropriation, or 'end of the law' is its repudiation or its replacement, or both, does not change the fact that all three moves are evident at different points in his letters.

It is possible to disagree with my understanding of some of the details and still see the three signature steps as characteristic of Paul's dance with the law. To my mind, along with engaging in careful exegesis, the biggest task for students of Paul is to clarify the sense in which, and the extent to which, the apostle *repudiates*, *replaces* and *reappropriates* the Law of Moses.

With respect to the law, Paul is like the restaurant proprietor who fires a waitress, replaces her, and then hires her as the maître d' and as the sommelier. Her function of serving tables would end and someone else would perform that role. But she would then carry out two different functions in the restaurant, as hostess and as manager of the wine service. To get the full picture of the status of this particular woman one needs to take all three moves into account, namely her termination, substitution and rehiring.

A hermeneutical solution

The solution to the puzzle of Paul and the law is hermeneutical. Rather than asking which bits of the law Paul retains and which he rejects, a hermeneutical approach starts by acknowledging the unity of the law and asks instead, when Paul speaks positively or negatively about the law, in which capacity the law is functioning. To illustrate, consider the two apparent inconsistencies noted in chapter 1, which apart from a hermeneutical approach remain inscrutible: Christ has abolished the law as law-covenant (Eph. 2:15), but faith in Christ upholds rather than abolishes the law as prophecy (Rom. 3:31); and Paul does not appeal to the commandment to obey one's parents as law (Eph. 6:1–2), but as advice concerning how to walk in wisdom (cf. Eph. 5:15).

The main task of this book has been to demonstrate that the hermeneutical solution to the puzzle of Paul and the law, where he repudiates the law as law-covenant, replaces it and reappropriates it as prophecy and as wisdom, is both exegetically compelling and comprehensive in its application across the range of material encountered in the Pauline corpus. Unlike other construals of Paul and the law, it embraces without reservation both the negative and positive things Paul says about and does with the law. It also takes seriously the complex character of the five-volume, multi-genre work that is the Law of Moses, giving due weight to its seminal prophetic and wisdom elements, along with its legal material.

Paul's teaching about the law reminds us that our standing with God is not based on our 'doing', but on what God has done for us in Christ. It also teaches us that to please God we do not live under a code of law but rather under the lordship of Christ. But the law, because it is God's law, remains a key resource for our moral teaching and admonition. Thus a hermeneutical solution to the problem of Paul and the law retains at full strength Paul's twin emphases on the free grace of God in salvation and the demand of God for holy living.

Along with its comprehensive exegetical reach, in the first two sections of this concluding chapter I wish to point to two other strengths of a hermeneutical solution to the puzzle of Paul and the law, namely its *pervasive presence* in Paul's letters and its *historical plausibility*.

The three signature steps across Paul's letters

While the details of the subject of Paul and the law can be debated, the big picture is clear. Paul consistently does three things with the law: he repudiates it, replaces it and reappropriates it. I have covered Paul's repudiation, replacement and reappropriation of the law in separate chapters throughout the book. In this section I wish to underscore the fact that the three moves are neither peripheral to Paul's thought, nor are they confined to just a few of his letters. The following tables illustrate the pervasive presence of the three moves across the Pauline corpus.

The three moves can be readily illustrated from nine of the thirteen Pauline letters. I have left out four of the shorter letters: 1 and 2 Thessalonians, Titus and Philemon. Some of these do contain one or two of the three of the moves in question, but the evidence is more implicit than is the case with the other nine. In order to keep the material manageable, no more than two examples for each move are displayed for each epistle. The examples are indicative rather than exhaustive, and are listed in their logical order (repudiation, replacement and reappropriation), rather than their sequential order in the letter (unless they appear in the same verse).[3]

Eight of Paul's letters exhibit all three moves, with six of these having both versions of reappropriation, namely the law as prophecy

---

[3] The chart for 1 Corinthians is repeated from chapter 1. All translations are mine.

and as wisdom. It is also noteworthy that repudiation and replacement appear in the same couple of verses on eight occasions in five letters (Rom. 6:15; 8:1–2; 1 Cor. 7:19; 9:20–21; 2 Cor. 3:6; Gal. 3:23–25; 5:18; Phil. 3:9), giving further confirmation of the polemical thrust of Paul's response to the law: Paul's rejection of the law as law-covenant is impressively vigorous.

Table 7.1 Paul and the law in Romans

Text	Repudiation	Replacement	Reappropriation as Prophecy	Reappropriation as Wisdom
6:15	believers are 'not under the law'	'but under grace'		
8:1–2	'you have been set free from the law of sin and death'	'by the law of the Spirit'		
4:1–3			Gen. 15:6, 'Abraham believed God . . . ', quoted to argue that Abraham was justified by faith, in connection with the promise in Gen. 12:1–3, which is now being fulfilled in Christ	
5:12–21			Adam as a type of Christ clarifies Christ's achievement	
12:19				Deut. 32:35, 'Vengeance is mine . . . ', quoted to support the call for non-retaliation

Table 7.2 Paul and the law in 1 Corinthians

Text	Repudiation	Replacement	Reappropriation as Prophecy	Reappropriation as Wisdom
7:19	'circumcision is nothing'	'Keeping God's commands is what counts' (my tr.)		
9:20–21	'I am not under the law'	'I am under the law of Christ'		
8:5–6			Allusion to Deut. 6:4 – 'there is but one Lord', establishing Christ as Lord	
15:45			Use of Gen. 2:7, 'the first Adam became a living being', to underscore the universal significance of Christ	
5:13b				Words from Deuteronomy quoted to enforce the expulsion of the incestuous man
9:9				Deut. 25:4, 'do not muzzle the ox . . .', quoted to support the argument for paying ministers
10:11				The exodus and wilderness wanderings 'were written down for our moral instruction'

Table 7.3 Paul and the law in 2 Corinthians

Text	Repudiation	Replacement	Reappropriation as Prophecy	Reappropriation as Wisdom
3:6	'he made us competent as ministers . . . not of the letter, for the letter kills'	'but of a new covenant, of the Spirit . . . the Spirit gives life'		
6:16			Lev. 26:11–12, 'I will live with them', quoted to identify Christians as the new people of God	
8:15				Exod. 16:18, 'the one who gathered much . . .', quoted in support of argument for material equality among God's people
13:1				Deut. 19:15, 'by the testimony of two or three witnesses', quoted to add force to the prospect of Paul's third visit

Table 7.4 Paul and the law in Galatians

Text	Repudiation	Replacement	Reappropriation as Prophecy	Reappropriation as Wisdom
2:5, 14		'the truth of the gospel'		
3:23–25	'we were held in custody under the law' but 'are no longer under the supervision of the law'	Christ and faith have now come		
5:18	'you are not under the law'	'if you are led by the Spirit'		
6:2		'fulfil the law of Christ'		
4:21–31			Exposition of Genesis narrative of Sarah and Hagar to contrast two covenants, two Jerusalems, slavery under the law and freedom in Christ	
5:14				'the entire law is fulfilled in keeping this one command: "Love your neighbour as yourself"'

Table 7.5 Paul and the law in Ephesians

Text	Repudiation	Replacement	Reappropriation as Prophecy	Reappropriation as Wisdom
2:15	'abolishing in his flesh the law with its command-ments and regulations'			
2:20; cf. 3:5; 4:11		'built on the apostles and prophets with Christ Jesus as the chief cornerstone'		
5:31–32			Gen. 2:24, 'the two will become one flesh', quoted to show that Christ and the church are one body	
6:1–3				Exod. 20:12, 'Children, obey your parents . . .', quoted as advice concerning how to walk in wisdom (5:15)

Table 7.6 Paul and the law in Philippians

Text	Repudiation	Replacement	Reappropriation as Prophecy
3:9	'not having a righteousness of my own that comes from the law'	'but that which is through faith in Christ – the righteousness that comes from God and is by faith'	
2:6–8			Paul's 'Adam Christology' exhibits an undeniable network of associations between Phil. 2 and Gen. 1 – 3
4:18			Exod. 29:18 allusion, 'a pleasing aroma, an offering made to the Lord', describing Christian service in priestly terms

Table 7.7 Paul and the law in Colossians

Text	Repudiation	Replacement	Reappropriation as Prophecy	Reappropriation as Wisdom
2:14	'[God] cancelled the written code, with its regulations that was against us and stood opposed to us; he took it away having nailed it to the cross'			
2:17		'the reality is found in Christ'		
1:6, 9–10			Paul applies the creation mandate in Gen. 1:28 to indicate that believers are a part of the inaugurated new creation and are beginning to fulfil in Christ what has been left unfulfilled in Adam	
2:8–23			Circumcision, festivals, sabbath days and dietary requirements prescribed in the law find their reality in Christ	
3:9–10				New creation lifestyle framed as discarding the clothes of Adam and putting on the clothes of the last Adam, alluding to Gen. 3

Table 7.8 Paul and the law in 1 and 2 Timothy

Text	Repudiation	Replacement	Reappropriation as Prophecy	Reappropriation as Wisdom
1 Tim. 1:8–9	'the law used lawfully (as law) is for the lawless'			
1 Tim. 1:11		'the glorious gospel of the blessed God, which he entrusted to me'		
1 Tim. 5:18				Deut. 25:4, 'do not muzzle the ox . . . ', quoted to argue for financial support of elders
2 Tim. 3:15			'the holy Scriptures, which are able to make you wise for salvation'	
2 Tim. 3:16–17				'All Scripture is useful for . . . training in righteousness . . . [to be] thoroughly equipped for every good work'

Paul and the pillars of Judaism

The subject of Paul and the law must be investigated as part of the larger question of Paul's relationship to Judaism. In Acts 21, when Paul arrived in Jerusalem after his third missionary journey, he was greeted with the charge that he was teaching against 'our people, our law, and this place' (Acts 21:28). The career of the apostle Paul, reminiscent of Samson with his hair cut, shook the three pillars of ancient Judaism: election, Torah and the temple.[4] And the biggest and most weight-bearing was the law.

---

[4] Other 'pillars' of Judaism, those distinctives that mark the ancient people of God, are sometimes suggested, including the land and the Shema. In both these cases too, analogous moves can be seen in Paul's letters.

It is difficult for Christians in the twenty-first century, with Christianity as a major world religion and Judaism a much smaller entity, to conceive of what it was like for Christians in Paul's day. When Paul wrote his letters, Judaism was an established religion in the Roman Empire, with estimates of adherents numbering in the millions, and the Christian faith was a tiny messianic movement sheltering precariously under its umbrella. The partings of the ways, as they are sometimes called, took decades and were anything but straightforward and uniform.

However, the nascent Christian movement was not alone in struggling to define itself over against the mother faith. Other Jewish 'sects', such as the Essenes, Sadducees, Pharisees and Zealots, also fought over questions of the identity of the people of God. Indeed, intra-Jewish polemic in the first century was rife and sharp.[5] To take note of this context for Paul's teaching on the law is not to reduce the subject to sociology and group behaviour. But the historical context is vital for understanding the dynamics of Paul's setting and it complements, rather than supplants, the contribution of his teaching about salvation history (see the section in chapter 2, 'The origin of Paul's view').

So what does a smaller group do with the iconic symbols of the mother group when the smaller group begins to break away? The Essenes at Qumran are a case in point. The sectarian documents of the Dead Sea Scrolls indicate that the sectaries reconfigured all three of the pillars of Judaism. First, they denied the validity of the Jerusalem temple and priesthood, asserting their own alternative in a new order and a spiritualized dwelling place of God. They asserted the superiority of their own interpretation of Torah and supplemented it with their own sacred interpretations. And they redefined the scope of the election of the nation, replacing it with a new definition of the sons of light and the sons of darkness. In other words, they repudiated, replaced and/or reappropriated the notion of election, the institution of the temple and the Law of Moses.

As the Christian movement emerges from the matrix of Judaism, Paul does similar things with 'the fundamental symbols of Jewish life', as Davies labels them (see the quotations of Davies and Horrell at the beginning of this chapter). It is not just the law that Paul repudiates, replaces and reappropriates.

Although Paul never explicitly rejects the Jewish temple and its priesthood and sacrifices, he implies as much in his use of cultic

---

[5] See the literature cited in Dunn 1993a.

imagery to refer to something else. In Romans, for example, Christ is the mercy seat and the sacrifice of atonement (3:21–26); the church is the temple (cf. cultic terminology in 12:1–2) and Paul offers 'priestly service' (15:17).

With respect to the election of Israel, in Romans Paul opposes the notion that the Jews, Abraham's sons, constitute the people of God: 'For not all who are descended from Israel are Israel' (9:6, my tr.). Instead, the church comprises the new people of God, whom he describes as the elect (8:33); called (1:6–7; 8:28, 30; 9:7, 12, 24–28); beloved (1:7; 9:25); saints (1:7); beloved children of Abraham (4:11–12, 16–17); and the true circumcision (2:28–29).

A hermeneutical solution to the puzzle of Paul and the law fits within the constraints of history and makes historical sense. The three moves of repudiation, replacement and reappropriation that Paul makes vis-à-vis the law are what would be expected of a new movement within Judaism. And what Paul does with the law is comparable to the moves he makes with two of the other pillars of ancient Judaism.

 Much more could be said on several related subjects. However, the simple point I wish to make here is that Paul's repudiation of the law as law-covenant, replacement of the law by the realities of the new age of the Messiah, and reappropriation of the law as prophecy of the new age and as wisdom for living fit very well in this context as a part of his polemical response to Judaism.

The usefulness of the law

By this stage of the book it will be apparent that I am using the book's subtitle, and the title of this concluding chapter 'Keeping the commandments of God', in a deliberately ambiguous manner. The allusion, of course, is to 1 Corinthians 7:19, a verse we explored at length in chapter 1. There I concluded that the 'commandments' the Corinthians were meant to 'keep', in the sense of 'observe', were not the laws of Moses, but rather Paul's own instructions. Paul did not think that believers in Christ are meant to 'keep', in the sense of 'observe', the law. But Paul most definitely does think that Christians are to 'keep', as in 'retain', the Law of Moses.

In terms of 'keeping the commandments of God', the law is useful to Christians in two ways. According to Paul, believers in Christ do not read the law *as law-covenant*, but rather *as prophecy* and *as wisdom*.

In the end there is nothing particularly novel about my view of Paul and the law. Most often when I explain my understanding of Paul and the law to Christian friends without a formal theological education, their response is along the lines of 'well of course'. The notion that Paul read the law as prophecy of the gospel and teaching for Christian conduct fits well with the normal Christian experience of reading the Pentateuch. Most Christians understand that even though we are not under the law, the law is still a part of Scripture, and must be read as the word of God, 'written for us'. Christians typically read the law as pointing in one way or another to the person and work of Christ and as providing guidance for everyday life. These two impulses correspond to prophecy and wisdom respectively.

As it turns out, 2 Timothy 3:14–17, Paul's most explicit and extensive explanation of the purpose of 'all scripture' (*pasa graphē*), an expression that includes the law,[6] mentions both of these positive uses:

> But as for you, continue in what you have learned and firmly believed, knowing from whom you learned it, and how from childhood you have known the sacred writings that are able *to instruct you for salvation* through faith in Christ Jesus. All scripture is inspired by God and is *useful for teaching* [us how to live], for reproof, for correction, and for training in righteousness, so that everyone who belongs to God may be proficient, equipped for every good work. (2 Tim. 3:14–17)

It is not, however, that Christians look only to the law (and the rest of Old Testament Scripture) for instruction in matters concerning salvation and for guidance on how to live in a manner pleasing to God. In the Pastoral Epistles, as Paul Wolfe points out, the same functions are assigned to the teaching of the apostles:

> The author [of the Pastoral Epistles] often ascribes to the tradition the same features and purpose that he explicitly ascribes to Scripture. In 2 Tim 3:15–17, he speaks of Scripture as being able to make one wise unto salvation and able to give guidance in a godly life. These are the exact same things that he says of the apostolic tradition (1 Tim 2:4; 4:16; 2 Tim 1:10–11; 2:9–10; Titus 1:1–2).[7]

---

[6] The only other reference to *graphē* in the Pastoral Epistles is in 1 Tim. 5:18, where it introduces a quotation of Deut. 25:4.

[7] Wolfe 2010: 215.

A final point about the Christian use of the law as prophecy and wisdom concerns the place of Jesus Christ. Christ is obviously the key to reading the law as prophecy. In short, Christ and the salvation he brings is the content of the prophecy. Paul states in Romans that the 'gospel of God which was promised through his prophets in the Holy scriptures *concerns his Son*' (Rom. 1:2–4, my tr.). Likewise, in Galatians the gospel of justification by faith in Christ is 'declared beforehand' by the scripture in Genesis 12:3 (Gal. 3:8). And, as we saw in chapter 5, Paul's example of reading the law in conjunction with the prophets as a witness to the gospel confirms this picture of the message about Christ as central to that to which the law bears testimony.

The relationship of Christ to the law as wisdom, while less overt, is nonetheless just as critical. As Paul affirms in Colossians 2:3, in Christ 'all the treasures of wisdom and knowledge are hidden'.[8] But, as Cameron explains,

> this statement should not be taken in an *ontological* sense, as if we need no longer to refer to anything else in the cosmos, whether the writings of the Old Testament, or the general ordering of the cosmos. The statement is *teleological*, describing the way it is that only through Christ and his eschatological purposes may we properly 'decode' the texts we read and the order we think we see.[9]

When reading the law as wisdom, we look not only to its meaning in relation to the created order, but also its meaning in relation to Christ. And the two are of course related, as Christ is 'the second man' (1 Cor. 15:47) and 'the last Adam' (1 Cor. 15:45). As Paul says elsewhere in Colossians, when shunning vice and donning virtue, we 'put on the new man [Christ], who is being renewed in knowledge according to the image of his Creator' (Col. 3:10, my tr.).

In Paul's own words (a summary and paraphrase)

The best test of any solution to the puzzle of Paul and the law is how convincing a reading of Paul's letters it engenders. Does it illumine Paul's many and varied interactions with the law? Does it allow him to make his points forcefully? Does it explain them, rather than

---

[8] Cf. 1 Cor. 1:30.
[9] Cameron 2008: 147, italics original.

explain them away? Does it impose a synthesis that is alien to his thought? Does it make sense in his ancient Jewish setting? Does it add depth to his expositions of the gospel? Does it make his moral exhortations more compelling?

In other words, 'the proof of the pudding is in the eating'. With this in mind, as a summary of the book and as an encouragement to readers to read Paul's life-giving letters, it is only appropriate to give Paul the last word. What does the Jewish apostle to the Gentiles say about the Law of Moses in relation to believers in Christ? (The following paragraphs are the summary paraphrases that closed chapters 2–6.)

Paul's explicit repudiation of the law as law-covenant

Unlike Jews, believers in Christ are not under the law, nor are they in the law or from the law. They are not imprisoned and guarded under the law, nor are they subject to the law as to a disciplinarian. Those who are under the law are under a curse and under sin. Even though the law promises life to those who keep it, it is evident that no one keeps the law. Consequently, no one receives life through the law. The law used as law is for the lawless. Christ has abolished the law with its commandments and ordinances.

Paul's implicit repudiation of the law as law-covenant

Paul never says, as he does of Jews, that believers in Christ rely on the law, boast about the law, know God's will through the law, are educated in the law, have light, knowledge and truth because of the law, do, observe and keep the law, on occasion transgress the law, or possess the law as letter or a written code, as a book, as decrees, or as commandments. Paul also never says, as he does of Jews, that Christians learn the law, walk according to the law, and expect good fruit and good works to flow from obedience to the law.

Paul's replacement of the law

Believers in Christ do not rely on the law, but on Christ; do not boast in the law, but in God through Christ; do not find God's will through the law, but in apostolic instruction, wisdom and the gospel; are not instructed by the law, but by the gospel; and are not obliged to obey the law, but rather must obey apostolic instruction.

Christians are not under the Law of Moses, but under the law of Christ, the law of faith and the law of the Spirit. We have died to the law, Christ lives in us and we live by faith in the Son of God. Above all else, including righteousness under the law, we value knowing Christ Jesus our Lord. We do not keep the law, but fulfil the law in Christ and through love. We do not seek to walk according to the law, but according to the truth of the gospel, in Christ, in newness of resurrection life, by faith, in the light and in step with the Spirit. Instead of the oldness of the letter, we participate in newness of life, the new life of the Spirit, and the one new humanity. What counts is not the law, but faith expressing itself through love, the new creation, keeping the commandments of God, and righteousness, peace and joy in the Holy Spirit.

Paul's reappropriation of the law as prophecy

The law was written for us Christians and is part of the prophetic writings which disclose my gospel and proclamation of Jesus Christ, which was a mystery kept secret for long ages, and is now made known to the Gentiles to bring about the obedience of faith. This gospel was promised beforehand through the prophets in the holy Scriptures, that is, through the law and the prophets. The law and the prophets testify to the message of the righteousness of God through faith in Jesus Christ for all who believe. When it comes to this gospel, the law is upheld and the word of God has not failed.

In particular, in Romans the law bears witness to Abraham's faith as a model for all believers, to the partial hardening of Israel that has accompanied the gospel, to righteousness by faith, to not all of Israel accepting the gospel, to the hardening of Israel, and to the Gentiles glorifying God as a result.

Paul's reappropriation of the law as wisdom

The law was written for us Christians to teach us how to live. It was written for our instruction and the events it records were also written down to instruct us. In fact, all of the law is useful for moral teaching, for reproof, for correction and for training in righteousness.

Bibliography

Athas, George (2008), 'The Creation of Israel: The Cosmic Proportions of the Exodus Event', in Brian S. Rosner and Paul Williamson (eds.), *Exploring Exodus: Literary, Theological and Contemporary Approaches*, Nottingham: Apollos, 30–59.

Avemarie, Friedrich (1996), *Tora und Leben: Untersuchungen zur Heilsbedeutung der Tora in der Frühen Rabbinischen Literatur*, TSAJ, Tübingen: Mohr.

Banks, Robert (1987), 'Walking as a Metaphor of the Christian Life', in E. W. Conrad and E. G. Newing (eds.), *Perspectives on Language and Text*, Winona Lake, Ind.: Eisenbrauns, 303–313.

Barclay, John M. G. (1988), *Obeying the Truth: Paul's Ethics in Galatians*, Edinburgh: T. & T. Clark.

—— (2011), *Pauline Churches and Diaspora Jews*, WUNT 275, Tübingen: Mohr Siebeck.

Barrett, C. K. (1968), *The First Epistle to the Corinthians*, Peabody, Mass.: Hendrickson.

Barth, Karl (1933), *The Resurrection of the Dead*, London: Hodder & Stoughton.

Barth, Markus (1974), *Ephesians 1–3*, vol. 34, New York: Doubleday.

Bassler, Jouette M. (2007), *Navigating Paul: An Introduction to Key Theological Concepts*, Louisville: Westminster John Knox.

Beale, G. K. (2005), 'The Old Testament Background of Paul's Reference to "the Fruit of the Spirit"', *BBR* 15.1: 1–38.

Beale, G. K., and D. A. Carson (2007), *Commentary on the New Testament Use of the Old Testament*, Grand Rapids: Baker Academic; Nottingham: Apollos.

Beetham, Christopher A. (2008), *Echoes of Scripture in the Letter of Paul to the Colossians*, Leiden: Brill.

Betz, Hans Dieter (1979), *Galatians: A Commentary on Paul's Letter to the Churches in Galatia*, Hermeneia, Philadelphia: Fortress.

Bird, Michael F. (2006), *The Saving Righteousness of God: Studies on Paul, Justification and the New Perspective*, Milton Keynes: Paternoster.

———— (2011), 'Progressive Reformed View', in James K. Beilby and Paul Rhodes Eddy (eds.), *Justification: Five Views*, Downers Grove: InterVarsity Press, 131–157.

———— (2012), 'Salvation in Paul's Judaism', in Reimund Bieringer and Didier Pollefeyt (eds.), *Paul and Judaism: Crosscurrents in Pauline Exegesis and the Study of Jewish–Christian Relations*, Edinburgh: T. & T. Clark, 15–40.

Blocher, H. (2004), 'Justification of the Ungodly (Sola Fide): Theological Reflections', in D. A. Carson, Peter T. O'Brien and Mark A. Seifrid (eds.), *Justification and Variegated Nomism*, vol. 2: *The Paradoxes of Paul*, Tübingen: Mohr Siebeck, 465–500.

Bockmuehl, Markus (2000), *Jewish Law in Gentile Churches: Halakhah and the Beginnings of Christian Public Ethics*, Edinburgh: T. & T. Clark.

Bruce, F. F. (1982), *The Epistle to the Galatians: A Commentary on the Greek Text*, NIGTC, Grand Rapids: Eerdmans.

———— (1984), *The Epistle to the Colossians, to Philemon, and to the Ephesians*, Grand Rapids: Eerdmans.

Brueggemann, Walter (2002), *Reverberations of Faith: A Theological Handbook of Old Testament Themes*, Louisville: Westminster John Knox.

Burridge, Richard A. (2007), *Imitating Jesus: An Inclusive Approach to New Testament Ethics*, Grand Rapids: Eerdmans.

Byrne, Brendan (1996), *Romans*, ed. Daniel J. Harrington, SP, Collegeville, Minn.: Liturgical.

Calvin, John (1975), *Institutes of the Christian Religion*, tr. Ford Lewis Battles, Grand Rapids: Eerdmans (1536 ed.).

Cameron, Andrew (2008), 'Liberation and Desire: The Logic of Law in Exodus and Beyond', in Brian S. Rosner and Paul Williamson (eds.), *Exploring Exodus: Literary, Theological and Contemporary Approaches*, Nottingham: Apollos, 123–153.

Campbell, Douglas A. (1992), *The Rhetoric of Righteousness in Romans 3.21–26*, JSNTSup 65, Sheffield: JSOT Press.

Carson, D. A. (2004a), 'Atonement in Romans 3:21–26', in Charles E. Hill and Frank A. James III (eds.), *The Glory of the Atonement: Biblical, Historical and Practical Perspectives: Essays in Honor of Roger Nicole*, Downers Grove: InterVarsity Press, 119–139.

———— (2004b), 'Mystery and Fulfillment: Toward a More Comprehensive Paradigm of Paul's Understanding of the Old and the New', in D. A. Carson, Peter T. O'Brien and Mark A. Seifrid (eds.), *Justification and Variegated Nomism*, Tübingen: Mohr Siebeck, 393–436.

Charlesworth J. H. (ed.) (1983–5), *The Old Testament Pseudepigrapha*, 2 vols., Garden City, N.Y.: Doubleday.

Childs, Brevard S. (2008), *The Church's Guide for Reading Paul: The Canonical Shaping of the Pauline Corpus*, Grand Rapids: Eerdmans.

Ciampa, Roy E. (1998), *The Presence and Function of Scripture in Galatians 1 and 2*, WUNT 2.102, Tübingen: Mohr Siebeck.

———— (2000), 'Galatians', in *NDBT*, 311–314.

———— (2007), 'Deuteronomy in Galatians and Romans', in M. J. J. Menken and Steve Moyise (eds.), *Deuteronomy in the New Testament*, London: T. & T. Clark, 99–117.

———— (2008), 'Paul's Use of Scriptural Language and Ideas', in Stanley D. Porter and Christopher E. Stanley (eds.), *As It Is Written: Studying Paul's Use of Scripture*, SBLSymS, Atlanta: Society of Biblical Literature, 41–58.

———— (2011), 'Flee Sexual Immorality: Sex and the City of Corinth', in Brian S. Rosner (ed.), *The Wisdom of the Cross: Exploring 1 Corinthians*, Nottingham: Apollos, 100–133.

Ciampa, Roy E., and Brian S. Rosner (2006), 'The Argument and Structure of 1 Corinthians: A Biblical/Jewish Approach', *NTS 52*: 205–218.

———— (2007), '1 Corinthians', in G. K. Beale and D. A. Carson (eds.), *Commentary on the New Testament Use of the Old Testament*, Grand Rapids: Baker; Nottingham: Apollos, 695–752.

———— (2010), *The First Letter to the Corinthians*, PNTC, Grand Rapids: Eerdmans.

Collins, Raymond F., and Daniel J. Harrington (1999), *First Corinthians*, Collegeville, Minn.: Liturgical.

Conzelmann, Hans (1975), *1 Corinthians: A Commentary on the First Epistle to the Corinthians*, Hermeneia, Philadelphia: Fortress.

Craigie, Peter C. (1976), *The Book of Deuteronomy*, London: Hodder & Stoughton.

Danby, H. (tr.) (1933), *The Mishnah*, Oxford: Oxford University Press.

Cranfield, C. E. B. (1975, 1979), *A Critical and Exegetical Commentary on the Epistle to the Romans*, 2 vols., ICC, Edinburgh: T. & T. Clark.

Das, Andrew A. (2001), *Paul, the Law, and the Covenant*, Peabody, Mass.: Hendrickson.

Davies, W. D. (1982a), *Paul and Rabbinic Judaism: Some Rabbinic Elements in Pauline Theology*, London: SPCK.

———— (1982b), 'Paul and the Law: Reflections on Pitfalls in Interpretation', *Paul and Paulinism*, London: SPCK, 4–16.

Dickson, John (2003), *Mission-Commitment in Ancient Judaism and in the Pauline Communities: The Shape, Extent and Background of Early Christian Mission*, Tübingen: Mohr Siebeck.

Dodd, C. H. (1952), *According to the Scriptures: The Sub-Structure of New Testament Theology*, London: Nisbet.

Donaldson, Terence L. (1989), 'Zealot and Convert: The Origin of Paul's Christ–Torah Antithesis', *CBQ* 51: 655–682.

Dunn, James D. G. (1988a), *Romans 1–8*, WBC 38a, Dallas: Word.

——— (1988b), *Romans 9–16*, WBC 38b, Dallas: Word.

——— (1993a), 'Echoes of Intra-Jewish Polemic in Paul's Letter to the Galatians', *JBL* 112.3: 459–477.

——— (1993b), *Epistle to the Galatians*, Peabody, Mass.: Hendrickson.

——— (1997), *The Theology of Paul the Apostle*, Grand Rapids: Eerdmans.

——— (1998), 'Paul: Apostate or Apostle of Israel', *ZNW* 89: 256–271.

——— (2003), *The Cambridge Companion to St. Paul*, Cambridge Companions to Religion, Cambridge: Cambridge University Press.

——— (2008), *The New Perspective on Paul*, rev. ed., Grand Rapids: Eerdmans.

——— (2009), *New Testament Theology: An Introduction*, Nashville: Abingdon.

Ellis, E. E. (1957), *Paul's Use of the Old Testament*, Grand Rapids: Baker.

Fee, Gordon D. (1987), *The First Epistle to the Corinthians*, NICNT, Grand Rapids: Eerdmans.

——— (1988), *1 and 2 Timothy, Titus*, NICNT, Peabody, Mass.: Hendrickson.

Fitzmyer, Joseph A. (1993), *Romans: A New Translation with Introduction and Commentary*, AB 33, New York: Doubleday.

Furnish, Victor Paul (1999), *The Theology of the First Letter to the Corinthians*, Cambridge: Cambridge University Press.

Gagnon, Robert A. J. (2000), 'A Comprehensive and Critical Review Essay of *Homosexuality, Science, and the "Plain Sense" of Scripture*, Part 1', *HBT* 22: 174–243.

García Martínez, Florentino (1996), *The Dead Sea Scrolls Translated: The Qumran Texts in English*, tr. Wilfred G. E. Watson, Leiden: Brill.

Garland, David E. (2003), *1 Corinthians*, BECNT, Grand Rapids: Baker Academic.

Gathercole, Simon J. (2002), 'A Law unto Themselves: The Gentiles in Romans 2:14–15 Revisited', *JSNT* 85: 27–49.

——— (2004), 'Torah, Life and Salvation: Leviticus 18:5 in Early Judaism and the New Testament', in C. A. Evans (ed.), *From Prophecy to Testament: The Function of the Old Testament in the New*, Peabody, Mass.: Hendrickson, 126–145.

Goldingay, John (2003), *Old Testament Theology: Israel's Gospel*, Downers Grove: InterVarsity Press.

——— (2010), *Key Questions About Christian Faith: Old Testament Answers*, Grand Rapids: Baker.

Hafemann, Scott J. (1993), 'Paul and His Interpreters', in *DPHL*, 666–679.

——— (1995), *Paul, Moses and the History of Israel: The Letter/Spirit Contrast and the Argument from Scripture in 2 Corinthians 3*, Tübingen: Mohr Siebeck.

Hafemann, Scott J., and Paul R. House (2007), *Central Themes in Biblical Theology: Mapping Unity in Diversity*, Nottingham: Apollos.

Hagner, Donald A. (2007), 'Paul as a Jewish Believer – According to His Letters', in Oskar Skarsaune and Reidar Hvalvik (eds.), *Jewish Believers in Jesus: The Early Centuries*, Peabody, Mass.: Hendrickson, 96–120.

Hamerton-Kelly, R. G. (1990), 'Sacred Violence and "Works of the Law." "Is Christ Then an Agent of Sin?" (Galatians 2:17)', *CBQ* 52.1: 55–75.

Hammer, R. (tr.) (1986), *Sifre: A Tannaitic Commentary on the Book of Deuteronomy*, New Haven: Yale University Press.

Hanson, A. T. (1968), *Studies in the Pastoral Epistles*, London: SPCK.

Harnack, Adolf von (1995), 'The Old Testament in the Pauline Letters and in the Pauline Churches', in Brian S. Rosner (ed.), *Understanding Paul's Ethics: Twentieth Century Approaches*, tr. George S. Rosner and Brian S. Rosner, Grand Rapids: Eerdmans, 27–50.

Harris, W. Hall (1996), *The Descent of Christ: Ephesians 4:7–11 and Traditional Hebrew Imagery*, AGAJU, New York: Brill.

Hays, Richard B. (1989), *Echoes of Scripture in the Letters of Paul*, New Haven: Yale University Press.

——— (1996a), 'The Role of Scripture in Paul's Ethics', in Eugene H. Lovering and Jerry L. Sumney (eds.), *Theology and Ethics in Paul and His Interpreters: Essays in Honor of Victor Paul Furnish*, Nashville: Abingdon, 30–47.

———— (1996b), 'Three Dramatic Roles: The Law in Romans 3–4', in James D. G. Dunn (ed.), *Paul and the Mosaic Law: The Third Durham-Tübingen Research Symposium on Earliest Christianity and Judaism*, WUNT, Tübingen: Mohr, 151–165.

———— (1997), *First Corinthians*, Louisville: Westminster John Knox.

———— (2005), *The Conversion of the Imagination: Paul as Interpreter of Israel's Scripture*, Grand Rapids: Eerdmans.

Hoehner, Harold W. (2002), *Ephesians: An Exegetical Commentary*, Grand Rapids: Baker Academic.

Holloway, Joseph O. (1992), *Peripateō as a Thematic Marker for Pauline Ethics*, San Francisco: Mellen Research University Press.

Holtz, Traugott (1995), 'The Question of the Content of Paul's Instructions', in Brian S. Rosner (ed.), *Understanding Paul's Ethics: Twentieth Century Approaches*, tr. George S. Rosner and Brian S. Rosner, Grand Rapids: Eerdmans, 51–71.

Horbury, William (2006), 'Monarchy and Messianism in the Greek Pentateuch', in Michael A. Nibb (ed.), *The Septuagint and Messianism*, Leuven: Leuven University Press, 79–128.

Horrell, David G. (2005), *Solidarity and Difference: A Contemporary Reading of Paul's Ethics*, Edinburgh: T. & T. Clark.

———— (2006), *An Introduction to the Study of Paul*, Edinburgh: T. & T. Clark.

Hubbard, Moyer V. (2002), *New Creation in Paul's Letters and Thought*, Cambridge: Cambridge University Press.

Hübner, Hans (1990), *Biblische Theologie des Neuen Testaments*, 3 vols., Göttingen: Vandenhoeck & Ruprecht.

———— (1997), *Vetus Testamentum in Novo*, vol. 2: *Corpus Paulinum*, Göttingen: Vandenhoeck & Ruprecht.

Hugenberger, Gordon Paul (1998), *Marriage as a Covenant: Biblical Law and Ethics as Developed from Malachi*, Grand Rapids: Baker.

Hurtado, L. W. (2004), 'Jesus' Death as Paradigmatic in the New Testament', *SJT* 57.4: 413–433.

Instone-Brewer, David (1992), '1 Corinthians 9:9–11: A Literal Interpretation of "Do Not Muzzle the Ox"', *NTS* 38.4: 554–565.

Jewett, Paul K. (1971), *The Lord's Day: A Theological Guide to the Christian Day of Worship*, Grand Rapids: Eerdmans.

Jewett, Robert (2007), *Romans*, Hermeneia, Minneapolis: Fortress.

Josephus (1926–65), Text and Translation, tr. H. St J. Thackeray (vols. 1–5), Ralph Marcus (vols. 5–8) with Allen Wikgren (vol. 8), and Louis H. Feldman (vols. 9–10), LCL, London: Heinemann; Cambridge, Mass.: Harvard University Press.

Kaiser, Jr., Walter C. (1978), 'Current Crisis in Exegesis and the Apostolic Use of Deuteronomy 25:4 in 1 Corinthians 9:8–10', *JETS* 21.1: 3–18.

Kampen, John (2011), *Wisdom Literature*, Grand Rapids: Eerdmans.

Keener, Craig S. (1993), *The IVP Bible Background Commentary: New Testament*, Downers Grove: InterVarsity Press.

Kelly, J. N. D. (1963), *The Pastoral Epistles*, Edinburgh: Continuum.

Kim, Chæong-Hun (2004), 'The Significance of Clothing Imagery in the Pauline Corpus', JSNTSup 268, Sheffield: JSOT Press.

Kim, Seyoon (1984), *The Origin of Paul's Gospel*, 2nd ed., Tübingen: Mohr Siebeck.

——— (2002), *Paul and the New Perspective: Second Thoughts on the Origin of Paul's Gospel*, Tübingen: Mohr Siebeck.

Koch, Dietrich-Alex (1986), *Die Schrift als Zeuge des Evangeliums: Untersuchungen zur Verwendung und zum Verständnis der Schrift bei Paulus*, Tübingen: Mohr.

Köhler, Ludwig (2001), *The Hebrew and Aramaic Lexicon of the Old Testament*, study ed., Leiden: Brill.

Kruse, Colin G. (1996), *Paul, the Law and Justification*, Leicester: Apollos.

Lincoln, Andrew T. (1990), *Ephesians*, WBC 42, Dallas: Word.

Lindemann, Andreas (1986), 'Die biblischen Toragebote und die Paulinischen Ethik', in Wolfgang Schrage (ed.), *Studien zum Text und der Ethik des Neuen Testaments*, Berlin: de Gruyter, 242–265.

Lindsay, Dennis R. (1993), *Josephus and Faith: Πιστις and Πιστευειν as Faith Terminology in the Writings of Flavius Josephus and in the New Testament*, Leiden: Brill.

Lock, Walter (1924), *A Critical and Exegetical Commentary on the Pastoral Epistles*, ICC, Edinburgh: T. & T. Clark.

Louw, J. P., and E. A. Nida (eds.) (1989), *Greek–English Lexicon of the New Testament: Based on Semantic Domains*, 2nd ed., New York: United Bible Societies.

Luther, Martin (1962), *Lectures on Galatians*, ed. J. J. Pelikan, tr. J. J. Pelikan, St. Louis: Concordia.

McNamara, Martin (1972), *Targum and Testament. Aramaic Paraphrases of the Hebrew Bible: A Light on the New Testament*, Grand Rapids: Eerdmans.

Marshall, I. H. (1996), 'Salvation, Grace and Works in the Later Writings in the Pauline Corpus', *NTS* 42: 339–358.

——— (1999), *A Critical and Exegetical Commentary on the Pastoral Epistles,* ICC, Edinburgh: T. & T. Clark.

Martens, John W. (2003), *One God, One Law: Philo of Alexandria on the Mosaic and Greco-Roman Law*, Leiden: Brill.

Martin, Dale B. (1995), *The Corinthian Body*, New Haven: Yale University Press.

Martin, R. P. (1993), 'Center of Paul's Theology', in *DPHL*, 92–95.

Meier, John P. (2009), *A Marginal Jew: Rethinking the Historical Jesus*, 3 vols., ABRL, New York: Doubleday.

Metzger, Bruce M., and United Bible Societies Greek New Testament Editorial Committee (1994), *A Textual Commentary on the Greek New Testament: A Companion Volume to the United Bible Societies' Greek New Testament*, 4th rev. ed., Stuttgart: United Bible Societies.

Metzger, Bruce M. (ed.) (1977), *The Oxford Annotated Apocrypha: Revised Standard Version*, New York: Oxford University Press.

Meyer, H. A. W. (1880), *Critical and Exegetical Handbook to the Epistle to the Ephesians and the Epistle to Philemon*, Edinburgh: T. & T. Clark.

Millar, J. G. (1998), *Now Choose Life: Theology and Ethics in Deuteronomy*, NSBT, Leicester: Apollos; Downers Grove: InterVarsity Press.

Moberly, R. W. L. (2009), *The Theology of the Book of Genesis*, Cambridge: Cambridge University Press.

Moo, Douglas J. (1996), *The Epistle to the Romans*, NICNT, Grand Rapids: Eerdmans.

Moritz, Thorsten (1996), *A Profound Mystery: The Use of the Old Testament in Ephesians*, NovTSup 85, Leiden: Brill.

Murray, John (1959), *The Epistle to the Romans*, NICNT, Grand Rapids: Eerdmans.

Neusner, Jacob (2002), *The Tosefta*, 2 vols., Peabody, Mass.: Hendrickson.

O'Brien, Peter T. (1999), *The Letter to the Ephesians*, PNTC, Grand Rapids: Eerdmans.

O'Donovan, Oliver (1986), *Resurrection and Moral Order: An Outline for Evangelical Ethics*, Grand Rapids: Eerdmans.

Oegema, Gerbern S. (1998), *Für Israel und die Volker: Studien zum Alttestamentlich-judischen Hintergrund der Paulinischen Theologie*, NovTSup 95, Boston: Brill.

Pedersen, Sigfred (2002), 'Paul's Understanding of the Biblical Law', *NovT* 44.1: 1–34.

Peterson, David G. (2012), *Transformed by God: New Covenant Life and Ministry*, Nottingham: Inter-Varsity Press.

Philo (1929–53), Text and Translation, tr. F. H. Colson (vols. 2, 6–10) with G. H. Whitaker (vols. 1, 3–5), and by Ralph Marcus (supplements 1–2), LCL, London: Heinemann; Cambridge, Mass.: Harvard University Press.

Plevnik, J. (1989), 'The Center of Paul's Theology', *CBQ* 51: 460–478.

Räisänen, Heikki (1987), *Paul and the Law*, 2nd ed., WUNT, Tübingen: Mohr.

Reinmuth, Eckart (1985), *Geist und Gesetz: Studien zur Voraussetzungen und Inhalt der paulinischen Paränese*, Berlin: Evangelische Verlagsanstalt.

Ridderbos, Herman (1975), *Paul: An Outline of His Theology*, Grand Rapids: Eerdmans.

Robertson, A. T., and Alfred Plummer (1911), *A Critical and Exegetical Commentary on the First Epistle of St Paul to the Corinthians*, Edinburgh: T. & T. Clark.

Rosner, Brian S. (1991a), 'Moses Appointing Judges: An Antecedent to 1 Cor. 6:1–6?', *ZNW* 82.3: 275–278.

——— (1991b), 'Temple and Holiness in 1 Corinthians 5', *TynB* 42.1: 137–145.

——— (1992a), '"*Ouchi mallon epenthēsate*": Corporate Responsibility in 1 Corinthians 5', *NTS* 38.3: 470–473.

——— (1992b), 'A Possible Quotation of Test[ament of] Reuben 5:5 in I Corinthians 6:18a', *JTS* 43.1: 123–127.

——— (1994), '"Written for Us": Paul's View of Scripture', *Pathway into the Holy Scripture*, Grand Rapids: Eerdmans.

——— (1995), *Understanding Paul's Ethics: Twentieth Century Approaches*, Grand Rapids: Eerdmans.

——— (1996a), 'The Function of Scripture in 1 Cor 5:13b and 6:16', *The Corinthian Correspondence*, Leuven: Peeters University Press, 513–518.

——— (1996b), 'The Origin and Meaning of 1 Corinthians 6:9–11 in Context', *BZ* 40.2: 250–253.

——— (1998), 'Temple Prostitution in 1 Corinthians 6:12–20', *NovT* 40.4: 336–351.

——— (1999), *Paul, Scripture and Ethics: A Study of 1 Corinthians 5–7*, Biblical Studies Library, Grand Rapids: Baker; first published 1994, AGAJU 22, Leiden: Brill.

——— (2004), '"With What Kind of Body Do They Come?"', in P. J. Williams, A. D. Clarke, P. M. Head and D. Instone-Brewer (eds.), *The New Testament in Its First Century Setting: Essays on Context* and *Background in Honour of B. W. Winter on His 65th Birthday*, Grand Rapids: Eerdmans, 190–205.

—— (2007a), 'Deuteronomy in 1 and 2 Corinthians', in M. J. J. Menken and Steve Moyise (eds.), *Deuteronomy in the New Testament*, London: T. & T. Clark, 118–135.

—— (2007b), *Greed as Idolatry: The Origin and Meaning of a Pauline Metaphor*, Grand Rapids: Eerdmans.

Sailhamer, J. (2009), *The Meaning of the Pentateuch: Revelation, Composition and Interpretation*, Downers Grove: InterVarsity Press.

Sanders, E. P. (1977), *Paul and Palestinian Judaism: A Comparison of Patterns of Religion*, London: SCM.

—— (1983), *Paul, the Law, and the Jewish People*, Philadelphia: Fortress.

Schlatter, Adolf von (1999), *The Theology of the Apostles: The Development of New Testament Theology*, 2nd ed., Grand Rapids: Baker.

Schnabel, E. (1985), *Law and Wisdom from Ben Sira to Paul: A Tradition Historical Enquiry into the Relation of Law, Wisdom, and Ethics*, Tübingen: Mohr Siebeck.

Schrage, Wolfgang (1991), *Der Erste Brief an die Korinther*, Zurich: Benziger.

Schreiner, Thomas R. (1993), *The Law and Its Fulfillment: A Pauline Theology of the Law*, Grand Rapids: Baker.

—— (1998), *Romans*, BECNT, Grand Rapids: Baker.

—— (2008), *New Testament Theology: Magnifying God in Christ*, Grand Rapids: Baker Academic; Nottingham: Apollos.

—— (2010), *40 Questions About Christians and the Biblical Law*, Grand Rapids: Kregel.

Segal, Alan F. (1990), *Paul the Convert: The Apostolate and Apostasy of Saul the Pharisee*, New Haven: Yale University Press.

Seifrid, Mark A. (2007), 'Romans', in G. K. Beale and D. A. Carson (eds.), *Commentary on the New Testament Use of the Old Testament*, Grand Rapids: Baker Academic, 607–694.

Silva, Moises (2005), *Philippians*, BECNT, Grand Rapids: Baker Academic.

—— (2007), 'Philippians', in G. K. Beale and D. A. Carson (eds.), *Commentary on the New Testament Use of the Old Testament*, Grand Rapids: Baker Academic; Nottingham: Apollos, 835–839.

Sloane, Andrew (2008), *At Home in a Strange Land: Using the Old Testament in Christian Ethics*, Peabody, Mass.: Hendrickson.

Söding, Thomas (1995), *Das Liebesgebot bei Paulus: Die Mahnung zur Agape im Rahmen der Paulinischen Ethik*, Münster: Aschendorff.

Sprinkle, Preston M. (2007), *Law and Life: The Interpretation of Leviticus 18:5 in Early Judaism and in Paul*, WUNT, Tübingen: Mohr Siebeck.

Stanley, Christopher D. (1992), *Paul and the Language of Scripture: Citation Technique in the Pauline Epistles and Contemporary Literature*, Cambridge: Cambridge University Press.

Stuhlmacher, Peter (1994), *Paul's Letters to the Romans: A Commentary*, Louisville: Westminster John Knox.

Thielman, Frank (1992), 'The Coherence of Paul's View of the Law: The Evidence of First Corinthians', *NTS* 38.2: 235–253.

────── (1994), *Paul & the Law: A Contextual Approach*, Downers Grove: InterVarsity Press.

────── (2007), 'Ephesians', in G. K. Beale and D. A. Carson (eds.), *Commentary on the New Testament Use of the Old Testament*, Grand Rapids: Baker Academic, 813–833.

────── (2010), *Ephesians*, BECNT, Grand Rapids: Baker.

Thiselton, Anthony C. (2000), *The First Epistle to the Corinthians: A Commentary on the Greek Text*, Grand Rapids: Eerdmans.

Tobin, Thomas H. (2004), *Paul's Rhetoric in its Contexts: The Argument of Romans*, Peabody, Mass.: Hendrickson.

Tomson, Peter J. (1990), *Paul and the Jewish Law: Halakha in the letters of the Apostle to the Gentiles*, Assen: Van Gorcum.

Towner, Philip H. (2000), 'The Pastoral Epistles', in *NDBT*, 330–336.

Tuckett, Christopher M. (2000), 'Paul, Scripture and Ethics: Some Reflections', *NTS* 46: 403–424.

Unnik, Willem Cornelis van (1960), 'Die Rücksicht auf die Reaktion der Nicht-Christen als Motiv in der altchristlichen Paränese', in *Judentum, Urchristentum, Kirche: Festschrift für Joachim Jeremias*, BZNW, Berlin: Töpelmann, 221–234.

Vlachos, Chris Alex (2004), 'Law, Sin, and Death: An Edenic Triad? An Examination with reference to 1 Corinthians 15:56', *JETS* 47.2: 277–298.

Wagner, J. Ross (1998), ' "Not Beyond the Things Which Are Written": A Call to Boast Only in the Lord (1 Cor 4.6)', *NTS* 44.2: 279–287.

Waltke, Bruce K., and Charles Yu (2007), *An Old Testament Theology: A Canonical and Thematic Approach*, Grand Rapids: Zondervan.

Watson, Francis (2004), *Paul and the Hermeneutics of Faith*, London: T. & T. Clark.

Wenham, Gordon J. (1991), 'The Old Testament Attitude to Homosexuality', *ExpTim* 102: 359–363.

———— (1997), 'The Gap Between Law and Ethics in the Bible', *JJS* 48: 17–29.

———— (2012), *Psalms as Torah: Reading Biblical Song Ethically*, Grand Rapids: Baker.

Westerholm, Stephen (1988), *Israel's Law and the Church's Faith: Paul and His Recent Interpreters*, Grand Rapids: Eerdmans.

———— (2004a), *Perspectives Old and New on Paul: The 'Lutheran' Paul and His Critics*, Grand Rapids: Eerdmans.

———— (2004b), 'The New Perspective at Twenty-Five', D. A. Carson, Peter T. O'Brien and Mark A. Seifrid (eds.), *Justification and Variegated Nomism*, vol. 2, Tübingen: Mohr Siebeck, 1–38.

Williams, H. H. Drake (2001), *The Wisdom of the Wise: The Presence and Function of Scripture Within 1 Cor. 1:18–3:23*, Leiden: Brill.

———— (2004), 'The Psalms in 1 and 2 Corinthians', in Steve Moyise and M. J. J. Menken (eds.), *The Psalms in the New Testament*, London: T. & T. Clark International, 163–180.

Williamson, William Andrew (2007), 'The Influence of You Shall Not Murder on Paul's Ethics in Romans and 1 Corinthians', PhD thesis, University of Western Sydney / Moore Theological College.

Winger, Michael (1992), *By What Law? The Meaning of Nomos in the Letters of Paul*, Atlanta: Scholars Press.

Wintermute, O. S. (1983), 'Jubilees', in James H. Charlesworth (ed.), *The Old Testament Pseudepigrapha*, Garden City, N.Y.: Doubleday, 1: 35–142.

Witherington, Ben (1995), *Conflict and Community in Corinth: A Socio-Rhetorical Commentary on 1 and 2 Corinthians*, Grand Rapids: Eerdmans.

———— (1998), *The Paul Quest: The Renewed Search for the Jew of Tarsus*, Downers Grove: InterVarsity Press.

———— (2010), *The Indelible Image: The Theological and Ethical Thought of the New Testament*, vol. 2, Downers Grove: InterVarsity Press.

Wolfe, B. Paul (2010), 'The Sagacious Use of Scripture', in Andreas J. Köstenberger and Terry L. Wilder (eds.), *Entrusted with the Gospel: Paul's Theology in the Pastoral Epistles*, Nashville: Broadman & Holman, 199–218.

Wright, Christopher J. H. (1992a), 'The Ethical Authority of the Old Testament: A Survey of Approaches', *TynB* 43.1: 101–120.

———— (1992b), 'The Ethical Authority of the Old Testament: A Survey of Approaches', *TynB* 43.2: 203–231.

———— (1995), 'Old Testament Ethics', in David J. Atkinson, David H. Field, Oliver O'Donovan and Arthur F. Holmes (eds.), *New Dictionary of Christian Ethics and Pastoral Theology*, Leicester: Inter-Varsity Press; Downers Grove: InterVarsity Press, 48–56.

Wright, David F. (1984), 'Homosexuals or Prostitutes: The Meaning of Arsenokoitai (1 Cor 6:9; 1 Tim 1:10)', *VC* 38.2: 125–153.

Wright, N. T. (1986), *The Epistles of Paul to the Colossians and to Philemon: An Introduction and Commentary*, TNTC, Leicester: Inter-Varsity Press.

———— (1991), *The Climax of the Covenant: Christ and the Law in Pauline Theology*, Edinburgh: T. & T. Clark.

———— (1996), 'The Law in Romans 2', in James D. G. Dunn (ed.), *Paul and the Mosaic Law: The Third Durham-Tübingen Research Symposium on Earliest Christianity and Judaism (Durham, September, 1994)*, Tübingen: Mohr, 131–150.

Zachman, Randall C. (2009), '"Deny Yourself and Take up Your Cross": John Calvin on the Christian Life', *IJST* 11.4: 466–482.

Zerbe, Gordon M. (1993), *Non-Retaliation in Early Jewish and New Testament Texts: Ethical Themes in Social Contexts*, Sheffield: JSOT Press.

Index of authors

Index of Scripture references